Evaluating and Measuring the Value, Use and Impact of Digital Collections

Evaluating and Measuring the Value, Use and Impact of Digital Collections

Edited by
Lorna M. Hughes

facet publishing

© This compilation: Lorna M. Hughes 2012
  The chapters: the contributors 2012

Published by Facet Publishing,
7 Ridgmount Street, London WC1E 7AE
www.facetpublishing.co.uk

Facet Publishing is wholly owned by CILIP: the Chartered Institute
of Library and Information Professionals.

British Library Cataloguing in Publication Data
A catalogue record for this book is available from the
British Library.

ISBN 978-1-85604-720-3

First published 2012
Reprinted digitally thereafter

Text printed on FSC accredited material.

Typeset from editor's files by Facet Publishing in 10/13pt
Garamond and Frutiger.
Printed and made in Great Britain by CPI Group (UK) Ltd,
Croydon, CR0 4YY.

Contents

Figures and tables

Figures

Tables

Foreword

This set of chapters on digital collections fills an important gap in the professional literature of the memory institutions: libraries, museums, and archives. While much has been written of late on the evolution of digital scholarship, most analyses are written by and for scholars. These chapters are written by librarians, archivists and scholars engaged in building, assembling and digitizing content for a range of audiences, largely in the humanities. As noted in the acknowledgements, the book emerged from an expert seminar in e-research. The result is a coherent arrangement of chapters from a group of authors collaborating toward a common goal of identifying metrics for digital collections.

They survey developments, concerns, best practices and criteria for evaluation in a wide range of projects across the United Kingdom, Australia and New Zealand – where these authors currently are based – with reference to projects in the United States and elsewhere. The comparison of efforts in libraries, museums and archives, which in turn serve universities, schools, theatres and other environments, offers a rich set of case studies. A number of policy issues cut across these environments, most notably intellectual property rights and provenance.

Information professionals, managers and students alike will find much of value in this volume. The current environment of accountability is particularly problematic for the humanities. The 'impact' or value of collections may not be evident for years, decades, or even centuries after the origin of the materials, yet funders demand immediate economic indicators. These chapters take a balanced approach, acknowledging the trade-off in short and long term assessment of value, and to whom.

In all fields, the availability of scholarly content in digital form makes possible new research questions, methods and uses. The humanities especially have benefited from the ability to digitize historic documents, to mine large corpuses of texts, audio and images, and to assemble widely dispersed cultural objects into common repositories for comparison and analysis. Yet digitization is a means for scholarship and learning, not an end in itself. Careful assessments are required of trade-offs between usability and honesty to original form, between image quality, speed of access and cost, and between assorted other project-specific factors. Managers must identify their goals clearly to steer their way through the sea of standards that apply to digital projects. The orientation towards assessing use and users is particularly valuable, as it is often under-appreciated in digital projects.

Some of the projects represented here go well beyond scholarship, making historical resources useful not only for research, teaching and learning, but also for 'enjoyment'. Would that all digital projects keep the joy of discovery at the centre of attention!

Christine L. Borgman
Professor and Presidential Chair in Information Studies,
University of California, Los Angeles

Acknowledgements

Many of the papers in this volume were initially developed at an Expert Seminar hosted by the Centre for e-Research at King's College London on 12 July 2010. Participants in that event presented their initial ideas for this book, and the discussions that followed shaped the content that has emerged. The participants were Sheila Anderson and Simon Tanner (King's College London), Ann Borda and Lyle Winton (University of Melbourne), Jean-Claude Guédon (University of Montreal), Andrew Prescott (University of Glasgow), Claire Hudson (the Victoria and Albert Museum), Ben Showers (Joint Information Systems Committee), Milena Dobreva (University of Strathclyde), Claire Warwick (University College London) and Monica Bulger (University of Oxford). From the discussions at that event, ideas emerged about other strands that could be included in the book, and I am grateful to Melissa Terras, Claire Ross, Vera Motyckova, David Robey, Andy O'Dwyer, Leo Konstantelos and Gillian Oliver for contributing chapters and additional material that have shaped and completed the content in this volume. I would also like to thank Marilyn Deegan, Harold Short, Andrew Green, Arwel Jones and Avril Jones for their assistance and much-valued input to the project.

I am grateful to my former colleagues at King's College, both in the Centre for e-Research and the Centre for Computing in the Humanities, for their collaboration over the five years I worked at King's. I would also like to express my thanks to my new colleagues at the National Library of Wales, who have been enormously supportive and encouraging of this project since I took up my new post at the Library in 2011. The National Library of Wales has been a pioneer in digitization, and working among their digital collections, and the experts who create, manage and sustain them, has been a supportive and intellectually stimulating environment in which to complete the editing of this book.

Thanks are of course also due to all those who made images available for use in this volume.

I'd also like to thank the team at Facet, Sarah Busby and Lin Franklin, for being extremely helpful and encouraging at all stages of the development of the text.

Above all, I'd like to thank Russell, Archie and Lachlan for their patience and support.

The contributors

Ann Borda has held strategic roles in academic and research organizations for 15 years. Ann is currently Executive Director of the Australian state-funded Victorian eResearch Strategic Initiative (VeRSI), which is a multimillion dollar programme providing a co-ordinated approach to accelerating the uptake of e-research by the use of advanced information and communication technology (ICT) to enhance research outcomes, support collaboration and improve access to data and resources. Previously, Ann worked with the Joint Information Systems Committee (JISC) where she was responsible for the quality delivery of government-funded projects in building a UK wide e-infrastructure to support research. Ann is an Honorary Principal Fellow at the University of Melbourne and she has published in the areas of virtual research collaboration, data modelling and information system design.

Christine L. Borgman is Professor and Presidential Chair in Information Studies at the University of California, Los Angeles (UCLA). She is the author of more than 200 publications in the fields of information studies, computer science, and communication. Both of her sole-authored monographs, *Scholarship in the Digital Age: information, infrastructure, and the internet* (MIT Press, 2007) and *From Gutenberg to the Global Information Infrastructure: access to information in a networked world* (MIT Press, 2000), have won the Best Information Science Book of the Year award from the American Society for Information Science and Technology. She is a lead investigator for the Center for Embedded Networked Systems (CENS), a US National Science Foundation Science and Technology Center, where she conducts data practices research. Current collaborations include Monitoring, Modelling, and Memory and the Data Conservancy project. She is a member of the US National Academies' Board on Research Data and Information, the US National CODATA and the Board of Directors of the Electronic Privacy Information Center, and a Fellow of the American Association for the Advancement of Science. She is also the 2011 recipient of the Paul Evan Peters Award from the Coalition for Networked Information, the Association for Research Libraries and EDUCAUSE, and the 2011 recipient of the Research in Information Science Award from the American Association of Information Science and Technology.

Milena Dobreva is a research fellow at the School for Creative Technologies, University of Portsmouth. Before joining the School, she worked for the University of Strathclyde where she managed the DiSCmap project (JISC, 2010b) funded by JISC, studying priorities in digitization for UK higher education institutions from the point of view of users (2008–9), the international Europeana user and functionality study (2009–10) and the local contribution to the Sustaining Heritage Access through Multivalent ArchiviNg (SHAMAN) project funded by FP7 of the European Community (EC) (2008–11). From 1990 she worked at IMI-BAS where she earned her PhD degree in informatics and applied mathematics. Milena was the founding head of the first Digitization Centre in Bulgaria (2004) and of the Humanities Informatics Department at IMI-BAS (2007). During 2002–5 she collaborated with the Humanities Advanced Techology and Information Institute (HATII) at the University of Glasgow on three Technology Watch reports on the application of new/core/emerging technologies in the cultural and scientific heritage sector for the DigiCULT project funded by the EC, and in 2007–8 she contributed to the work on the policy and quality domains within the DELOS Network of Excellence on Digital Libraries' Digital Libraries Reference Model (DLRM). She also served as chair of the Bulgarian national committee of the Memory of the World programme of UNESCO. Her interests are in user studies for digital libraries, long-term preservation and e-culture.

Claire Hudson is Head of Collections Management for the Victoria and Albert (V&A) Museum's Department of Theatre and Performance. She is a qualified librarian whose career began in public libraries; she then moved to the academic sector before she joined the V&A Theatre Museum (now the Department of Theatre and Performance) in 1987. Since then, her responsibilities have expanded into managing in their entirety the museum's highly diverse performing arts collections. They include library material, archives, manuscripts, works of art, costume, museum objects, photographs and video collections, and form the UK's national collection for the performing arts. With an emphasis on making the collections accessible to the research community and to the general public, her role also encompasses responsibility for digital projects. The department was an early adopter of digitization, beginning with a successful lottery-funded project in the late 1990s.

Claire is actively involved in national and international networks of performing arts curators, librarians and archivists, serving as President of SIBMAS – the International Association for Libraries and Museums of the Performing Arts – between 2004 and 2010.

Lorna M. Hughes is the University of Wales Professor of Digital Collections at the National Library of Wales. She took up her appointment in January 2011, and leads a research programme based around the Library's digital collections. Prior to moving to the National Library of Wales in Aberystwyth, Lorna worked at King's College, London, most recently as Deputy Director of the Centre for e-Research. From 2005 to 2008, she was Programme Manager of the Arts and Humanities Research Council (AHRC) ICT Methods Network, based in the Centre for Computing and the Humanities (CCH). She has worked in digital humanities at New York University, Arizona State University, Oxford University and Glasgow University. She is the author of *Digitizing Collections: strategic issues for the information manager* (Hughes, 2004) and the co-editor of *Virtual Representations of the*

Past (Greengrass and Hughes, 2008). She is the Secretary of the Alliance of Digital Humanities Organizations (ADHO).

Leo Konstantelos is a Preservation Researcher in HATII at the University of Glasgow and in the School of Creative Technologies at the University of Portsmouth. He holds a PhD on user requirements for born-digital art in digital library environments, and an MSc in information technology. Leo is the HATII Principal Investigator of the JISC-funded Preservation Of Complex Objects Symposia (POCOS) project. He has worked extensively in digital preservation projects, delivering innovative research in the area of digital/new media arts preservation requirements and in alternative manners for preserving dynamic and interactive material. He co-authored the Preservation and Long-term Access through NETworked Services (Planets) report on emerging digital art characterisation techniques (McHugh, Konstantelos and Barr, 2009), producing a vocabulary for context classification of dynamic, interactive and ephemeral digital artworks. He has worked for the EC-funded project SHAMAN. Leo recently joined the Keeping Emulation Environments Portable (KEEP) project team at the University of Portsmouth.

Vera Motyckova completed an MA in electronic communication and publishing at University College London (UCL) in 2010. During her studies she carried out research in collaboration with UCL and the British Museum focusing on the non-academic users of the British Museum's Collection Database Online. She also worked at the British Museum on the development of new online research catalogues. Currently, Vera is part of the online editorial team at the British Broadcasting Corporation (BBC) in the Learning Department.

Andrew O'Dwyer is a Technologist/Project Manager at the BBC, working on digitization activities for preservation and access to audiovisual collections. He also works on a number of European Union (EU) collaborative projects to bring archives online for public and academic use. He is a member of the Television Studies Commission of FIAT, www.fiatifta.org, promoting academic use of audiovisual material, and a member of the European Television History Network (http://cms.hum.uu.nl/ethn). He is also a contributing author of the book *A European Television History* (Bignell and Fickers, 2008).

Gillian Oliver is currently Senior Lecturer in Archives and Records Management at the School of Information Management, Victoria University of Wellington, New Zealand. Her doctoral degree is from Monash University, Melbourne, Australia. Her professional practice background spans libraries (mainly in the health care sector), records management and archives. Most recently she was actively involved in establishing digital archiving capability at Archives New Zealand. Her teaching experience includes the development and delivery of online education for records and information management at The Open Polytechnic of New Zealand. Her research interests encompass record-keeping perspectives on digital preservation and organizational cultures.

Andrew Prescott is Professor of Digital Humanities at King's College London, and until recently was Director of Research at the Humanities Advanced Technology and Information Institute, University of Glasgow. He was formerly a curator in the Department of Manuscripts at the British Library, where he was a library contact for a number of pioneering digitization projects, such as Electronic Beowulf. He edited, with Leona Carpenter and Simon Shaw, the account of the British Library's first digital and network programme, *Towards the Digital Library: the British Library's Initiatives for Access programme* (Carpenter, Prescott and Shaw, 1998). From 2000 to 2007, he worked in the Humanities Research Institute, University of Sheffield, where he was Founding Director of the Centre for Research into Freemasonry, the first academic centre in the UK devoted to the history of Freemasonry. From 2007 to 2010, Andrew was Librarian of the University of Wales Lampeter, serving latterly as Pro Vice Chancellor. His publications include *English Historical Documents* (Prescott, 1988), *The British Inheritance* (Hallam and Prescott, 1999) and *The Benedictional of St Aethelwold* (Prescott, 2002).

David Robey currently holds the position of Arts and Humanities Consultant at the Oxford e-Research Centre. Until recently he was Director of the Arts and Humanities Research Council's ICT in Arts and Humanities Research Programme. He has been University Lecturer in Italian at Oxford and Fellow of Wolfson College, then Professor of Italian at Manchester, then Professor of Italian at Reading. He has published on 15th-century Italian humanism (educational and poetic theory), language and style in Dante and Renaissance narrative poetry, the computer analysis of literature, and modern critical theory. He has authored a computer-based study on sound and structure in Dante's *Divine Comedy* (Robey, 2000), later extending this work to include the major narrative poems of the Italian Renaissance. He has also completed a major online analytical database on 'Sound and Metre in Italian Narrative Verse' (www.italianverse.rdg.ac.uk). He was joint editor of *The Oxford Companion to Italian Literature* (Hainsworth and Robey, 2002, now translated as the *Enciclopedia della Letteratura Italiana*, Oxford/Zanichelli), and joint author of the forthcoming *Very Short Introduction to Italian Literature* (Hainsworth and Robey).

Claire Ross is a PhD student and researcher at the UCL Centre for Digital Humanities. Her research focuses on user evaluation and user centric design of social media applications, and digital museum content and online collections. Formerly, she held the position of E-Learning Development Project Manager working on a collaborative project with the University of Exeter and Geevor Tin Mine Museum. She is Chair of the Digital Learning Network, formerly the E-Learning Group For Museums, Libraries and Archives. She is also a member of the committee for Ignite London. Her research interests include usability studies, web 2.0 applications, social media, museum e-learning, digital heritage and digital repositories.

Ben Showers is a programme manager with the Digital Infrastructure team at JISC with responsibility for the Library Infrastructure programme. Ben manages a number of programmes of work, including library systems, user experience, mobile library services nd shared services. Prior to this Ben worked with the e-Content team at JISC, working on a number of digitization and digital scholarly resource programmes helping to explore innovative new models of content creation and curation including crowdsourcing and user-generated content. Ben holds an MA in philosophy and an MA in library and information science from University College, London.

Simon Tanner is the Director of Digital Consultancy at King's College London (www.kdcs.kcl.ac.uk). He is also a senior academic in the Department for Digital Humanities at King's and co-Director for the MA in digital asset management. He authored the book *Digital Futures: strategies for the information age* with Marilyn Deegan (Deegan and Tanner, 2001). Simon previously led in information technology (IT), management and library roles for the Higher Education Digitisation Service (Senior Consultant), Loughborough University (Systems Manager) and Rolls-Royce and Associates (Head of Library Services).

Melissa Terras is the Reader in Electronic Communication in the Department of Information Studies, University College London. She has a background in classical art history and English literature, and computing science. Her doctorate (University of Oxford) examined how to use advanced information engineering technologies to interpret and read the Vindolanda texts. Publications include *Image to Interpretation: intelligent systems to aid historians in the reading of the Vindolanda texts* (Terras, 2006) and *Digital Images for the Information Professional* (Terras, 2008). She is a general editor of *DHQ: Digital Humanities Quarterly* and the Secretary of the Association of Literary and Linguistic Computing. Her research focuses on the use of computational techniques to enable research in the arts and humanities that would otherwise be impossible.

Lyle Winton is eResearch Analyst and Policy Manager at VeRSI, University of Melbourne. His responsibilities include managing engagements with VeRSI stakeholders and the research community, exploring opportunities and solutions that align with VeRSI aims (advancing research, collaboration and sharing through ICT and e-research practice). His general interests lie in research informatics, research data management, distributed collaboration, service oriented architecture, and training and education with respect to all of these areas.

1

Introduction: the value, use and impact of digital collections

Lorna M. Hughes

Background and context
The aims of this volume

A key motivation for developing this volume was the need to address the 'use', 'value' and 'impact' of digital collections in the context of an expanding mass of digital content with tremendous potential. Specifically:

- How can we understand how digital collections are being used, and by whom?
- How do we assess their value, and add value over time, in order to make decisions about which collections to digitize or make available, and how?
- How do we assess their impact on scholarship, on knowledge transfer and on information management and access?
- How do we 'measure' value? What can be measured, and how?
- Is it possible to ensure their sustainability, value and impact over time?
- How might we apply indicators of use, value and impact to inform funding decisions and policy making for the future?

The explosion of digital initiatives

This volume of essays is, in many respects, a follow up and companion to *Digitizing Collections: strategic issues for the information manager* (Hughes, 2004).[1] Since its publication, digitization initiatives have continued at a tremendous pace in libraries, archives and museums, as well as in higher education. Digitization of existing library, museum and archive collections is still a major priority, where funding can still be found for these initiatives. The National Library of Wales is continuing to digitize two million pages of historic Welsh newspapers and journals in a three-year project that will conclude in 2012, with funding from the Welsh Government.[2] The British Library is partnering online publisher Brightsolid to digitize up to 40 million pages of newspapers. In the USA, the Smithsonian Institute has a remit to digitize its entire collection: a challenge considering that the Smithsonian is home to 137 million objects, 100,000 cubic feet of archival material and 1.8 million library volumes.[3] In the UK, the Joint Information Systems Committee (JISC) has launched a new phase of digitization via its e-Content programme, for projects that will be completed in 2012. This is the era of Google, and mass digitization initiatives to put our cultural heritage online are flourishing. This has been described as a 'data deluge' (Hey and Trefethen, 2005), and it has a huge impact on scholarship, teaching and public engagement.

Digitization in an economic downturn

This is an auspicious time to take stock of this mass of digital content, and consider its impact, value and use. The global economic decline that began in 2007 has led to serious cuts in funding for almost all humanities and cultural heritage initiatives, including the development of, and support for, digital collections. In the arts, humanities and cultural heritage world, especially in the UK, the threats to funding have become a reality, with the closure of the Museums, Libraries and Archives Council (MLA), cuts to the Arts Council, and to Research Council funding overall. In the USA, there have been calls to withdraw federal funding from the National Endowment for the Humanities.[4] This economic 'austerity' has created significant institutional and societal pressures on cultural heritage and higher education organizations.

Partly as a consequence of the reduction in funding, we have seen a sharper emphasis on the need to demonstrate the 'impact' of publicly funded resources and research, as a means of quantifying the value of the investment in their creation. Research councils and funding agencies, notably the Arts and Humanities Research Council (AHRC) in the UK, have placed an increasing emphasis on 'impact' and 'evidence of value' of all research that they fund (AHRC, 2006) for several years. This focus on understanding the 'evidence of value and impact' of digital research and collections in the arts and humanities was one of the reasons that AHRC ICT Methods Network was funded from 2005 to 2008. This was a national organization that provided a forum for the exchange and dissemination of expertise in the use of information and communication technologies (ICTs) for arts and humanities research. In its final evaluation report, the Methods Network was able to provide a considerable body of evidence that there was indeed 'evidence of value' of the use of digital collections for scholarship and research in the arts and humanities:

> The new research that has been enabled by ICT . . . has depended upon the development of new kinds of resources, such as large corpora in literary, linguistic, musicological, and television and film studies domains, the digitization and digital-encoded representation of materials in classics, history, literature and history of art, and the creation of databases in archaeology and the performing arts. This recognition that the future generations of scholarship in the arts and humanities will depend upon the accessibility of a vast array of digital resources in digital form is becoming more widespread.   (Hockey and Ross, 2008)

Since then, the Browne review (Browne, 2010) has called for evidence of the 'value' of the arts and humanities to society, and there is increasing pressure for scholarly research to demonstrate economic and social impact, despite the fact that the 'economic benefit of the arts and humanities' is a topic for which there is little hard evidence at this time. Nonetheless, the AHRC has produced two publications that set out the arguments for the 'value' of the arts and humanities, in the recent publication edited by Jonathan Bate, *The Public Value of the Humanities* (Bate, 2010) and in the AHRC report *Leading the World: the economic impact of UK arts and humanities research* (AHRC, 2009). A noteworthy web-based initiative, 4Humanities (http://humanistica.ualberta.ca), organized by leading digital humanities scholars, has also been set up as an advocacy organization for the value of digital collections and methods in the humanities.

2

The need for open and useable digital collections

Another recent development that provides part of the background to this volume is the increasing focus on the value and use of 'open' scholarly resources for research. While publicly funded research outputs are intended to be freely available (even if this is not always the case, and as Robey discusses in this volume, the demise of the Arts and Humanities Date Service in the UK in 2008 has made it harder for publicly funded resources to be used and sustained), digitization that has been funded by commercial entities is frequently subject to licensing and use restrictions. Notably, in the UK the digitization and redistribution of the census materials and similar 'name rich' resources has been made possible by commercial entities including Ancestry.com and Find My Past.

While these efforts have digitized and made available an enormous range of primary source materials, there is some concern that resources that are not 'open' are less valuable for scholarship. This is of particular concern, as the availability of large-scale, distributed collections allows new approaches to scholarship in a number of disciplinary areas.[5] The idea of taking a 'big picture' approach to historical and cultural issues, working with large-scale data across disciplines, is gaining ground in scholarly enquiry once more. This is the type of research highlighted in the American Council of Learned Societies report, emphasizing the opportunities 'to reintegrate the cultural record, connecting its disparate parts and making the resulting whole available to one and all, over the network' (ACLS, 2006). Underpinning this re-integration, of course, is the principle of freely available and open data for aggregation, use and reuse: 'the full range of online content needs to be made available to all, quickly, easily and in a form appropriate to individuals needs' (JISC Strategic Content Alliance, 2010).

Some organizations have made the principle of providing freely available digital content where possible (see Prescott's discussion of the National Library of Wales in this volume), but this is not always possible, especially in the current economic climate. There are various approaches: can data be chargeable for a time to recover the costs in making it? Under what conditions can cultural heritage content be monetized? This volume is not about business models for digital content, but there is an implicit understanding that 'price' and 'value' could become interconnected – people may have to pay for valuable resources. There are also issues related to sustainability – the digital content must be sustained as long as charging models are in place – which adds to their cost. In a related development, commercial entities have raised concerns about digitization of out of copyright materials in libraries (Sabbagh, 2010). However, these discussions lack the evidence of the actual economic 'value' of digital resources, and work is under way to address this balance, developing a 'deeper understanding of the social and economic impact of digitization' (Hargreaves, 2011).

The cost of digital creativity

While the economic data is incomplete – and this volume is not a quantitative analysis of business models for digitization – one thing that is very clear is that digital collections are expensive to develop, manage and sustain over the long term. This has been documented in two reports commissioned by the AHRC: its *Resource Enhancement Scheme* (AHRC, 2005) and *Sustainability of Digital Outputs from AHRC Resource Enhancement Projects* (Denbo, Haskins and Robey, 2008). The latter report demonstrated that 'The average grant to projects with digital outputs was £228,155, as against £153,090 to those without: the total amount invested in those with digital outputs was therefore almost £40m.' Furthermore, there are hidden costs to developing digital resources – institutional overheads in keeping collections online and visible, and in the allocation of resources to digital programmes, frequently at the cost of other activities. In academia, the costs are less hidden – there is a body of evidence (see, for example, Raban, 2007) demonstrating that the development of digital resources by academics can hinder their career progress, and even jeopardize promotion or tenure. It is notable the research findings presented in this volume by Ross, Terras and Motyckova show that the largest numbers of academic users of the British Museum Collections online database were either postgraduate students or professors – either those just starting out, or those secure in their promotions. Impact, of course, can be negative as well as positive, so it is timely to assess the pressures that developing, sustaining and using digital collections can place on organizations and individuals.

Protecting the digital investment

Given the current economic climate, and the pressure on funding for digital collections, addressing these issues is crucial in order to make the case for protecting existing digital heritage, and for increased digitization. New digital projects must have compelling and visible impact. It is necessary to be creative about the sort of funding available, and to look further afield, both internationally and in disciplinary focus, for funding. In this regard, the economic downturn has been a way of incentivizing collaboration, enhancing existing resources, and aggregating content, as well as consolidating expertise in a few centres. Research Council funding in the UK has also been mostly contingent on developing digital resources that are driven by research challenges, rather than resource enhancement or access, which may well create resources that have more demonstrable 'value' for scholarship. This has been a 'carrot and stick' approach – the carrot being the opportunity to apply for the limited funding still available, the stick being that this is the only way that funding can be awarded. Equally pragmatically, as it becomes more difficult to get funding for digital collections, there is a need to make better use of those we have, and to ensure that they are fully embedded in research, teaching and public engagement. There is a need to show clearly – to funders, to the public and to those responsible for their long-term sustainability – that digital resources can enable scholarship that generates new research questions and findings; that they make it easier and more efficient to carry out 'traditional' scholarship through better and enhanced access to resources (Lehmann and Renfro (1991) and Wiberley (2000) suggest that humanities scholars are receptive to technology as long as it demonstrates adequate savings in time or effort); and that they extend the evidence base for research. By expanding the cultural heritage collections available to the public, they also have economic and societal impacts. However, this evidence is not readily available, as outlined in the keynote address at the Digital Humanities Conference in 2010 (Terras, 2010), where the case was forcefully made for better, more readily available exemplars of the use and value of digital collections and research.

Evidence of use and impact

Some evidence exists for the use of digital resources for research, education and public engagement, thanks to initiatives like the JISC e-Content programme; the Methods Network; and the National Endowment for the Humanities Office of Digital Humanities, notably the 'Digging into Data' initiative, which seeks to use large digital corpora to address key research challenges in the humanities (see hwww.diggingintodata.org). The AHRC ICT Methods Network produced a body of evidence (documented in the final evaluation of the programme) that demonstrated that digital resources were having a transformative effect on scholarship, and that this was a vibrant, fast-expanding area. However, as the final evaluation stressed, the full impact of the Methods Network and, indeed, the impact of digital resources in the arts and humanities, will be over the longer term (Hockey and Ross, 2008). But, since the demise of the Network, there has been no attempt to systematically address these issues across the disciplines. A longitudinal, multi-disciplinary study on use and impact of digital resources is still needed.

Value

One of the key issues is being able to provide a definition of 'value'. Digital resources are valuable to different audiences for different reasons, and some value may not be realized immediately. Digital collections come about for different reasons. Many research projects, for example, have produced digital images or digital text as a by-product of scholarship, and a need to put these digital images online for public access may not be the first priority of the project team. For example, 'The Visual Culture of Wales' Project (based at the University of Wales Centre for Advanced Welsh and Celtic Studies) was funded mainly through the Arts Council of Wales Lottery Unit and the University of Wales from 1996 to 2003, as a publication project. The photographic archive contains digitized photography of around 3000 works of art, dating from the fifth century up to the 1960s, in a wide variety of media. The database for the images was subsequently made available online, with minimal funding, as a by-product of the research publication project. Similarly, name-rich sources (parish records, census records, baptism records) have been digitized by the Church of Latter Day Saints for theological reasons. The digital files may be invaluable for family history, or demographic research, but this was certainly not the motivation for their creation. Other digital resources, including born-digital materials, are being preserved for future use – the Library of Congress, for example, has archived the Twitter archive, which could prove just as useful to scholars of the early 21st century as 19th-century newspapers online have proved to political, social and cultural historians of the newspaper era. In this regard, digital resources are just like any other cultural artefact – historical resources that are used for research were seldom intended to be 'historical resources'; they were administrative records, ephemera or cultural artefacts. They tell us more than they were ever intended to. This is a useful truth to apply to digital content. As we create more and more digital content – as part of conscious attempts to digitize analogue materials, as by-products of research or as part of our daily digital mode for work and communication – we are creating, maintaining and sustaining 'digital content' that may have value to future scholars.

A digital text may be valuable to a scholar because it enables the use of text mining tools to undertake historic research, or it may be valuable to family historians as it mentions an ancestor, or to scholars of material culture through its description of objects. It may gain value if linked to other digital content through 'virtual reunification', where collections held in disparate archives around the world can be combined in digital facsimiles. Value is subjective, changes over time and has different meanings that are contingent on external factors. Value of digital collections, and digital humanities in general, is particularly difficult to assess as 'Digital Humanities is not a unified field but an array of convergent practices' in multimedia configurations; using digital tools, techniques and media have altered the production and dissemination of knowledge in the arts, human and social sciences, creating 'digital models of scholarly discourse for the newly emergent public spheres of the present era (the www, the blogosphere, digital libraries, etc.), to model excellence and innovation in these domains, and to facilitate the formation of networks of knowledge production, exchange, and dissemination that are, at once, global and local' (Schnapp and Presner, 2009).

This is, of course, a common issue across the arts and humanities: funded research often does not show its 'value' until it is broadly disseminated, shared, cited and becomes common across the disciplines. This can take time. It is the same with digital resources, and funders often fail to appreciate that the 'value' of digital collections and the scholarship they enable may take time to emerge. The chapters by Prescott, Hudson and Oliver are interesting in this regard as they take a longer view of the impact of digital collections and programmes on the institutions that host them.

Some of the factors that make digital collections 'valuable' to libraries, archives, museums and higher education were addressed in *Digitizing Collections: strategic issues for the information manager* (Hughes, 2004). These included:

- access, both broader access to a global audience via the internet, and enhanced access, by making aspects of collections searchable, findable and linked to related materials
- supporting preservation, by providing digital surrogates of rare and fragile materials
- collections development, by enabling organizations to develop cataloguing and records management around digital objects, and by enabling the 'virtual reunification' of collections that are physically separated
- institutional and strategic benefits, such as professional development of staff; the prestige and PR value to the institution; and enabling the institution to fulfil its goals of access and outreach

- supporting research and education across the disciplines.

The book also investigated the impact of digital collections on institutions, including:

- the need for new business models to support and develop digital collections, and how this was forcing institutions to consider the institutional costs and benefits of digital collections, grappling with the contradiction that there can be indirect cost savings from digital delivery of services, but that these are offset by the increased costs of digital access and preservation
- the resources and intellectual implications of changes to the way that information is used and managed
- the implications of supporting entirely new approaches to scholarship and access.

The book concluded that there was no definitive evidence base that could provide concrete numbers about the economic 'value' of digital collections, but there were some interesting debates around the topics at the time, for example, 'The Economics of Digitizing Library and Other Cultural Materials', which identified the 'costs' of digitization: institutional, technological and legal (Waters, 2004).

The structure and content of this volume

This volume has three parts. The first, 'Digital transformations in libraries, museums and archives', describes the use and impact of digital collections in libraries, museums and archives. Andrew Prescott, Claire Hudson and Gillian Oliver provide valuable examples that capture practice and experience in a variety of organizations, discussing ways that the digital revolution has transformed the mission and organization of services and collections. The second part, 'Understanding and measuring the use, impact and value of digital collections', presents different approaches to measuring and understanding value. Ben Showers describes some approaches developed through the JISC e-Content programme to measure impact and to embed digital collections more thoughtfully within user communities. Milena Dobreva, Andy O'Dwyer and Leo Konstantelos present a series of approaches to user testing that can inform the development of more valuable resources, and discuss how this can impact the development of business models. Claire Ross, Melissa Terras and Vera Motyckova discuss a survey of users of the British Museum Collections Online Database, and develop an analysis of the use of digital content by academic researchers. Simon Tanner concludes this section with an overview of the opportunities and impacts that digitized resources have made for learning, teaching, research and society.

The third part, 'Enhancing the future impact and value of digital collections', presents some approaches that can add value to digital collections: Lorna M. Hughes describes ways in which they can effect transformative research via the use of ICT tools and methods; Ann Borda and Lyle Winton discuss the ways in which e-infrastructures can enable collaborative scholarship and shared resources, considering how preservation and research infrastructures and strategies developed for the sciences can be applicable to other disciplines, and citing the exemplary work that has been funded in Australia in order to support this; and David Robey discusses sustainability and the long-term value of digital resources.

A concept with considerable impact is the 'holistic' approach to digitization, which sees the whole digital life cycle as significant and interdependent, rather than as a series of individual phases or stages. For illustrations of the concept, see, for example, the work of the Digital Curation Coalition in the UK (www.dcc.ac.uk), and the recent report by the Strategic Content Alliance, *Developing Digipedia: a guide to the digital content lifecycle* (JISC Strategic Content Alliance, 2010). Taking this approach at the outset of a digitization project should make the resource more 'valuable', as it will enable use and reuse to be embedded into the resource at each phase of development (Hughes, 2008). However, many digitization projects do not develop this approach. Therefore, at a practical level, this volume covers a number of useful and valuable things that the managers of digital collections can do at any stage of the digital life cycle in order to develop a better understanding of, and to increase, the use, value and impact of their resource. In terms of documenting resources, making their impact more visible and providing badly needed use cases (and guidelines for use, which are equally important) to demonstrate the transformative effect of digital collections, the five modes of value suggested by Tanner are an extremely useful taxonomy that could be useful for categorizing and documenting projects and their outputs. This model could well be adopted as a means of documenting 'impact' while projects are in progress, or applying to published digital collections retrospectively. Similarly, the 'impact framework' that Showers describes could well be adopted by project managers as an internal documentation exercise, or for dissemination. Showers also describes the implementation of the useful Toolkit for the Impact of Digitised Scholarly Resources (TIDSR) toolkit by projects funded by the JISC e-Content Impact and Embedding Programme. This is an easily adoptable methodology for using both qualitative and quantitative methods for assessing the use of a digital resource, which can produce useful findings. Similarly, the information manager might adopt the approach described in detail by Ross, Terras and Motyckova to understand user information-seeking behaviours, in order to get a deeper sense of usage patterns. Ross, Terras and Motyckova, and Showers describe approaches that can be applied at any time after a resource has been published, while Dobreva, O'Dwyer and Konstantelos describe in detail the value of applying usability and user engagement methods into the development of a digital resource. The importance of this cannot be underestimated, as usability is inconsistently factored into the project development cycle.

However, it is also possible to make resources more valuable and useful after they have been publicly available for some time. The JISC projects described by Showers are examples of ways in which projects can be enhanced by becoming more embedded in research, teaching and public engagement. Hughes describes some of the ways in which digital resources can underpin scholarly use through the application of ICT tools and methods. From a strategic perspective, Borda describes how data management and use can be supported through research infrastructures and in virtual research environments, to foster collaborative and individual use and reuse of existing collections. At the heart of all this work is of course the expectation that resources are open to allow use and reuse for unforeseen purposes. It also supposes that the resources will be available to all. The FEDORA (Flexible Extensible Digital Object and Repository Architecture) commons community (http://fedora-commons.org) now favours the term 'durability' to describe robust digital resources that are sustained and preserved over the long term for use by many communities and purposes – and this approach would indeed add 'value' to digital resources. Sustaining durable digital resources over the long term will add institutional overhead costs to digital collections. However, the visibility of digital collections means that they must be addressed, unlike the forotten 'unseen' costs to libraries of preserving and managing the monograph.

Conducting user assessments and studies, developing use cases and developing ways of embedding digital collections more effectively in teaching and research are, of course, activities that require the time and effort of staff, and therefore additional investment after a resource has been published. This is often a daunting prospect – digital projects are usually developed through short-term funding, with staff on short-term contracts. Therefore, after they are launched, they are seldom given any more than the most cursory technical attention. The projects described by Showers have attempted to redress this, by providing small amounts of JISC funding to 'revisit' projects to enhance usability or embedding, and this approach is an extremely useful one. Institutions may look to ways that they can themselves underwrite this sort of activity – possibly by using volunteers, interns or students[6] to work on the enhancement of digital collections. It is also the sort of activity that users themselves can contribute to – every project has a core community of users, and identifying who they are and working with them to enhance resources could be a valuable opportunity to create a 'virtuous circle' of collaboration, engagement and outreach, integrating people and collections.

At the heart of the volume is the theme of digitization as a process with many stages – a digital life cycle – during which issues related to use, value and impact can be factored in. Digital culture is far more complex and encompasses more realities than textual cultures. At an Expert Seminar at King's College London where preliminary ideas for the volume were discussed, Jean-Claude Guédon introduced this idea with the useful analogy that working with digital documents brings us back to the ways of working that were more familiar in a pre-print time, especially that of individual processing of documents, rather than mass printing. The production of medieval manuscripts is also a useful metaphor for the process of developing digital materials. In the world of manuscripts, communities took responsibility for maintaining texts carefully as a collective endeavour, as texts and the effort that had gone into their creation were easily lost. Texts were maintained due to the efforts of the community to sustain them. Churches had a role as supporters of these communities to preserve texts, and community involvement was essential for preservation: an early prototype of 'collective intelligence' before Wikipedia. 'Use' was key to sustainability of the resources – texts from antiquity were preserved as they were used as grammars, demonstrating how a community often adds value to material. To continue the analogy, digital collections need to be tended, *pace* the concept of digital collections as 'processes' rather than 'products'. Diffuse communities use collections in different ways – and memory organizations create these relationships between the objects and the public.

Conclusion: future strategic directions

There are some key strategic themes discussed in this volume that still need to be addressed. In order to more fully embed use, value and impact into the development of future digital collections, strategic input from funders is required, especially with regard to recommending that projects they fund take a more robust approach to evaluating and demonstrating the impact, value and use of digital collections. Implementing a form of 'peer review' for digital resources, as suggested here by Robey, could contribute to this agenda. Documenting and measuring value and impact should be built into project planning and funding: an impact assessment should be carried out while the project is in development, and then funding made available for a summative piece several years after the publication of the digital resources. The value, impact and use of collections take time to evolve and to be understood, and this needs to be reconciled in a world of responsive, short-term funding opportunities. Similarly, while the underlying technical infrastructure should support aggregation and use of content across collections and organizations, a human infrastructure is also needed enabling and supporting the use, citation and durability of digital collections. This sort of collaboration, through networks and partnerships, must be supported over the long term to develop and disseminate the evidence of the use and value and impact of digital collections.

Notes

1 Part of the Digital Futures series, edited by Marilyn Deegan and Simon Tanner.
2 See www.llgc.org.uk/index.php?id=4723.
3 See www.smartplanet.com/people/blog/pure-genius/smithsonian-secretary-plans-to-make-massive-collection-available-to-all/3126/.
4 See the website of the National Humanities Alliance for updates on these and other issues: www.nhalliance.org/.
5 An AHRC funded network (http://historicweather.cerch.kcl.ac.uk/) is investigating integration of historical archives for the analysis of weather records and data over time, working in partnership with the Met Office ACRE project, which is carrying out digitization and analysis of historic weather data, primarily from ships' logbooks (www.met-acre.org).
6 The JISC funded Shipping Archives and Integrated Logbooks of Ships (SAILS), a linked data project, was extremely successful in working with maritime history MA students to develop transcriptions of data for the project (http://sailsproject.cerch.kcl.ac.uk).

Part 1
Digital transformations in libraries, museums and archives

2
The digital library

Andrew Prescott

Introduction

This chapter takes the long view of the digital library, and reflects on the historical context of library developments, identifying some of the key ways in which digital transformations have enabled libraries around the world to educate, inform and delight their readers. These developments are then considered in a case study that highlights ways in which these changes have been implemented at the National Library of Wales, illustrating the ways in which these changes are impacting research in the arts and humanities.

A celebration of the library

The Argentinian bibliophile Alberto Manguel possesses a huge private library, which he has installed in a 15th-century barn at his home in the Loire Valley. In his book *The Library at Night* (2008), Manguel describes the magical atmosphere of his library at night-time, when pools of light over the library desks expunge the outside world, so that sounds become muffled and the very thoughts in the books seem clearer and louder. The comforting smells of the wooden shelves and the musky leather bindings permeate the library, and these smells seem to convey connections with ancient human knowledge and dreams. In this private world of public knowledge, connected through its books to countless other cultures and literatures, Manguel's mind roams through other great libraries, from the great building at Alexandria to the private collections of authors such as Dickens or Borges.

Manguel's book is a celebration of the library as a space for study, reflection, exploration, inspiration, privacy and sharing. Whether it is an ancient room lined with oak bookcases, a large and extravagant Edwardian municipal building, or a clean and functional modern block, the library is an evocative space where the mind can take wing, finding new connections and discerning new possibilities. It is a space that is at once private and public, where people of all social classes, intellectual accomplishments and enthusiasms can discover new thoughts and intellectual vistas. The library is one of the most potent of all spaces created by humanity, eliciting deeply personal reactions from all those who encounter it, from members of the public to wizened researchers. The architect of the British Library at St Pancras, Colin St John Wilson, expressed this library fever very well when he declared that 'To every scholar the library is a realm of secret topography' (Losh, 2004, 378). For Wilson, a library was the modern equivalent of a medieval cathedral, whose sacral potency was enhanced rather than detracted by modern technological developments. He declared that 'A great library is like a coral reef whose exquisite structure as it grows proliferates a living network of connectedness, and its ramification is all of a piece, like knowledge itself – the knowledge that bridges the endless curiosity of the human mind, from the first pictogram to the latest microchip' (McCarthy, 2008).

The changing library

Libraries are an aspect of the ecosystem of humanities scholarship where the impact of digital and networking technologies has already been profound, and if there is one area in which the working practices of humanities scholars have been utterly transformed as a result of new technologies, it is the use of the library. Humanities academics who are, like me, in their late fifties have witnessed an astonishing transformation of the library space. At the heart of the traditional library space with which I grew up was the physical catalogue – as can be seen from the way in which the huge General Catalogue of the British Museum stood in a great arc at the centre of the Round Reading Room, like the cortex of a huge brain. The catalogues of large British libraries like the British Museum were published, but for many smaller academic libraries an up-to-date catalogue was only available on-site and the availability of particular items could only be established by a personal visit, which in the case of libraries at a distance might first necessitate lengthy correspondence. From the 1970s, the gradual conversion of catalogues into machine-readable form, then their availability online, increasingly through aggregated resources such as COPAC (the online public access catalogue of CURL, the Consortium of University Research Libraries) for British research libraries, or the international WorldCat developed by the OCLC (Online Computer Library Center) library consortium, transformed the logistics of tracing and consulting the rare books, manuscripts and archives with which many humanities scholars work. The libraries I used as a young scholar were dominated by serried dusty ranks of printed journals, and a journal search was a lengthy and physically arduous prerequisite of any new research project. Today, I rarely consult a printed journal, since articles are so much more readily and conveniently made available through a variety of repositories ranging from multi-publisher archives such as JSTOR and Project Muse, gateways developed by journal suppliers such as SwetsWise and the packages offered by the journal publishers themselves. Above all, as a historian I now have direct access to images and editions of primary sources online. If I wanted as a young man to consult newspapers, it usually necessitated a journey to the out-of-the-way suburban idyll of the British Library Newspaper Reading Room at Colindale. Nowadays, I can sit late at night, hunched at my laptop in a pool of light as evocative as that of Manguel's library in the French countryside, ranging through newspapers covering every conceivable quirk and foible of British society in the 18th century.

Of course, it is not just access to British materials that have been transformed. One of the reasons that I became a British historian was because of the balance of library provision when I was a young man; the barriers for a scholar researching European history in the London of the 1970s were considerable. These restrictions have been greatly eased. If I tire of British periodicals, I can turn to the French titles made available by the Bibliothèque Nationale de France through Gallica or cross the Atlantic to trace the footsteps of Wyatt Earp in the *Tombstone Epitaph* available through the Library of Congress. The Victorian founders of the modern British Library such as Anthony Panizzi and his lieutenant Thomas Watts dreamed of creating a great imperial library in London in which the best collection of English books in the world would be allied to the best collections of Russian books outside Russia, the best collection of German books outside Germany, and so on (Hill, 1953, 38). In building the circular British Museum Reading Room, surrounded by state-of-the-art industrial iron bookshelves designed to accommodate such a huge library and make it speedily available, Panizzi and Watts created a potent cultural symbol of Victorian Britain. This was predicated on the idea that at the heart of the largest city in the world should be a library that gathered together the world's culture. This collection instinct – the idea that the function of a library was to pull in material from as far afield as possible – was fundamental to the traditional library. Although in the pre-network age there were some remarkable experiments in making more widely available the information stored in large national libraries, such as the book box scheme by which the National Library of Wales provided duplicate items to adult education classes in the 1930s (Baggs, 1997), these pale by comparison with the transformation wrought by the availability of digital and network technologies since 1980. Although librarians have always been fascinated by ways in which technology can reduce costs and streamline services, with Victorian librarians experimenting with early forms of duplication in cataloguing and the use of pneumatic tubes for transmission of book and other requests, the engagement of librarians and libraries with technology is nowadays more profound than ever.

'The Battle of the Books'

The transformations are evident to anyone who haunts libraries, but, while the movement of the tectonic plates of scholarship is clearly evident, it is much more difficult to characterize and quantify the nature and impact of these changes. How can the impact of the digital transformations in the library be succinctly encapsulated? Do the new resources give the arts and humanities scholar unparalleled access to primary materials or does the deluge of data risk undermining the traditional relationship of arts and humanities research with books, archives and manuscripts? In 1993, at a time when many humanities scholars were still unfamiliar with the internet, Robin Alston gave a remarkable inaugural lecture as Director of the School of Library Archive and Information Studies at University College London entitled, after Swift's satire on the 18th-century controversies about ancient and modern forms of learning, 'The Battle of the Books' (Alston, 1993). As Director of the Eighteenth-Century Short Title Catalogue project in the British Library from 1977, Alston, by supervising the creation of a machine-readable catalogue of printing in English-speaking countries to 1800, laid the foundations for many of the online resources that are today most familiar to humanities scholars, such as Early English Books Online and Eighteenth-Century Collections Online. Nevertheless, Alston is far from an uncritical technophile, and in his inaugural lecture issued a warning against those who declared that:

> the library has become less a nursery of knowledge than a play-room in which those with antiquarian obsessions indulge their fantasies and must be transformed into electronic warehouses invisibly connected to all other warehouses; that there can be no real progress until every scrap of paper has been digitized and rendered tractable to electronic manipulation and distribution via the telecommunication networks being built in space.
>
> (Alston, 1993)

Such an approach, Alston declared, 'may be a fine prospect for faculties of engineering, and the makers of electronic devices on which the librarian is increasingly dependent, but it might have serious consequences for a balanced view of who we are, where we came from, and where we are going'. Alston stressed that 'the reduction of analogue information to digital form, and the transformations which are then possible, is without doubt a process as fascinating as anything in the history of technology', but felt that the view that libraries and archives simply comprise 'so much information', ignoring the complex bibliographical and physical character of the historical materials in research library collections, posed immense intellectual and cultural dangers. For Alston, these concerns related not simply to obvious logistical issues such as cost, preservation and copyright, but also to the way in which fundamental questions about the value of digitization had not been fully discussed:

> Of course it is possible to digitize and index the contents of all the world's important libraries and archives. In the 1930s Eugene Power demonstrated that it was possible to persuade libraries that what they needed was microfilm and created that juggernaut of unselective micropublishing University Microfilms. The question we must answer is, who could benefit from such a colossal enterprise? Commerce or knowledge? Are libraries in the control of visionaries or are they in the control of irresistible economic forces which we ignore at our peril?
>
> (Alston, 1993)

The real danger, as Alston saw it, was to the books themselves, and to the engagement with the physical culture of the book that is at the heart of much scholarly thinking in the humanities. To avoid these perils, Alton foresaw the need for:

> enlightened and imaginative librarians able to develop within a hostile political environment a model which can adapt to the evolving needs of research in all disciplines. Those needs will, within a decade, include access to information in a wide variety of databases, electronic archives of images and sounds, as well as the cultural inheritance in print and manuscript, most of which will, I am certain, remain in its present form for the foreseeable future. One

consequence of this is the self-evident need for librarians in the future to develop both ancient and modern skills. The notion that knowledge can prosper by creating vast knowledge warehouses based on the hypermarket model – you can buy it if you can find it – is sheer fantasy as well as being intellectually suspect. (Alston, 1993)

Mass digitization initiatives

Alston's 1993 warning against the hypermarket model seems particularly prescient today in the light of the subsequent development of Google Books and other cloud-based repositories such as the HathiTrust (Malpas, 2011). Alston's lecture is an impassioned plea for a strategic approach to digitization, informed by awareness of the structure, history and physical characteristics of the collections being digitized. In his concern about the risks posed by commercial interests to the public character of the cultural heritage of libraries, books and archives, Alston was anticipating by many years the recent articles by Robert Darnton, the President of Harvard University Libraries, drawing attention to the dangers posed by the development of Google Books. Like Alston, Darnton's concern is not simply that 'Google will enjoy what can only be called a monopoly – a monopoly of a new kind, not of railroads or steel but of access to information' (Darnton, 2009a) but also that the Google project is dominated by technical experts with little involvement of librarians or bibliographers, who would have avoided the 'missing pages, botched images, faulty editions, omitted artwork, censoring, and misconceived cataloging that mar Google's enterprise' (Darnton, 2009b). The recent call by Darnton (2010a, 2010b) for the creation of a Digital Public Library of America looks very much like a belated attempt to shut a stable door behind a horse whose escape was noted 17 years ago by Robin Alston. It is striking how many of the anxieties described by Robin Alston in his inaugural lecture remain current. In particular, the question most forcefully posed by Alston, of the need to consider the purpose and value of digitization before embarking on large-scale investment and the creation of digital libraries, remains inescapable, and is still rarely addressed. Alston's comment that 'A close examination of the products currently available in electronic form might well suggest to an unprejudiced mind that we have a wonderful solution in search of problems' (1993) sadly perhaps still holds true today. In 1993, Alston was unable to discern any immediately tangible benefits in digitization work in libraries.

Revisiting the 'Battle of the Books' after nearly 20 years, which have seen major funding programmes, the development of new technical facilities and the appearance of new services such as Google, it is surprising how we far still lack tools or analytical approaches that can effectively measure or model the impact of digital resources on arts and humanities research. While statistics collected by libraries document major changes in provision since 1993, they give little sense of the extent to which these developments have reshaped or enhanced humanities scholarship or developed new audiences. The most striking shift in the nature of library provision since 1993 is that the bulk of the acquisition budgets of university libraries in the UK are today used for the purchase of access to electronic resources. In 2007–8, over 40% of expenditure on information service provision in British universities was on electronic resources (if journals purchased in both print and electronic forms are included in the figure) (British Library, 2010, 9), and for the research-intensive Russell Group universities, the proportion was considerably higher. Notoriously, of course, the nature of the expensive and complex licences for online journal bundles means that commercial publishers have in effect hijacked large parts of university library budgets (so that recently the University of California threatened to cancel its subscription to *Nature* and to boycott peer reviewing activities for the journal) (Howard, 2011). Nevertheless, it is clear that there has been a major and radical shift in provision.

Given the nature of the large bundled journal subscriptions, it is difficult to disentangle the extent to which this pattern of expenditure reflects shifts in provision for the humanities, but changes in user behaviour are more easily documented. A survey in 2006 by Stephen Brown and Mark Greengrass (2010, 13) found that over 60% of a sample of arts and humanities researchers regarded digital resources as essential to their research, with 89% using the web on a daily basis. Focus groups conducted by Brown and Greengrass found that researchers considered that the greater speed with which material could be located and accessed had transformed the way in which they conducted research. Researchers felt that, as a result of these developments, new scholarship and ideas were circulating more quickly in the humanities, although they were vague as to the type of innovative thinking generated by these more active dialogues. Unfortunately, studies such as those by Brown and Greengrass or by Claire Warwick et al. (2006) are concerned with general patterns of humanities use of online resources, and do not tend to distinguish between specialist digital humanities resources and the more generic packages procured through libraries such as Early English Books Online, but there are indications in the study by Brown and Greengrass that these generic packages are the most important to library users. The British Library's Online Public Access Catalogue was first made available online in 1997. By 1999, it was receiving more than five million hits a year. In 2009–10, the overall British Library website received more than 74 million hits. This represents a major widening of access to the library: in 2010 there were over 500,000 on-site visits to the British Library, a tiny amount compared with the huge figures for online access. In 1979, the British Library Lending Division received over two million requests a year, about 80% of which were satisfied, usually by manual means. In 2009–10, over ten million items were supplied to users by the British Library, the vast majority of these online (British Library, 1979–2010).

While figures like these illustrate the transformation that has occurred in library use and provision over a short time, they do little more than indicate that the infrastructure of humanities scholarship has changed. The usage statistics compiled by libraries tend to cover all disciplines, and it is difficult to disaggregate figures for humanities users from them. Moreover, the patterns of change are complex, and it is difficult to reach straightforward conclusions about the impact on humanities scholarship. For example, the digitized version of the *Codex Sinaiticus* was made available by the British Library in July 2009, and received over one and a half million hits during the following few months

(British Library, 1979–2010). Some of these hits were doubtless from biblical scholars but the vast majority were apparently from curious members of the public. While the digitization of the *Codex Sinaiticus* has demonstrably enhanced public engagement with the original manuscript, it is more difficult to quantify its impact on scholarship in the field. Moreover, simply to focus on statistics for the production of digital images as a measure of the impact of digitization is misleading, since the process of digitization covers a variety of activities within the library, and these different activities have had varied purposes, audiences and impacts. Digitization has not been restricted to rare books and manuscripts. JSTOR is the digitization of a large back catalogue of periodicals. Likewise, the conversion of printed and card catalogues to a machine readable form is also a form of digitization (indeed, in the British Library, the first attempt to convert the printed British Museum catalogue involved the early use of a form of optical character recognition (OCR)). It is striking that humanities scholars seem to take the availability of automated catalogues and searchable back runs of periodicals for granted, and it could be argued that to date these represent the major impact of digitization on the engagement of humanities scholars with libraries.

The impact of digital transformations in the library

In seeking to find a framework to analyse and explore the nature and character of these changes, it is perhaps worth returning to the idea at the heart of Manguel's reflections in his *Library at Night*, namely the library as space and the way in which technology changes this space. The digitization of catalogues is a powerful reminder of how changes in libraries reflect changes in configuration in space. To digitize a catalogue and make it internationally available fundamentally alters the relationship of a library to the outside world. The catalogue, instead of being a map of the enclosed restricted space of the individual library, becomes instead a means by which this space is linked to the outside world, and, through such links to other libraries, the isolated library suddenly becomes part of a network. This important theme was explored by Lorcan Dempsey (1999) in a reflection on digital information spaces, which although it was published more than ten years ago is still worth re-reading. Dempsey emphasized how the traditional library was place-based, comprising the management of multiple individual physical repositories (the strict division of the historic British Library into departments based on particular media exemplifies this). By contrast, suggested Dempsey (1999, 54):

> In digital information spaces, there will continue to be repositories of information but the emphasis shifts to the flows between them and between them and their users. These repositories may contain metadata – catalogues and other data which assists in the discovery, use and exploitation of resources – or resources themselves. In this environment, the activities of discovery, locate, request, and deliver, currently carried out in multiple incompatible circuits need to be brought into a common framework of communicating applications.

The implications of this spatial readjustment of the library described by Dempsey are still barely worked through, particularly in research and university libraries. As well as different flows of information, the patterns in which information is held have also fundamentally shifted. The traditional library was primarily concerned with pulling in the widest range of information possible, and this is still an important feature in a digital environment. However, increasingly libraries are concerned with the curation of local information and pushing that information out to the network. This is a relatively new role, and one whose implications for scholarly work practices are still not yet wholly evident. One expression of this new concern is the institutional repository, whose origins lay in an attempt to undermine the monopolies of publishing houses on the dissemination of research produced in universities, but which is being increasingly used by universities as a means of managing and curating information about the research output of the university. For university libraries – and indeed universities – to take a direct role in managing and making available the research produced in the university has radical implications for scholarly practice that have only just begun to be explored. Two influential American scholars and commentators on libraries, Robert Darnton (2010b) and Jerome McGann (2010), have recently emphasized the profound impact on the academic career structures of the collapse in sales of academic monographs by American university presses, causing publishers to withdraw completely from certain subject areas. Possibly the increasing availability of doctoral theses through institutional repositories may make the production of such monographs redundant. Perhaps repositories may ultimately become the means by which niche academic writing is eventually disseminated (MacMahon, 2009). It is difficult to say at present, but certainly the humble institutional repository, by involving universities directly in the curation and dissemination of the research work of members of the university, has the potential completely to reconfigure the spaces of scholarly production and communication.

In concluding his 1999 article, Dempsey pointed out the paradox that, at the time the British Library was undertaking its first experimental programme of digital and network activities, it was also constructing at St Pancras 'one of the most significant library "places" the world will have seen, a building in which the main objective is to create "an easy commerce between the lone scholar and the huge building mass required to house the collections, all the fellow (rival?) researchers and the general public"' (Dempsey, 1999, 58). Dempsey noted the need for the new British Library building 'to organise a social and learning space within the emerging global space of flows'. The success of the British Library building says much about the continuing demand for a physical space for work, reflection and investigation within the global space of flows, and the way in which the restaurants and cafés of the British Library have accommodated what St John Wilson called 'the wandering scholars of the laptop' suggest that the British Library building, designed long before the internet, is impressively adaptable to these new flows.

The transformation of library space

The growth of network services has led to a reconfiguration of physical space in the library, not its disappearance. While online services have grown apace in recent years, library building has also boomed. Partly this reflects the fact that the production of printed books has continued unabated: Robert Darnton (2010b) calculates that there will soon be a million new titles published worldwide each year, adding that 'I have been invited to so many conferences on the "Death of the Book" that I suspect it is very much alive'. Likewise, far from becoming more marginal places, university libraries have been under pressure to increase their opening hours, with many British university libraries now staying open into the small hours or even, in a few cases, 24 hours. Although principally a library designed mainly to serve scientists who make increasingly less use of printed resources, nevertheless demand by Imperial's students for a flexible study space led to an 11 million pound refurbishment of Imperial College's Central Library, which opened in 2008, and has proved immensely popular with students. Imperial College is not alone in its investment in new library buildings. The past few years has seen the opening of new university library buildings in Leicester, Sheffield, Coventry, Glasgow Caledonian University and elsewhere, while major new developments are currently under way in, for example, Aberdeen and Manchester (Designing Libraries, 2011). However, many of these library buildings are radically different from those that were constructed during the period of university expansion in the 1960s. Features of these developments include the integration of many different types of information, with online provision being given particular prominence. These libraries are just as much social hubs, for meeting, talking, sharing information, as they are places of study. The coffee bars are as important as the quiet study rooms – the buildings are highly zoned. Correspondingly, many of these new forms of library also provide access to other university services, particularly student services. Above all, librarians are less evident as gatekeepers. This partly reflects the use of self-service technologies, but also the reconfiguration of support services, which have been placed in help desks or reconfigured as roving assistants.

Some of these developments, such as the new emphasis on group work, are driven more by pedagogical than technical considerations. However, it is clear that a major force in shaping these new libraries and learning spaces was the demand for online access in a variety of forms alongside more conventional library resources. The corporate university information services (whether converged or not) play as important part as the library in designing these new facilities. As Diana Oblinger has observed in a recent publication by Educause on new learning spaces:

> Information technology has changed what we do and how we do it. It would be hard to identify a discipline in which IT is not a necessity. Collecting, analyzing, displaying, and disseminating knowledge typically involves IT. Retrieving information has become an IT function; students consider the Internet, not the library, their information universe. And, rather than trying to know everything, students and faculty rely on networks of peers and databases of information. What impact, if any, should this have on learning space design? Technology has also brought unique capabilities to learning. Whether by stimulating more interaction through the use of personal response systems or by videoconferencing with international experts, IT has altered learning spaces. (2006, 1.2)

It might be asked how far this new breed of library building is an attempt to save the concept of a library fatally wounded by the delivery of information services to student homes and staff desks, but the demand for designated learning spaces of this sort is strong and evident: in the case of Sheffield, Martin Lewis (2010, 176) has noted that 'The biggest challenge faced by the I[nformation] C[ommons] is that of its own success … Maximum occupancy is regularly achieved and the most common complaint from students is inability to find a seat, despite the delivery of a substantial net gain in overall study space capacity on the campus'.

Such new learning spaces have a varying relationship to the library. In some cases, such as the Learning Grid at Warwick University, the new learning space supplements the central library; in others, most notably the Saltire Centre at Glasgow University, the library has been transformed into a social hub for the entire campus. In many other cases, existing buildings have been remodelled and reshaped. A good example of the refurbishment of older library buildings to meet new needs is the Library and Information Centre at the University of Swansea. The main reading areas of an older building have been refurbished to provide access to banks of computers adjacent to a coffee shop and with various student service points close by. The immediate impression on entering the Swansea Library and Information Centre is of noise, interaction and social exchange. Research libraries have begun cautiously to import some of this thinking: the recent refurbishment of the North Reading Room of the National Library of Wales has introduced into a formal reference reading room from the 1930s group study areas, informal seating, extended provision of personal computers (PCs) and wireless access. These new library spaces are the most striking expression of the impact of digital technologies in the library. However, by focusing on these spaces, there is a danger of falling prey to older perspectives of the library, and to think of individual libraries as autonomous and disconnected spaces. It is in the flows of information between libraries and the way in which new connections are developed between them that the transformations in libraries are more evident. This requires a study of libraries based on national and international links. For larger countries such as France or the USA, this would necessitate a major study, but the transformational effects of digital technologies can be more readily discerned in small countries. The way in which, for example, the national libraries of Finland and Sweden enthusiastically pioneered the use of digital technologies in the 1980s and 1990s shows how digital and networking technologies can provide business, educational and cultural benefits in countries where a small population is dispersed and the physical geography makes face-to-face communication difficult. In Great Britain, this 'small country' model can be seen at work in the development of library provision in Scotland and Wales.

Case study: Library initiatives in Wales
Introduction and background
In order to get a sharper idea of the extent to which changes in libraries are reshaping research in the arts and humanities, Wales provides a very interesting case study.

Formidable barriers of physical geography and the resulting difficulties in communication have been major issues in the development of Wales since the middle ages, and the persistence of the Welsh language despite the intense competition from English is partly a reflection of the physical isolation of parts of Wales. Even today, travel between north and south Wales is very difficult, and improving links between the different parts of Wales in order to create a greater sense of shared nationhood has been a priority of the Welsh Government since its establishment (as the Welsh Assembly Government) in 1999. The communication difficulties in Wales have encouraged the development of decentralized and federal institutions. The University of Wales is perhaps the best known example of a federal national institution in Wales, while the Welsh Government has been at pains since its creation to ensure the establishment of an extended network of regional offices. While Cardiff became the home to such Welsh national institutions as the National Museum of Wales and the Registry of the University of Wales during the period before the First World War, it was not designated as the capital of Wales until 1955, and even then other towns such as Caernarfon vied for the honour. The pattern of cultural and administrative provision in Wales remains very dispersed. The National Library of Wales for example was established in the small western coastal town of Aberystwyth at the insistence of its major benefactor, Sir John Williams, who was anxious to see the library placed in a Welsh-speaking area. The National Library is thus located in an area that, as the present National Librarian of Wales Andrew Green (2007a) has commented, is 'well populated with animals but less well endowed with humans. There are about 4.5m sheep in our hinterland, compared with only 180,000 people, and to make matters worse not all of the sheep are yet fully literate. We're seventy miles from any major town or city.'

Collaborative frameworks in Wales

The need to transcend these physical barriers meant that the National Library and other Welsh institutions took an early interest in digitization. While this is readily understandable, what is striking about the Welsh experience is the extent to which it was underpinned by a strong collaborative framework. Much of this has been directly driven by the Welsh Government, which has since its creation consistently emphasized the need for reconfiguration and collaboration in Welsh public institutions. This led, for example, to the creation in 2004 of CyMAL as a policy division of the Welsh Government to foster collaboration between libraries, museums and archives (Atkinson and Kensler, 2004, 51–2). Among the development activities taken forward by CyMAL has been the creation of an integrated portal for Welsh libraries (http://library.wales.org) featuring CatCymru, which allows the cross-searching of all publicly accessible library catalogues in Wales. CyMAL has also facilitated the provision to all library members of online resources such as Newsbank. Another major focus of cooperation has been the Welsh Higher Education Libraries Forum (WHELF), comprising the librarians of higher education institutions in Wales together with the National Library (Atkinson and Kensler, 2004; www.whelf.ac.uk). These collaborative activities have been actively facilitated and promoted by the National Library, and the active role of the National Library perhaps helps explain why patterns of library provision in Wales are less fragmented than in some other areas of the UK. The extent and effectiveness of collaboration among the Welsh libraries is very striking and suggests that strategically directed partnerships can be very important in developing successful digitization projects that achieve major impact.

One focus of Welsh collaborative activity has been joint procurement of commercially produced digital resources. The most striking digital divide at present is between members of universities, who have access to commercial journal bundles and such packages as Early English Books Online or British Library Newspapers, and the general public for whom the cost of access to such resources is prohibitively expensive. For most university-based researchers in the UK, the effectiveness of the agreements negotiated by the JISC for discounted access to commercially produced journal bundles and databases means that there is little recognition of the high cost of these resources. In the USA, there is no such national procurement, so that many smaller colleges find the cost of online journal packages prohibitive, leading to a digital divide between small colleges where the provision of electronic resources is patchy and larger universities, which have invested heavily. Although UK university researchers benefit from the national agreements brokered by JISC, the general public are still frequently excluded from access to the main online resources on which researchers rely. Like the National Library of Scotland, the National Library of Wales makes available to all its registered readers who have a Welsh postcode a portfolio of electronic resources including many of those most familiar to humanities researchers in universities. Although any member of the Welsh public can become a registered reader, Andrew Green (2007b) has expressed his ambition to 'increase the size of this digital collection, and to extend its reach far beyond registered readers'. For Green, the establishment of such a service 'will mean a radical rethink of what it means to be a Library member . . . the result being a truly national online knowledge service available freely to every Welsh citizen'. Green points out the parallels between this vision and the model adopted by the National and University Library in Iceland, which provides free access to over 8000 full-text journals and databases for all Icelandic citizens. The creation of these 'small country' online national libraries may also be seen as prefiguring the recent discussion initiated by Robert Darnton (2010b) for the creation of a Digital Public Library of America. The recent Research Information Network (2011) report on e-journals has documented the various ways in which these have transformed scholarly practice, yet this revolution remains in many ways effectively confined to university researchers, and this knowledge is perhaps less widely accessible to other parts of society than it was in the print era. The initiatives adopted in Wales and other small countries to open up access to these online resources are a vital part of the way in which libraries are renegotiating their role as knowledge brokers in the online world.

These activities of the National Library of Wales have been complemented and extended in the higher education sphere by various initiatives of WHELF. Particularly notable was the creation of a shared Welsh university collection of e-books, which was launched in the autumn of 2007 with over 500 e-books on OCLC's Netlibrary (Atkinson and Riley, 2009). The experience gathered through this shared e-book project will be important in negotiating future access to new forms of e-books as these become more widely available. The value of a collaborative approach in ensuring a strategic approach to new services is also apparent in WHELF's Welsh Repository Network project, which created an integrated network of repositories in all Welsh universities, enabling many advantages such as the development of a cross-searching facility and the development of a service for storing and harvesting electronic theses produced in Wales, which it is hoped will increase the visibility and usage of Welsh theses and give Wales a research advantage (Knowles, 2010). A more recent WHELF initiative has emulated the pioneering work of its Scottish opposite number, SCURL (Scottish Confederation of University and Reserarch Libraries), in securing joint licences to e-journals to create a Scottish Higher Education Digital Library.

The digitization of Welsh cultural heritage

While on the one hand both WHELF and the National Library have collaborated in realigning audiences for digital resources through innovative procurement activities, perhaps more pertinent for the themes of this volume is the role of both WHELF and the National Library in digitizing historical collections in Welsh libraries. While the physical location of the National Library was certainly one incentive for its early interest in digitization, another was the very wide range of media held by the National Library. As well as books, manuscripts and maps, the National Library also houses the *de facto* national archive of Wales, its national photographic collection, its screen and sound archive, and its second largest art collection. Indeed, it was the presence of the screen and sound archive that provided the initial impetus for the National Library of Wales to experiment with digitization, with a project to create stills from films for the Welsh language television channel S4C (Green, 2007a). The Library took an early decision to use mainstream National Assembly funding to support its digitization programmes; Andrew Green points out that this contrasts with the British Library, which has never used core funding for digitization but relies on external funding and outsources major digitization operations. Green (2007a) adds, 'We wanted to develop a body of internal practice in the art and science of digitisation: not just data capture, but the entire workflow, from selection to presentation. We built up small teams of scanners and metadata experts, and added others to contribute in other areas, such as preservation and online presentation.' Because of this stress on integrated management of digitization process, including metadata, the Library pioneered in the UK the Metadata Encoding and Transmission Standard (METS) schema developed by the Library of Congress.

Much of the National Library's early work in this sphere comprised a series of projects designed to promote awareness of the Welsh cultural heritage, which were administered through Culturenet Cymru, a limited company owned by the Library and dedicated to promoting online culture in Wales. Among the largest projects undertaken by Culturenet Cymru was Casglu'r Tlysau/Gathering the Jewels (www.gtj.org.uk), a People's Network project containing over 30,000 images from over 140 libraries, museums and archives around Wales. The involvement of the three domains of libraries, museums and archives mean that the subjective experience of using Casglu'r Tlysau is immediately very different from that of a conventional library. The materials made available via Casglu'r Tlysau range from a Welsh woman's hat of the 19th century, stuffed animals from West Wales and aerial photographs of hill forts to the first known recording of the Welsh national anthem and manuscripts by Iolo Morganwg that recorded his invented Druidic histories. Such a description might make Casglu'r Tlysau sound like a digital equivalent of a rambling antiquarian museum, but the effect is far more integrated and powerful and it is not an exaggeration to describe it as a reinvention of Welsh national culture on the web. While there can be no question about the popular impact of Casglu'r Tlysau, there is far less evidence of its impact on scholarly and research activities. Casglu'r Tlysau makes available full facsimiles of some manuscripts but, like its Scottish counterpart, SCRAN (Scottish Cultural Resources Access Network), its focus is on supporting learning and in increasing general awareness of the resources of Welsh museums, libraries and archives.

This community emphasis of the National Libraries digitization programme was taken a stage further by another Culturenet Cymru project, Your Past Their Future (www.tpyf-wales.com). This project was linked to a touring exhibition commemorating memories of the Second World War, and recorded the recollections of Welsh people about the war. Items from their personal collections, such as photographs, ration books and letters from the front, were digitized and added to the website to form a virtual archive of the Welsh experience of the war. Again, like Casglu'r Tlysau, the main function of this activity is in the area of community engagement, and its direct value in arts and humanities research appears comparatively limited. Projects such as Your Past Their Future and Casglu'r Tlysau also have a major function, in a devolved administration, of assisting in nation building. This aspect is even more strongly apparent in Casgliad y Werin Cymru/People's Collection Wales, which was launched in August 2010 as a result of a specific commitment in 'One Wales', the agreement governing the coalition of the Labour Party and Plaid Cymru in the Welsh Assembly Government at the time. Casgliad y Werin Cymru offers seamless access to digital images from the National Library of Wales, the National Museum of Wales, the Royal Commission on the Ancient and Historical Monuments of Wales as well as to Casglu'r Tlysau. Cross-searching of this type between museum, library and other collections can potentially be very beneficial for research purposes, but the structure of Casgliad y Werin Cymru is much more geared to popular access and engagement. Members of the public can add their own images, create exhibitions that they can share online, create their own family stories, and map out walks and tours. Notwithstanding the strongly popular emphasis of the site, usage appears to be comparatively limited: a visit to the site in March 2011, 18 months after the launch of the site, showed that it had attracted only 1249 contributors.

A holistic approach: management of the digital life cycle

While these figures may seem to suggest that the impact of Casgliad y Werin Cymru has so far been comparatively limited, it is important to note that it forms part of an integrated approach to digitization by the National Library of Wales. Such holistic management of digitization and the storage of digital data is important in achieving the maximum use and impact from digital resources. The wide range of media within the National Library posed pressing issues with the management of digital data from an early stage in the library's digitization programme. The National Library had to address not only the storage of images of historic books and manuscripts but also the management of large quantities of digital recordings of Welsh-language television programmes and increasingly the deposit of born-digital information. Such born-digital acquisitions can be very large; on the closure of a Cardiff media company in 2006, the Library acquired a shared drive containing the records of the company, which contained 26.2 gigabytes (Gb) of data (Robson, 2010). It is also usually necessary to transfer such born-digital data from physical carriers that may already be faulty by the time they reach the Library; in a deposit of compact discs (CDs) by Cliff McLucas and Brith Gof Theatre Company, 20% of the CDs from McLucas and 60% of the CDs from Brith Gof could not be read on arrival in the Library (Robson, 2010). In order to manage the ingest, metadata, storage and access of this wide range of materials, the National Library implemented a digital asset management system (DAMS) using the Vital institutional repository system (www.vtls.com/products/vital), which is based on the open source FEDORA (Flexible Extensible Digital Object Repository Architecture) software (Bevan and Robson, 2008).

The quantity and variety of material already handled by the National Library's DAMS is extremely impressive. By February 2009, the DAMS was holding for example over 800,000 images of 186,000 wills dating from between 1543 and 1858, amounting to some 2.5 terabytes (Tb) (Robson, 2009). At the same time, over 1000 television programmes were being automatically recorded and ingested into the system. From the point of view of the researcher, the value of the DAMS lies in the way in which it integrates digital objects with the library's conventional collections. Geoff Charles (1909–2002) was a newspaper photographer who over 50 years produced a vivid and distinctive portrait of Welsh life, and his archive of 120,000 photographs is now one of the National Library's treasures. In the late 1990s, it was noticed that some of the cellulose acetate negatives in Charles' archive were suffering from 'vinegar syndrome', and a programme to digitize the affected negatives was established so that the original negatives could be frozen to stabilize their condition. Over 14,000 images from the Geoff Charles archive were digitized, producing 2294 images and over 16,000 FEDORA objects (Bevan and Robson, 2008). The fact that these objects are held within the DAMS means that they can be made available in a variety of ways: the Charles archive is one of the prominent components of Casgliad y Werin Cymru; it features in the 'digital mirror' section of the Library's website; it supports the National Library's contribution to the Flickr Commons site, which allows users to comment on and tag photographs from major museums, libraries and archives (www.flickr.com/photos/llgc); and a search on the Library's catalogue of terms such as Wrexham will also produce images by Charles, integrated into the catalogue record. The use of a DAMS to manage the Geoff Charles images is a small but important example of how the impact of digitization activities can be maximized. By holding the images in a digital repository, they can be made available in a variety of contexts, meaning that they can be used to address the needs of different audiences.

Public engagement and access with the Geoff Charles archive can be promoted through sites such as Casgliad y Werin Cymru, while at the same time researchers may use the archive in a more structured fashion through the Library's catalogue.

Among the key lessons that Glen Robson, the manager of the DAMS at the National Library, has drawn from experience thus far is that digitization should be organized around 'workflows not projects' (Robson, 2010). The benefits of integrating the digitization of a particular archive into a wider workflow are already apparent in the case of the Geoff Charles archive. Treating digitization activities as a series of discrete projects requires customization in respect of such elements as metadata or web presentation for each project. A focus on workflows means that much the same approach can be used for handling the digitization of wills as was used for the Geoff Charles archive, potentially reducing costs and increasing impact. However, researchers in some disciplines may feel uneasy about the stress on generic workflows. While librarians tend to be doubtful about the value of 'boutique digitization', arts and humanities researchers are often much more interested in comprehensive and scholarly editions of particular manuscripts and books. Another of the early fruits of the National Library's digital work was the creation of a 'digital mirror' comprising high quality digital facsimiles of some of the treasures of the library, such as an illustrated 13th-century copy of *Laws of Hywel Dda*, the first book printed in Welsh from 1546, and Dylan Thomas's map of Llareggub. Unlike the British Library, the National Library has consistently made complete facsimiles of the treasures available, so that the digital mirror in effect forms a small online manuscript library. Hitherto, the 'digital mirror' has been presented as a separate section of the National Library's website. An advantage of the DAMS is that the material in the 'digital mirror' will be presented in a different format in future and more closely integrated with other digital collections.

Manuscript digitization

Among the material presented on the 'digital mirror' are images of manuscripts of poems attributed to the celebrated 14th-century Welsh poet Dafydd ap Gwilym. These images were supplied for an interdisciplinary project at Swansea University directed by Professor Dafydd Johnston, which produced a comprehensive online edition of the poems of Dafydd ap Gwilym and was launched in 2007 (www.dafyddapgwilym.net). By presenting the manuscript evidence for these celebrated Welsh poems online, Dafydd Johnston and his team were able to show how readings for many well known lines were questionable. The online edition of Dafydd ap Gwilym is, from a scholarly point of view, an exemplar of how an online edition can deliver concrete research results. However, there can be no doubt that it falls into the category of 'boutique digitization'. Another of the National Library's great treasures, the early manuscript of Chaucer's *Canterbury Tales*, Peniarth MS 392D, was also the subject of a similar digital edition by Estelle Stubbs (www.sd-editions.com/hengwrt/index.html). Stubbs' work helped to contribute to the proposed identification of the London scrivener Adam Pynkhurst as the scribe of the manuscript, and has proved very influential on scholarship in the field. However, the CD edited by

Stubbs is another example of 'boutique digitization'. While from the point of view of the creation of a digital library, the advice offered by Glen Robson to focus on workflows not projects has a great deal to commend it; the stress in much humanities scholarship on the importance of the edition means that much digitization work in the arts and humanities will inherently need to be project-based if it is to achieve scholarly impact.

Mass digitization in context

There is potentially a tension between the requirement of scholars for project-based work and the need for libraries to emphasize workflows. The importance for librarians of workflows and a strategic approach to digitization has becoming more pressing in recent years. This is partly due to the arrival of the Google Books programme at the end of 2004. If projects like Dafydd ap Gwilym and the Hengwrt Chaucer represented 'boutique digitization', then the arrival of Google Books represented what Andrew Green (2007a) (in an echo of Robin Alston's comment about hypermarkets of knowledge) has called the IKEA era of digitization. According to Green, since the advent of Google Books 'most libraries have aspired to – if they haven't always found the means to realise – much larger-scale, mass production projects . . . Selection is simplified: whole collections can be treated, without worrying about making choices. Volume sometimes wins over quality, speed over care: but the end result can have more utility' (Green, 2007a). A more particularly pressing problem for national libraries in countries such as Wales is the way in which Google Books effectively excludes the literature of small countries. The library partners in Google Books are dominated by large American university libraries. The only British partner is the University of Oxford. While there are libraries from other major European language areas such as Germany and France (and one university from Japan), there are no representatives of countries such as Denmark, The Netherlands, Finland or any Balkan countries. This means that Google Books gives an inherently distorted view of the printed inheritance, so that many early Welsh books (including apparently the first Welsh Bible of 1588 that was critical in ensuring the survival of the Welsh language) are either completely invisible in Google Books or only present through later reprints and facsimiles.

Of course, while Google Books has increased awareness of 'big digitization', it is by no means the only approach to large-scale digitization of libraries, as Andrew Green pointed out in an important lecture to the Digital Resources in the Humanities and Arts Conference (2009). The Open Content Alliance was established in 2004 in response to Google Books, but has not been active in scanning of material since the withdrawal of Microsoft from the alliance in 2008. The Internet Archive has been active as a repository of open access material and the Open Library in many respects provides more extensive coverage than Google Books. Other libraries and archives have preferred to work with commercial partners in developing large-scale digital projects. The National Archives has used commercial partners to digitize British census returns, recouping costs by charging users. Likewise, the British Library is using a commercial partner in the digitization of out of copyright newspapers.

For Andrew Green, such a commercial approach presents great problems:

Those who advocate this approach point to its potential to make rapid progress, and to provide sustainability to a continuing digitisation programme – assuming, of course, that the commercial model itself holds water. The major disadvantage is the loss, at least for a considerable period, of either the wide public access that lies at the heart of the mission and indeed justification of national public institutions, or the free use of information that is also one of their central characteristics – or both. Libraries then become indistinguishable in their functions from publishers. An alternative is to view both the creation and provision of digitised knowledge as a public good. Public libraries were established and still flourish as a means of ensuring that all members of society, irrespective of their circumstances, could have access to all published knowledge. Traditionally their method of achieving this goal was to offer a place where any citizen could read and usually borrow any printed publication. The 21st century equivalent is surely to offer citizens free access, where possible online, to publications in digital form. It follows that, in the case of those publications already in print, libraries – in particular, I would suggest, national libraries, that have a duty to preserve and give access to their countries' published output – should do their best to arrange for their online public accessibility. (Green, 2009)

Green pointed to the ambition of the national libraries of countries such as New Zealand, Slovakia, Norway, Finland and The Netherlands to digitize as much of their collections as possible, and pointed to this approach as a means of achieving a network level of impact for the libraries and literature of those small countries 'of little interest to the global giants of Google'. The National Library of Wales has committed itself to a similar vision for Wales. The achievement of this vision will inevitably be a slow process, but a major first step is *Cylchgronau Cymru Ar-lein*/Welsh Journals Online, which was launched in February 2009. *Cylchgronau Cymru* makes available online 52 periodicals from Wales, including titles in both Welsh and English. It contains 400,000 pages altogether, with 180,000 pages in Welsh, representing the largest single corpus in the language available on the web (Locock, 2009, 5). While the material in *Cylchgronau Cymru* is exposed to Google, fully structured metadata in a MAchine-Readable Cataloguing (MARC) 21 format was also prepared for each article in the journals in the project, producing a very rich bibliographical record, and the provision of this metadata proved to be one of the most demanding aspects of the project.

Two other features of the project are of particular note. The first is that most of the journals date from the 20th century and consequently most of the articles in them were in copyright. Copyright agreement was obtained on a case-by-case basis. This occasionally proved controversial (Meredith, 2008) but agreement was obtained for the overwhelming majority of articles, although, since no payment was offered, works by Dylan Thomas, Robert Graves and R. S. Thomas are not included in the online resource. (The project manager, Martin Locock (2009, 5), notes that given that the cost of web publication was about £2 per page, the payment of even minimal copyright fees would transform the economics of mass digitization.) The result of this work in obtaining clearance for the reproduction of work in copyright is that *Cylchgronau Cymru* is an addition, rather than a rival to, Google Books, which does not fully reproduce material in copyright. The second notable feature of the project is again its collaborative character. The project was not simply a National Library project, but was undertaken under the aegis of WHELF, and indeed the active support and involvement of the WHELF libraries was essential not only in securing the necessary access and agreements for the digitization but also in ensuring funding under the JISC capital programme. Some funding for *Cylchgronau Cymru* was also provided by the Welsh Government, and this paved the way for additional funding through its Strategic Capital Investment Found the lion's share of the funding for a second larger project, now under way, to digitize newspapers and periodicals from the 19th century (Green, 2009).

Projects such as *Cylchgronau Cymru* have been carefully designed in order to make a strategic impact that both ameliorates the cultural issues raised by large resources such as Google Books and provides structured access to core elements of the Welsh printed heritage. This strategic approach is pursued collaboratively through bodies such as WHELF with the aim of creating an integrated and comprehensive resource that Andrew Green (2007a) has designated 'The Theatre of Memory'. More importantly, such initiatives will themselves ultimately feed through to larger resources. The National Library is among the institutions contributing to the Europeana programme, a web portal that will bring together digital collections from a variety of institutions across Europe (www.europeana.eu/portal/index.html). Currently, the National Library of Wales is contributing content through the eContentPlus Programme under the theme of 'travel', and is digitizing 574 drawing volumes, containing over 35,000 drawings and watercolours, from the amateur sketches of wealthy travellers to the field sketchbooks of professional artists (http://nlwales.blogspot.com/2010/10/contributing-to-europeana-web-portal.html).

Recent developments in digitization in Wales provide some strong pointers as to how the impact of digital resources can be maximized. One key lesson appears to be the importance of what Andrew Green called a 'whole process approach', in which digitization is seen as 'an integrated series of operations, starting with selection and preservation, moving through image and data capture and metadata addition, and ending with presentation' (Green, 2007a). In this context, impact is enhanced if projects are designed to make a strategic impact in terms of the current and developing landscape of digital provision. In successfully achieving this, a strong collaborative and cooperative framework is desirable. Close alignment with the funding priorities of government and other bodies is also essential in securing financial resources for these programmes. The Welsh record is particularly impressive in terms of its success in securing financial support for digital programmes. While questions of cost occasionally loom, as with copyright payments for authors like Dylan Thomas or R. S. Thomas in *Cylchgronau Cymru*, they are not particularly prominent. This is partly because the integration of digital processes into overall workflows in the library has proved extremely cost-effective (as is evident from Locock's calculation (2009, 5) that the web publication cost of *Cylchgronau Cymru* is about £2 per page). While Locock notes that the creation of metadata can be very expensive, it does not appear that the cost is much greater than with conventional library materials. The success of the Welsh programme in securing financial resources to date also reflects to a large degree the strong strategic alignment of the programme, and particularly the way it links to Welsh Government priorities. The extent to which the current crisis of funding in the public sector will affect the programme in the future remains to be seen.

Supporting digital scholarship in Wales

However, the stress of the National Library and WHELF on 'big digitization' raises questions as to the continuing role of scholarly projects such as the Dafydd ap Gwilym and Hengwrt Chaucer editions. Where do such scholarly resources fit into this picture? Has the National Library succumbed to the dangers outlined by Robin Alston in 1993 and decided to focus on the creation of a Welsh bibliographical hypermarket to the exclusion of the smaller scale scholarly investigation of the bibliographical and textual characteristics of manuscripts and rare books? Andrew Green has stated that he believes that small-scale digitization 'has an assured future – possibly not as end in itself but simply as a natural by-product of another process, such as an academic research project' (Green, 2009). However, it is clear that he sees such activities as remaining on a cottage scale, and therefore of limited impact. Indeed, it seems that he sees the future of cyberscholarship as lying more in the exploration of the larger data sets produced by bodies such as the National Library:

> In future, as techniques for searching, text mining, document recognition and automated translation become more sophisticated, as the semantic web develops and as 'cyberscholarship' becomes more common, these great reservoirs of text will yield new knowledge, and perhaps even generate new research fields. As interest in this kind of specialist analysis grows it will ask complex questions about the digitised material itself: how, for example, might it be possible to extract consistent and structured information about places, people or dates out of a large mass of unstructured and heterogeneous data; how, in the absence of detailed structured metadata, might relevant items be recalled or grouped successfully; how OCR techniques might be improved or supplemented to achieve greater accuracy. (Green, 2009)

While Green paints a picture of many enticing research vistas, there are many other areas of humanities research that might require different digital techniques. Paleographers, for example, might be more concerned with the way in which different scribes form their letters; art historians might wish to compare brush techniques in paintings; landscape historians might wish to compare and overlay details in different maps. These all require specialist studies that inherently must frequently comprise projects rather than workflows, and which sometimes it can be very difficult to integrate into workflows.

It is here perhaps we sharply encounter one of the main issues identified by Robin Alston in 'The Battle of the Books'. 'Big digitization' projects treat the contents of books as so much information; the concern of humanities scholars is frequently with the historical context of that information. For a palaeographer, an art historian, a textual editor or a historian the information cannot be separated from the medium in which it occurs. It is fundamentally affected by the physical character of the manuscript, book, painting, print or recording in which the information occurs, and for many humanities scholars it is the study of the physical characteristics of that medium that are the focus of their research. As projects like the Dafydd ap Gwilym or Hengwrt Chaucer editions illustrate, part of the attraction of digital technologies is the ability minutely to explore in new ways the characteristics of manuscripts, printed books and other historical artefacts. It was for this reason that Alston so forcefully reminded his audience that traditional bibliographical skills would continue to be important in the new technological era. Yet it is difficult to see how the approach of the digital humanities, which emphasizes this close examination of texts, manuscripts and books, can be scaled up to produce the impact achieved by 'big digitization'.

Robin Alston felt that this reflected the inherent difficulty of measuring the impact of humanities research, asking:

> What useful purpose is served by disproving the existence of Phalaris? Or that Athens could not have been supplied with grain from the Black Sea because the Bosphorus flows at an average of 5 knots and their best sailing ships could only just manage that speed, so that while they could come down they had no way of going up? (Alston, 1993)

The success of the National Library of Wales and its partners in convincing the Welsh Government of the value of spending three million pounds on digitizing 19th-century Welsh periodicals and newspapers suggests that it is possible to convince government and funding bodies of the importance of such research, and that the secret of success in achieving this lies partly in a strategic alignment with government priorities, an approach which may come more naturally to librarians than academic researchers. Alston imagined that, in the new era of libraries, the need for librarians who could mediate between the new technologies and the older forms of bibliographic understanding would be greater than ever. Certainly it does seem that, in order to achieve greater impact in the digital sphere, it is essential for academic researchers to forge new, closer methods of working with librarians and curators. This reflects the view expressed by Andrew Green on the future role of librarians who he feels will hold a unique set of functions in the new digital economy of knowledge, in particular by acting as a mediator between existing 'stored culture' and the re-creation and production of new living culture and knowledge (Green, 2007b).

Conclusion

Reading in his library late at night, bathed in pools of light and comforted by the familiar smells of his books, Alberto Manguel is seized by an elegiac mood. The libraries he loves seem to him doomed, and his book is to a large extent a lament for a remarkable human institution that he feels will soon disappear. The danger signs are certainly there, and were there when Robin Alston described the new Battle of the Books in 1993. It is a common fear, described again by Andrew Green (2007b):

> An apocalyptic forecast might run like this. Libraries and archives have no future except as museums of the written word. Future generations will get their knowledge online and direct, either free from its originators or on payment from giant aggregators like the fictional 'Googlezon'. Even what libraries used to call 'special collections', historic or rare publications and unique archives, will have been electronically cloned and networked long ago by commercial organisations.

> Our reading rooms will empty. Even when it is libraries that provide access to online information, its users will be unaware of the fact. Skills for which librarians and archivists used to be valued, such as metadata creation, will have been undermined by further improvements in search engine technology. Long before the bicentenary of the National Library of Wales in 2107 the last reader will have been escorted out, and the building sealed, preserved like the statue of Ozymandias in the sands to remind travellers of the absurdity of monumental ambition.

Just as Alston argued that librarians have a special role to play in helping to ensure that the Battle of the Books does not lead to their destruction in favour of cloud repositories, so Green suggests that libraries can lead a process of reinvention and re-creation that reinterprets such traditional forms of knowledge as bibliography or codicology in a digital world, and can help usher in new forms of public culture. The many recent developments in libraries, from the creation of new forms of library space to the advent of major digital projects such as *Cylchgronau Cymru* and Europeana, shows that this process of reinvention is proceeding apace, and that, despite initial appearances in some places, such as Wales, the Battle of the Books is being won. In order to achieve similar impact and to play their part in the Battle of the Books, humanities academics need to forge closer alliances with librarians and to show an equal willingness to develop new working relationships and public roles.

3
The digital museum

Claire Hudson

Introduction

UK museums have experienced an interesting and sometimes frustrating journey since the arrival of affordable digitization technology. Until very recently, the impact and value of museum collections, especially for the research community, has not been fully recognized, and this has tended to hamper the speed and extent of museum digitization projects. Gradually, museums have not only generated a significant body of digital content themselves but have also become partners in higher-education-funded research projects with digital outputs, encouraging wider awareness not only of the value of their collections but also of the expertise they can contribute to the creation of research resources.

Despite this, there is still a great deal of unexploited potential. A recent study by the Comité des Sages (20011) on the online accessibility of Europe's digital cultural heritage identifies the museum sector as an area requiring greater investment. The physical characteristics of many museum artefacts have also tended to inhibit digitization. Frail materials, large objects, collections housed in off-site stores, or items of costume that need three-dimensional mounting to convey a true picture of their purpose and design all present time-consuming challenges for digitization that add to project costs.

This chapter will present a case study based on the experiences of digitization at one specific organization, my own, followed by 'the bigger picture', some more generalized perspectives on the implementation of digitization within UK museums as a whole.

Case study: A learning journey
New Opportunities Fund – the NOF-Digitise programme
Introduction

The V&A Museum's Department of Theatre and Performance is by no means a leader in the field of digitization but has been a very active player, with a track record stretching over ten years – almost back to prehistory in digitization terms.

In common with many UK heritage organizations, the journey started in the late 1990s when the V&A Department of Theatre and Performance was still known as the Theatre Museum, a branch of the V&A, located in its own premises in London's Covent Garden. Although dependent on the parent organization for many of its support services (IT, human resources (HR), conservation, etc.) it maintained its own website, which at the time, in common with the websites of most UK museums, was the responsibility of its marketing department, and was designed primarily as a means of attracting visitors to the museum building. Online information about the collections was rudimentary and in no way equated to an actual catalogue or database of holdings. However, a successful application to the New Opportunities Fund's NOF-Digitise programme provided the Theatre Museum with the chance to use the web to make its collections accessible to a wider audience, and at the same time to develop expertise and an awareness of the demands of this new medium of communication.

The NOF-Digitise programme offered a total of £50 million for heritage organizations to digitize areas of their collections and make them available to new audiences. To qualify for funding, the websites created with this funding had to be geared towards young people, families, lifelong learners and those who were socially excluded due to their cultural or socio-economic background. Organizations such as museums, archives and libraries were identified as guardians of very rich collections but it was felt that there were barriers preventing wider use of these materials.

PeoplePlayUK

The Theatre Museum was well placed to respond to the call for applications. It held very large collections of highly visual material in a wide range of formats, spanning stage costume, photographs, designs, ephemera, ceramics, posters, puppets and more. Even better, much of this material was free of intellectual property rights (IPR) constraints, either by virtue of its age or because the rights were owned outright by the museum. It also had access to

professional stage performers who formed the museum's animation and interpretation team. Since we wished to exploit a 'theatrical' look and feel for the project and enliven the content by including audio recordings of music and spoken word specially commissioned for the site, this provided us with a valuable advantage.

The museum took the objectives and aims of the NOF-Digitise programme very seriously, carefully considering the target audiences and their needs. The website we devised, called PeoplePlayUK, would provide a combination of packaged content about our most popular subject areas (pantomime, musical theatre, drama, dance, music hall, opera, etc.) with a database of 1500 objects, each with an 'object story' (see, for example, Figure 3.1) to engage the visitor. Rather than merely providing a physical description of an

Figure 3.1 *Example of a PeoplePlayUK object story (copyright Victoria and Albert Museum)*

object, this story would also try to draw on the 'human interest' associated with it.

The souvenir booklet of Barnum & Bailey's circus tour of America, 1897, is cut in the shape of an elephant. It features diary details of the day-to-day life of the circus on tour. Even the births of a leopard and of a sheep are recorded. The booklet gives a fascinating glimpse into the huge operation of mounting a tour. Fifty-three people are listed as selling tickets and acting as ushers. There are departments for railroad and baggage, men to erect the tents, special staff to care for the animals, others to maintain costumes and wigs. This souvenir may have been intended as an advert for the circus but also acts as a tribute to James A. Bailey who formed the circus partnership with P. T. Barnum in 1881.

For the specified audience, we felt that it was necessary to provide a rich mix of lively content, interpretation, glossaries, links and a multimedia approach to encourage visitors to engage with the content and explore the site.

Additional benefits

The project would not only provide an ideal means of showcasing the collections and of providing useful information of a high quality to its audience, it would help the museum to increase its efficiency by allowing visitors to answer their own enquiries rather than by using the museum's overloaded e-mail and telephone enquiry services. After a two-stage application process that began in 1999 the museum was successful in being awarded £330,000, and the project was ready to begin in January 2002. The Theatre Museum's PeoplePlayUK project was just one of 150 similar projects funded by NOF, some larger, some smaller. Most participants were novices, all starting to learn about digitization and website design at the same time. Although we had good technical advice from NOF's technical advisory service, and within the V&A we could draw on highly expert IT and photographic departments, we had to design and manage the entire workflow, from the initial selection of objects through to quality control and user testing of the site, with no prior experience. Rather than using an external digitization bureau, all our scanning was done on our own premises (and still is) because moving museum objects off-site can be administratively complex. As an example of how basic it got, our scanners were selected from recommendations in *What Scanner* magazine.

NOF-Digitise was very much a public access project and not a retrospective cataloguing initiative. All projects had to employ Dublin Core-compliant metadata but at an early stage we realized that there would simply not be time to create records of the standard required by the V&A's in-house cataloguing systems. We wished to use a mix of museum objects, library items, ephemera and archives to enliven the content and link very diverse materials. By rights, these materials would need to be catalogued in three different V&A systems. The added time and expense this would involve was prohibitive, so instead we created a dedicated database to contain the 1500 object records, their stories and their image metadata.

The PeoplePlayUK site was extremely popular with users – it achieved high visitor figures, averaging 170,000 visits per month at a time when the Theatre Museum's own website was achieving barely a third of that figure. Although it was created for the nonspecialist it had many devotees among academics and experts because the quality of the information was very high, even though it was packaged in an accessible style.

Conclusion

By early 2009 security flaws were beginning to emerge that allowed hackers to launch malicious e-mails purporting to come from the V&A – a form of e-hijacking, and the V&A was told by the Joint Academic Network (JANET) to take the site offline because it posed a major risk. Since then, the V&A web team has been migrating the PeoplePlayUK content to the V&A website but minus some of the original site's features and its separate branding.

The PeoplePlayUK project provided us with a very effective training experience that taught us all the basic skills needed for online publishing – workflow design, writing accessibly for the web, the creation and use of a style sheet to ensure consistent use of language, image manipulation, logical structuring of content and quality control. We also experimented with combining diverse materials in a complementary way and presenting them in a lively fashion, for example, by having an actor read a newspaper report rather than simply digitizing the press cutting.

The biggest and hardest lesson we learnt from this project was that it is essential that digital content resides within core institutional systems so that metadata can be updated in one single location, and content reused for other projects. It also ensures that it will be preserved alongside the organization's other digital assets.

The enduring benefits of the NOF-Digitise £50 million total investment have been hotly debated. For the Theatre Museum, the investment was of undisputable value. Fifteen hundred of the Theatre Museum's best objects were digitized to a high resolution and are still available for reuse from the V&A's digital asset management system. Most of the museum objects digitized through this project have now been incorporated into the V&A's online object catalogue, and the content written for the original website has been reused in publicly accessible web content. Not only was the content highly appreciated by its intended audience, it continues to be actively used, albeit through different channels of delivery.

The experience also vastly increased the Theatre Museum's capacity for engaging with subsequent digital projects.

JISC-funded collaborative project: the East London theatre archive

Introduction

In 2006 the department was approached by the University of East London (UEL) and invited to participate in an application for a large-scale digitization project to be funded by the JISC. The focus of the project would be East London Theatre. The suggested partnership comprised our two organizations plus a number of theatrical venues and companies, including the Theatre Royal Stratford East, Hackney Empire, Hoxton Hall and the Half Moon Children's Theatre. The technical partner was the Arts and

Humanities Data Service (AHDS) Executive at King's College London (which became the Centre for e-Research in 2008). The successful application resulted in a two-year digitization project that produced over 15,000 digital images (10,000 sourced from the V&A Theatre and Performance collections) plus a theatre gazetteer, interactive map and a series of introductory essays on themes such as animal performers, East End immigration and nautical drama.

Exploding the myths

The project began in March 2007 and the website (www.elta-project.org) was launched in March 2009. Of approximately £500,000 of project funding, the V&A received around £200,000, which allowed us to catalogue and digitize material that had been severely under-exploited in the past. Some of the 19th-century playbills we digitized had been inaccessible for years because of the fragility of the paper on which they were printed. In terms of resource discovery and access, this was therefore a very successful project. Traditionally, research interest has always focused on West End theatre. The East London theatre archive (ELTA) project exploded several myths concerning the nature of performance in East London (which was by no means confined to music hall and variety) and opened up new research opportunities for scholars in many disciplines including social, economic and urban history, as well the more obvious disciplines of English literature and drama. This time we created standardized MARC catalogue records using the V&A's bibliographical system, Horizon, from where they can be migrated when that system is ultimately superseded.

Conclusion

One of the more challenging aspects of this exercise, especially for the project managers at UEL, was the diversity of the partner organizations, all of whom were different in their size, status, aims and in what they could contribute to the project. Some were very small organizations with no member of staff designated to care for their archives. The partners' degree of copyright awareness was also very uneven. UEL is to be congratulated for maintaining a productive partnership to the end of the project, despite the disparate aspirations and abilities of the participant organizations. Imposing deadlines for project milestones can be difficult if this essentially not-for-profit work conflicts with an organization's commercial imperatives.

One interesting area of tension was the need to create an authoritative and scholarly resource for use by the research community while at the same time presenting the content in an accessible style. Primary sources such as playbills and account books do need a degree of interpretation to make them useful. The thematic essays certainly provided a way into new areas of research for those new to a subject area, and further work on using the site's content for creating teaching and learning resources, and for evolving new works of performance inspired by the archive, is currently being carried out under a follow-up, JISC-funded initiative, called CEDAR (Clustering and Enhancing Digital Archives for Research, www.uel.ac.uk/lls/resources/CEDAR.htm). This initiative will encourage the addition of user-generated content, and will present case studies illustrating the potential uses to which the digitized material can be put in order to create new resources

V&A-funded digitization programme

Since 2007, the Department of Theatre and Performance has additionally received internal funding to digitize areas of its collections. Initially the intention was to balance the outputs between the mass digitization of largely two-dimensional copyright-free material, such as theatrical prints and photographic collections, and the creation of 'value added' learning packs in the style of PeoplePlayUK. The latter would provide web pages explaining and illustrating a specific aspect of performance history or practice. The first subject chosen was one we knew held great interest for audiences – that of designing, making and wearing theatrical costume. The project entailed selecting 50 of our most interesting costumes from a collection of around 3000, having them mounted on mannequins and photographed (converted in some cases to 360-degree animations), writing authoritative essays, captions and presenting the material in a logically structured package with links to related objects such as stage photographs and costume designs. Although we succeeded in completing the pack, the project was extremely time-consuming and was inevitably dependent on the intervention of the museum's Web Team to code and publish it. The iterative process between web designer and client of presenting and signing off content worked well under the PeoplePlayUK model because it was fundamentally a commercial relationship defined by a formal contract. It was simply not appropriate when working in-house with a small and hard-pressed web development team, under constant pressure from competing internal projects such as web content relating to exhibitions, events and other time-specific activities.

By contrast, the department's mass digitization projects, which have produced almost 50,000 digital images and associated catalogue records over the last three years, have been easier to accomplish. A simple workflow ensures that objects are photographed, catalogued to a minimum standard and published to the web without requiring input from the web design team. The launch of the V&A's award-winning 'Search the Collections' initiative (http://collections.vam.ac.uk) has provided an effective and rapid system for connecting the public with descriptions and images of its objects.

National Video Archive of Performance recordings

One further area of digitization undertaken by the department has been that of the recordings made by V&A's National Video Archive of Performance. Founded in 1992, the project has produced around 250 full-length recordings of major UK stage productions, recorded professionally to archive standard. Over this period, changes in video media have resulted in recordings being created in several different formats, for both long-term preservation and for viewing purposes. The digitization project will even out any inconsistencies and make the collection easier to manage and exploit in the future.

My organization has been fortunate in the range of digitization projects it has been able to undertake but our experiences have been far from unique. The following section will set our findings within the broader context of the UK museums sector.

The bigger picture – digitization in UK museums

Over the past 15 years, UK museums have been engaged in digitizing their collections, with widely differing outcomes. In 1999, the National Museum Directors' Conference published its landmark report, *A Netful of Jewels: New Museums in the Learning Age*. It foresaw a digital future for museums established on the foundations already being built. This would comprise a broad spectrum of digital initiatives, including:

- relevant participatory galleries and digital exhibits
- digital cameras, smart cards and other media for use during a visit
- content created by visitors as well as by museum staff
- facilities for searching the collections in ways that are relevant to visitors
- trained staff to help visitors learn
- interactive websites and online services
- online information to help in planning visits
- connections between the actual and the virtual museum, and with other cultural resources locally and worldwide.

The remaining section of this chapter will look at how far this vision has been fulfilled after a decade of significant investment in museum digitization initiatives.

Why digitize museum collections?

In analysing which areas of this vision have and have not been delivered and why, it may perhaps be useful first to consider what philosophical, operational and economic motives underpin museums' efforts to digitize their collections. For example, the absolute requirement for museums to be accountable for all their objects, to know their exact location at all times, is not fully understood outside the sector. Digitization is a powerful tool in the auditing process and explains why museums may well seek to digitize their collections exhaustively, rather than focusing only on specific object types or themes.

An altruistic desire on the part of curators to make their collections widely accessible to audiences has to be the most obvious answer to this question of motivation. Although some museums reportedly still struggle with the conflict between making their collections accessible online and a feared reduction in real visitor numbers to their museums, the experience of those that have actively published their collections via the web is that this only builds their reputation and profile, and leads to larger numbers of visitors wishing to engage with the real objects and to participate in the events and activities designed around them.

Museums with a strong and well-populated web presence also enhance their reputations as centres of expertise. Most web visitors arrive at content through search engines, not through the home page, so a site that is rich in content optimized for search engines will achieve high visitor numbers. Larger museums, including the national museums, which have well developed websites, are also much more likely to attract approaches from the academic sector and other potential partners proposing funded research projects and other collaborative activities.

For the organizations designated as national museums in the UK and directly funded by the Department for Culture, Media and Sport (DCMS), their funding agreements with DCMS are based on a set of key performance indicators (KPIs), which may also influence their strategic direction. It is interesting to note that the key mandatory indicator associated with museums' online activities simply asks for the total number of website visits to be reported. There is no obligation to report the progress being made on providing access to digital images of objects in the collections. And, arguably, the key indicator for both the museums and their funding bodies still remains the number of visitors through the doors.

Auditing the collections is only one in-house operation to which digitization can make a valuable contribution. Providing public access to material that is fragile or notoriously difficult to make accessible through traditional means is also a major benefit (see Figures 3.2 and 3.3). Digital images may be inferior to direct physical access but are still far better than there being no access at all to objects such as large, rolled textiles, objects in remote stores, or to natural history specimens and other organic materials needing specialized storage environments such as freezers or preservation tanks.

The ability to present accompanying images of conservation processes provides complementary information about the scale and condition of the object.

Have museums fully exploited the online environment?

To return to *A Netful of Jewels*, it would seem that many of the elements expressed in its vision have yet to be fulfilled or developed. There are some impressive examples of digital museum initiatives to be seen. For example, it is comparatively easy to find examples of 'relevant participatory galleries and digital exhibits' connecting physical exhibitions and galleries with content specifically created for the online environment. Several good examples can be found on the website of the Pitt Rivers Museum (www.prm.ox.ac.uk), linking current displays and exhibitions with web resources that expand on the physical galleries.

However, there is huge variation in the degree to which the UK museums sector as a whole has been able to digitize its collections and manipulate that digital material. The following comments made by the Strategic Content Alliance relate as much to the museum sector as to other areas of the public sector:

> Public sector initiatives have so far been largely fragmented. Coordination has not taken place on any significant scale between initiatives to share expertise, identify suitable content and avoid duplication of effort. The uncoordinated nature of the activities to date is resulting in a patchy network of online content with different management and business models, with no comprehensive gap analysis or tools to support previous, current or planned activity.
>
> (www.jisc.ac.uk/whatwedo/themes/content/contentalliance/contentframework.aspx)

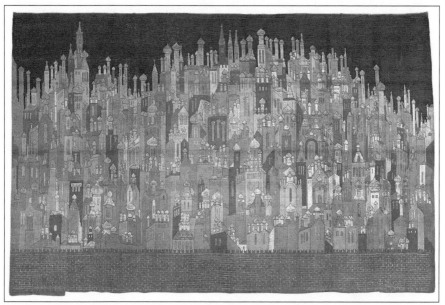

Figure 3.2 *Theatre backcloth designed by Natalia Goncharova for a 1926 production of* The Firebird *at the Lyceum Theatre (copyright Victoria and Albert Museum). The cloth measures over 10 metres by 15 metres and is consequently rarely displayed*

Figure 3.3 *Theatre backcloth designed by Natalia Goncharova on display in the V&A (copyright Victoria and Albert Museum)*

Very few UK museums and galleries have achieved the basic target of publishing images and descriptions of all the objects in their collections. Many still have no form of illustrated searchable catalogue available on their websites at all, relying simply on static pages broadly summarizing the content of their collections.

A major challenge for museums is that, unlike sites created for the research community, museum websites have to engage with a very wide audience, from the scholar who may simply want unmediated access to information about the museum's objects, to schoolchildren or others who may need a greater degree of assistance in interpreting the content. Many museums make a conscious effort to engage with audiences through interactive features on their websites but 'interactivity' is often quite limited and, at best, any user-generated content tends to be carefully corralled into areas of the website where there is no risk of it being mistaken for the authorized, museum view. Social networking channels (Facebook, Twitter, Flickr) and i-Phone apps are also useful tools for popularizing and disseminating content to audiences, and as a means of building a relationship with visitors who want a more active involvement with a museum's website than simply checking opening hours or accessing catalogue entries. Routine digitization of collections and more creative interactive initiatives need to run in parallel but in some museums it is felt that they compete for scarce resources that cannot support both types of output. Many local authority museums dependent on their council's IT department for any web content at all might well consider that dilemma a luxury compared with their own situations.

Providing 'facilities for searching the collections in ways that are relevant to visitors' deserves more attention. Although the 'typical museum visitor' may be impossible to identify, museums could make greater efforts, through user testing and focus groups, to discover from visitors what they would like to see, and how they would like to be able to search our collections. Very often, museums tend to describe their objects in terms of region, period, maker, style or material but don't cater for those who want to interrogate their collections by subject, activity or the incidental content within an image.

Perhaps the least developed part of that 1999 vision is the establishment of 'connections . . . with other cultural resources locally and world-wide'. *A Netful of Jewels* predicted that: 'National or regional museums [would] join digitally with local museums, and with other institutions that have related or complementary collections such as libraries and archives.' There is huge potential for museums to connect related collections, and to enrich their objects by linking them to material derived from outside the museum sector. In my experience of managing an integrated, cross-sectoral collection (museum objects, archives, library material) our visitors greatly appreciate the ability to access a wide range of complementary materials. This was also borne out by the success of PeoplePlayUK. They tend to be less concerned about the format of the material delivered to them as long as it is relevant to their field of interest. SCRAN (www.scran.ac.uk) led the way in aggregating content across the museum, library and archives domains; regional projects such as Black Country History (http://blackcountryhistory.org) work in a similar way to overcome the artificial obstacles between related collections.

Looking at the aspirations expressed in *A Netful of Jewels* it is clear that many museums are lagging some way behind that vision and that there has been a lack of consistent and systematic digitization across the sector. This is not only depriving general audiences of access to museums' collections. The potential research value of this material is enormous. There is a well recognized tendency for scholars to use only resources that are available to them online, and even to assume that a high proportion (or even all) of the material they should be using is accessible online. And yet so few UK museum collections, many of them comprising unique items of immense research value, are actually digitized. Even at the V&A, which has made serious investment in its digitization programme, only around 20% of its million-plus online catalogue records are as yet accompanied by a digital image.

Obstacles to museum digitization

Despite the enormous value of museum collections to learning and research (in its widest sense) there have been relatively few funding opportunities for digitization within the sector. *A Netful of Jewels* predicted in 1999 that, predicated on the availability of appropriate funding 'by 2007 all museums should be able to play their full role in the National Grid for Learning, from the very smallest museum, managed by a dedicated team of volunteers, to the largest national museum'.

This prediction has clearly not been realized.

Lack of available funding to support museums' strategic aims in the area of digitization has been and continues to be a major obstacle to progress. Projects have tended to respond to funding opportunities, rather than to follow a rational strategy for developing content in a logical or systematic way. In some cases, museums have realized that this opportunism has actually conflicted with their ability to meet other defined strategic goals because it has diverted staff time into delivering projects whose longer term public benefits were possibly questionable. Project funding has also led to problems with sustaining a web initiative once the funding has expired and the project staff have moved on.

Since the closure of the NOF-Digitise programme, much of the funding available for partnership digitization projects has come from the higher education sector, especially from the JISC. Since the lead partner in these projects has to be a university, museums have not necessarily been able to use this funding to design projects that directly meet their own key strategic goals. Museums can even find themselves locked out of projects to which they've contributed material because the online resource created is available only through licensing agreements or accessible only via secure academic networks.

As the JISC's Strategic Content Alliance has stated in its *A Guide to the Strategic Content Alliance* (Dempster, 2010):

> Organisations in different sectors are making significant amounts of online content available to their respective communities – in health, education, museums, archives, research, public libraries, and so on. However, the barriers between sectors means not all this content is accessible to all who might need it, or want it. Too much remains hidden amongst the low-

quality information that clutters the web and behind technical, commercial and administrative barriers.

It is not only in the role of digital content creators where museums have been placed in a less advantageous position than universities. As consumers of this content they stand outside the academic sector and are often deprived of access to sophisticated online research resources. Research is a core activity in most museums and yet the continuing professional development of their staff is seriously obstructed by these barriers. This not only impacts negatively on the ease with which curators and others can produce research for exhibitions, publications and acquisitions, it impacts on the way in which museums plan their own in-house digital projects. They are unable to see in full the information landscape in which they need to operate, making it difficult for them to design complementary digitization initiatives that fill gaps and avoid duplication with what already exists.

Lack of resources has also impacted on museums' ability to repurpose content, perhaps originally created through NOF-Digitise funding. Here at the V&A we have been extremely fortunate to have been able to reuse our PeoplePlayUK content very successfully. Furthermore, the V&A has a sophisticated digital asset management system ensuring the preservation of its assets and facilitating their use in other applications. Many museums are still using portable drives or even CDs to store digital files, where they are vulnerable to loss and are difficult to access.

To return to the issue of enabling users to access museum collections in the way they may wish to, this facility is of course dependent on appropriate metadata being in place to support that search function. Where object descriptions are rich and detailed, free text searching may well allow appropriate objects to be retrieved but the degree to which controlled language and terminology has been embedded in metadata can be highly inconsistent, leading to searches that retrieve fuzzy results and which cannot be refined effectively. Metadata relating to an object's IPR status has tended to be omitted at the point of digitization and then often becomes a significant challenge later, when the position on IPR for large collections of diverse assets has to be established retrospectively, rather than as a routine element of the workflow process.

Perhaps this is an appropriate point at which to look at the place of digital content creation within the culture of museums. The degree of interest or knowledge encountered in senior curators or even at management level can result in uneven coverage of a museum's subjects. Some departments can almost appear to opt out, while others, where enthusiasm for building online content is present, romp ahead.

Professional training for curators devotes scant time to the subjects of information management or digital asset management. Career progression for curators is still highly dependent on producing exhibitions and traditional publications such as books, catalogues and journal articles. There is seemingly little scope for a curator's online work to be recognized or rewarded. The abiding supremacy of visitor numbers as the key performance indicator for museums supports initiatives that directly result in increased

Figure 3.4
Costume for Swan Lake, *designed by Alexandre Golovine, Moscow 1901 (copyright Victoria and Albert Museum). A complex costume such as this requires thorough mounting and preparation in order to convey an accurate impression of its effect on stage.*

attendance. The impact of enriching a museum's digital image resources is far more subtle than, say, opening a new exhibition on a popular theme, with all the publicity and marketing opportunities which that presents.

Practical obstacles can also militate against applying a purely strategic or systematic approach to the digitization of museums' collections. Unlike most document collections, museum objects often require special preparation, handling or mounting before they can be photographed. For example, an item of dress or costume will usually need to be assessed for suitability, transferred to a photo studio, unpacked, mounted on a figure, and padded to create a three-dimensional effect before photography can take place (see Figure 3.4). The process is then repeated in reverse.

In these cases, the creation of the digital image is only a small part of the overall workflow. The search for quick wins can mean prioritizing what is easily and most economically captured (especially if published catalogues exist from which text can be easily migrated). These may not comprise a museum's most popular objects or those that are of greatest interest to the public.

Other objects are excluded because of IPR restrictions or uncertainty on the part of the museum on their right to release photographs of these objects into the public domain. At the start of our PeoplePlayUK project we sought authoritative advice on which types of objects would be subject to IPR restrictions. Some areas were clear but this was not the case for others, such as stage costumes, advertisements and puppets, for example. At the time, we were advised that we should not be overly risk-averse as the law appeared to be open to interpretation. Ten years later and it is still not easy to obtain broad authoritative guidance on the IPR situation. Objects really need to be assessed on a case-by-case basis but this is a time-consuming approach. Some larger museums appear to be bolder in their willingness to take risks; others express the view that they cannot afford to be sued for infringing copyrights and simply deselect complex cases from their digitization programme.

Conclusion: a way forward

In a period of economic restraint it is even more essential that the UK's digitization strategy for cultural heritage is well founded and robust. As discussed in this chapter, while there are significant benefits to digitization programmes in museums, there are also considerable obstacles to the implementation, management and sustainability of these initiatives. A strategic approach, including an audit of what already exists and an analysis of where the greatest potential lies, would be highly desirable, and make the opportunities clearer for museums. A key part of the Strategic Content Alliance's mission is to identify priorities, gaps and opportunities in publicly funded digital content and it is to be hoped that this will comprise a thorough assessment of the museum sector.

More creative partnerships are needed between academia, libraries and museums, to nurture and develop curatorial knowledge and also to ensure that museums fully benefit from the partnership projects to which they've contributed. Encouragingly, the vision recently published by the JISC's Resource Discovery Taskforce (JISC, 2011) clearly indicates a desire to integrate museums' digital collections within the research materials available to scholars. However, museums also need digitization funding that is dedicated to their sector and allows them directly to fulfil their own strategic aims and provide for the long-term preservation of their digital assets, so that they can serve future purposes.

Museums need to embrace the opportunities to pool skills and expertise in areas such as IPR and digital rights management. They also need to be in touch with opportunities provided by aggregating initiatives such as Culture Grid and Europeana (www.europeana.eu). To support their involvement with these developments they need to be well informed on current work in standards convergence and look hard at the quality of the metadata they create, and there needs to be greater cooperation and partnership between museums, libraries and archives, not only on management, standards and preservation issues but also on linking and enhancing content. This does, however, add significantly to the skills required by the current and future generation of museum curators, and the impact of this need for professional development and support for collaboration initiatives should be considered.

The phrase 'a netful of jewels' may have been coined in 1999 to link museum collections with the concept of online publication. Greater focus now on devising a national strategy for digitizing museum collections will help to prevent those jewels from remaining buried treasure.

4
The digital archive

Gillian Oliver

Introduction

The purpose of this chapter is to present an overview of digitization activities and issues in the archives domain. The vast new digital collections that are being developed provide striking examples of impact both internally and externally, that is, on the workflows and functions of archival institutions and on global communities of users.

Archival institutions keep records – but only those records that are considered to be worth preserving in perpetuity. Archival records are therefore those that have enduring value, as evidence for accountability as well as perhaps also having intrinsic informational value not simply today, but also far into the future. The ability to make digital copies of archives available via the internet has had far-reaching influences on archival services, and on users' perceptions and experiences of archival records. Traditionally, archival institutions have been the exclusive preserve of specialist researchers, but changing societal norms and information needs, particularly relating to family history research, have been instrumental in changing that focus. Digitization has played a key role, being both a consequence of, and motivator for, those changing requirements.

This chapter focuses on projects to make paper records available in digital form. It will not cover current activities to develop repositories and strategies to manage born-digital information. Challenges in that domain are quite distinct; particularly important are the activities that take place when information is created and captured into record-keeping systems. Significant areas of concern centre around the extent to which everyone has to be aware of record-keeping responsibilities. Attempting to cover both born-digital and digitized information within a single chapter would not do justice to either.

The structure of the chapter is as follows. First, the drivers for digitization in archives are identified and discussed, followed by consideration of the issues that arise. The impact of digitization on traditional archival functions and services and the emergence of new organizational forms are described. The chapter concludes by summarizing the impact of the ability to digitize on archival services.

Drivers for digitization

There are three main influences on digitization activities in archives: the changing usage and user profile of archives; reformatting as a preservation strategy; and the ability to crowdsource and harness 'user power'.

Archives – the new users

The nature of many archival materials as evidence of transactions (e.g. voluminous bureaucratic records) has meant that traditionally services have been targeted at scholars, rather than the general public. Changes in society relating to requirements and abilities to access information have resulted in interest in archival records now coming from very different sectors of the community, with family historians by far the largest user group. So service provision has had to change drastically; Susan Tucker highlights this by comparing the challenges archivists are facing now with those of public libraries 100 years earlier: suddenly having to work out how to respond to the many and varied needs of the general public (Tucker, 2007, 141). As can be imagined, this shift in focus has not been a straightforward or easy adjustment: archives have had to shift from responding to the needs of a small elite group of academics to a mass market of users with widely different backgrounds and information literacy skills. The needs of genealogists have even been perceived in some quarters as being detrimental to the core mission of archives. The language and tone of the following quote with its emphasis on 'recreational' conveys the view of family historians as being of lesser importance than other users: 'the extraordinary proliferation of recreational historians, especially in local repositories, has meant that those trying to use archives to broaden social and community understanding and to inform contemporary social policy (in the case of twentieth-century medical, economic and social historians) have had to compete with those using archives for their own pleasure' (Mortimer, 2002, 61).

Unfortunately this attitude still lingers in some institutions. Similarly, Elizabeth Yakel mentions the 'historically antagonistic' dimensions of relationships between family historians and memory institutions, and points out the two sides of this situation by referring to mutual suspicion between these users and archivists (Yakel, 2004).

However, there is also emerging a greater awareness of complex, personal reasons for researching family histories, and the significance of this for the understanding of self and identity. Sociologist Arlene Stein, for instance, describes the research conducted by children of Holocaust survivors to reconstruct their genealogies, stating, 'The contemporary expansion of genealogy represents a search for identity and social location in an uncertain world' (Stein, 2009, 294). The digital world enables this search for identity to become much more attainable, with archival collections providing essential components.

Reflection of the involvement of archivists in these searches for identity leads Judith Etherton to discuss the increasing awareness of our need to know our histories given that the traditional sources of information (i.e. the individuals concerned) may not be available to ask (Etherton, 2006). For instance, the children of non-biological families (perhaps adopted or born from donor insemination) are very likely to have particular needs to find out more about their biological ancestors for health reasons, whether relating to mental or physical well-being. Thus it is important to emphasize that the pursuit of family history cannot be simply dismissed as a recreational pastime, but that it is an important feature of our contemporary society that should be acknowledged and responded to appropriately by archivists and archives.

Elizabeth Shepherd reports that the first market research survey of readers' needs was commissioned by the UK's Public Records Office in 1970. At that time, just 25% of users were pursuing leisure interests including family history (Shepherd, 2009, 86). Later studies in Europe and North America reveal that genealogists account for 50–90% of all users (Tucker, 2007). Thus it can be seen that the shift from serving a very elite group to a much more egalitarian focus has occurred relatively recently, within a comparatively short period of time.

Digitization has served to highlight the magnitude of the family history phenomenon, and also motivates its ongoing growth. In January 2002, Britain's digitized 1901 census was made publicly available via the internet. Such was the volume of users (1.2 million per hour) that the website had to be closed, and remained unavailable to the public for another ten months (National Audit Office, 2003). Similarly, seven years later the release of the digitized 1911 census resulted in a 'family history frenzy' with 3.4 million searches conducted on the first day (National Archives, 2009).

The involvement of so many people in researching their family history, and their desire to access relevant records as easily as possible, preferably without having to travel to a physical repository, is a hugely significant driver in digitization projects. A key player in this landscape is the Church of Jesus Christ of the Latter Day Saints (LDS), often referred to as the Mormon church, headquartered in Salt Lake City, Utah.

The LDS church is undoubtedly the source of most digitized family history records. The genealogical function of the church was previously known as the Genealogical Society of Utah, but their public-facing web presence is now 'FamilySearch'. FamilySearch is described as a service of the church, and claimed to be the largest genealogical organization in the world. Their website explains the church's involvement in family history as follows:

> Our commitment to helping people connect with their ancestors is rooted in our beliefs. We believe that families are meant to be central to our lives and that family relationships are intended to continue beyond this life. We therefore believe that all family members – those living, those past, and those future – share an enduring bond that reaches across the generations. (FamilySearch, n.d.)

These beliefs motivate far-reaching worldwide activities to digitize and index records that contain information that is relevant to family historians, regardless of religion or ethnicity. For example, most of the digitized records available documenting the births, marriages and deaths of Jews in pre-war Eastern Europe are the result of LDS activity.

These activities have not been without controversy, however, as they have been associated with posthumous baptism, that is, making the long-deceased subjects of these records members of the LDS church. See the Jewish Genealogy website JewishGen for an account of the outrage associated with the baptism of Holocaust victims (JewishGen, n.d.).

In practice, archival institutions are likely to work in partnership with the church on digitization projects. For instance, Archives New Zealand worked with FamilySearch to digitize immigration records (Archives New Zealand, 2010a). After digitization, images are uploaded to the FamilySearch website and made available to volunteers for indexing. If an individual is seeking family in a particular community or country they may be motivated to volunteer to index relevant records. The list of record series available shows just how extensive, and global, these activities are, with projects taking place worldwide.[1]

Digitization as a preservation strategy

'Digital access to original collections obviates their uniqueness – perturbing a singular characteristic that has been both defining and limited. Original materials are fragile, and must be consulted in person and on-site; digital materials appear robust, are readily duplicated, and can be transferred anywhere the network reaches' (Trant, 2009, 374).

Not surprisingly, the uniqueness characteristic of archives has been a significant factor in determining usage constraints. The ability to make digital copies available therefore has been welcomed by some archivists as a strategy to assist in protecting those vulnerable originals. There is a challenge though in ensuring that there is understanding of the role of digitization as a reformatting, but not as a replacement, strategy.

In referring to digitization as a preservation strategy one runs the risk of fuelling the misconception that digitization in itself is a means of preserving the information artefact. As the quote from Jennifer Trant above makes clear, the contrast between the obviously fragile and seemingly robust is striking as well as misleading and anecdotal evidence suggests that in some instances digitization has indeed been perceived as a means of preservation, with originals destroyed after imaging. However, the challenges and uncertainties of digital preservation are well established, and it is clear that the complexity required to preserve digital objects far exceeds the known requirements for the preservation of analogue materials.

So it is important to stress that digitization must only be viewed as a preservation strategy in the sense that it provides a surrogate that can be used to facilitate access, and therefore enables the original to be protected more than would otherwise be possible. By minimizing the extent to which a fragile document has to be exposed to light and handled, risks that will impact on its ongoing preservation can be minimized.

However, digitization has had unexpected consequences in terms of promoting the existence of original records and therefore increasing requests for access to them. This is discussed further below, in 'Issues in digitization'.

Harnessing the power of users

Making digital copies of archives available via the web also facilitates the use of social networking tools to capture the knowledge of users to enhance and enrich archival description. For instance, Archives New Zealand has developed an online exhibition of its war art collection,[2] which consists of digitized images of about 1500 artworks (mostly paintings and drawings) created to document the involvement of New Zealanders in military conflict. As would be expected for an archival collection, a detailed description has been created for the series, but for the individual artworks often only minimal

Figure 4.1 *At Island Command by Allan Barns-Graham. Reproduced by permission of Archives New Zealand (Archives New Zealand/Te Rua Mahara o te Kaawanatanga Wellington Office AAAC 898 NCWA 316)*

additional information is provided (for example the name of the artist, the name of the campaign, physical dimensions and materials used). This digitized collection includes the functionality to allow users to add tags and/or further information, which provides the opportunity for people to contribute any specialist knowledge.

In one notable instance the son of the artist concerned has provided commentary that vividly evokes the context in which a particular painting was created. *At Island Command* by Allan Barns-Graham shows a dark and overcast jungle setting with soldiers wearing heavy-looking capes, obviously wet weather gear (see Figure 4.1).

The comment added to the online digitization of this painting is as follows:

My father said that this scene was re-created after an action the previous day. The participants were required to stand and pose in this position for some considerable period of time in the tropical heat while my father sketched the scene, and to make it look more authentic, he threw buckets of seawater over them. You can imagine the types of comment he received from his subjects at the time!'[3]

A project carried out by researchers at the University of Michigan also focused on capturing the knowledge of the local community to add context to military historical records. The Polar Bear Expedition Digital Collections are digitized records documenting a First World War incident when US forces (mostly from Michigan) were sent to combat on Russian soil. Given the ability to comment, users have provided additional information about individual soldiers, or corrections to existing data (Yakel, 2007).

The Jeremy Bentham Project, based at University College London, provides an example of harnessing user power to make accessible a non-family history-based project. 'Transcribe Bentham' is a participatory, online initiative that has been established to make a digitized collection available to scholars. The objective is to transcribe the archives of Jeremy Bentham, the 19th-century English scholar who developed the philosophy of Utilitarianism and the principle of the 'greatest happiness of the greatest number'. Bentham was a prolific writer, reported as producing 20–40 sheets of manuscript per day over a 40-year period (Bentham Project, n.d.). The legacy of his thought therefore is voluminous in terms of sheer quantity of written records. In order to make this legacy accessible, researchers and students interested in the works of Jeremy Bentham are invited to transcribe the content of his manuscripts, using digital images and an online text editor.

The virtual transcription centre contains a plethora of tools and devices to attract the interest of would-be transcribers and to build a community of practice. For instance, there are forums so that transcribers can discuss problems encountered, a 'Benthamometer' to provide a visual display of progress and, at the time of writing (25 November 2010), a banner headline at the top of the page proclaimed: 'Two new boxes uploaded! Box 73 and Box 96 contain interesting manuscripts on drunkenness, swearing, adultery and much more.'[4]

Similarly, the Old Weather project (www.oldweather.org) uses digitization to enable a fascinating collaboration between science and archives. This initiative uses crowdsourcing to transcribe weather data from the log books of First World War ships, to enable the development of a model to predict future climate (Old Weather, n.d.). The project is a collaboration between Galaxy Zoo, based at Oxford University, and the international Atmospheric Circulation Reconstructions over the Earth (ACRE) initiative based at the Met Office Hadley Centre.

Just as with family history digitization, the distinguishing feature of the Bentham and Old Weather projects is the sheer quantity of records involved. Without digitization, and without being able to mobilize external expertise through Citizencyberscience collaborative work, the information and data in these records would be largely inaccessible, or only retrieved serendipitously.

Issues in digitization

In addition to the undoubted benefits that the ability to digitize has brought to archives, there are a number of problem areas that need to be highlighted. These can be grouped into three categories: firstly the risks relating to potentially removing information from its context, secondly the resource implications and finally increased demand by users to consult originals.

Removal from context

Archives provide evidence of activity, and are thus described in terms of context rather than the content of the information they may contain. This point is critical in understanding the importance of documenting and preserving the context of the creation of records. Discussion papers from a Collections Council of Australia workshop to determine the characteristics of significance for the cultural sector provide a vivid example of the different attitudes on the part of librarians and archivists to the same document. The document in question was a playbill advertising the first theatre performance in Sydney, Australia. This was saved as a souvenir by a Canadian tourist and subsequently formed part of her scrapbook documenting her travels. The library perspective of this document was presented as follows:

> The ephemeral playbill advertising the performance of the melodrama Jane Shore –
> produced in Sydney in 1796, hand printed in a small edition, perhaps intended to survive just
> a couple of weeks – thanks to its generous repatriation by the Canadian government as an
> official APEC gift to the Australian Prime Minister, now enjoys exalted status as the earliest
> surviving document of Australia's print heritage.   (Burns, 2008, 1)

From the archival perspective however, this repatriation was regarded very differently:

> In the context of private archives, the removal and return of Australia's earliest playbill from
> a Canadian scrapbook to Australia was . . . an archival crime in terms of the removal of this
> item from its broader context of preservation.   (Anderson, 2008, 2)

This example highlights the importance accorded to context and helps to explain why, when archivists describe (catalogue) archives, the focus is rarely on a discrete object. The risk posed by the rush to digitize archival records is that individual items such as photographs may be digitized and made available in isolation, i.e. without cognizance of their provenance, the context of creation and use. Thus Joanna Sassoon argues that digitization encourages a focus on content, which 'can lead to pressure for individual items to be selected more for their aesthetic content than their archival values' and furthermore that 'digitization is creating a databank of orphans which have been removed from their transactional origins and evidence of authorial intent' (Sassoon, 2007, 139).

A related issue is the need to add sufficient metadata to the digitized information in order to not only make contextual relationships explicit but also to facilitate the retrieval of information content. As explained above, archival descriptive practice does not traditionally focus on the item level so normally extensive additional indexing will be required for information retrieval purposes. So although the process of scanning may appear to be quick, the addition of relevant metadata is labour intensive and time-consuming.

Resource implications

The volume of records involved in an archival digitization project is likely to be very large. The records that are of interest to family historians will include those that record names and personal details, for example the extensive documentation that is collected over time such as census returns, and shipping lists that show people's homes, ages, family members, occupations and details of travel. Some insight into the magnitude of effort involved in digitizing is provided by Shauna Hicks in her account of a Public Records Office Victoria (PROV) digitization project. The objective of this project was to digitize just four file series: wills (1841–53 and 1853–1924), probates (1841–1924) and inquests (1840–1924). These series were estimated to comprise about five and a half million images, and digitization was predicted to take five years (Hicks, 2008). In another recent project, digitizing the 270,000 pages of shipping lists recording migrants to New Zealand took two people 15 months to complete. This did not include indexing, which was a separate project (Archives New Zealand, 2009). In both the above projects, LDS volunteers performed all digitization tasks. But even when volunteers can be utilized to perform most of the work involved, supervision will still be an issue that will need to be addressed.

There are therefore significant costs associated with digitization, some of which are long term and may not be immediately apparent. As technology costs decrease, so it appears that digitization is within the capability of small, community archives with minimal resourcing. Digitization may appear to be a way in which to raise the profile of the archives and to attract more support and therefore funding. However, even short-term costs may be significant, taking into account the need to invest considerable time in adding metadata. Add to that long-term considerations relating to the need to ensure that technological features are appropriate for storage even over a time span as limited as five years, and it can be appreciated that the ongoing costs of digitization are by no means insignificant. Since the 1980s record keepers have been at the vanguard of those raising awareness of problems inherent in digital longevity (Bearman, 2006, provides a comprehensive review of this literature). Consequently much activity is being invested worldwide in developing digital archival repositories – the means to preserve digital records for the long term. However, the rush to digitize holdings to facilitate access seems to be taking place in a parallel universe with little awareness of concerns about even the medium-term sustainability of the digital surrogates that are being created, let alone the long-term considerations.

Various standards have been developed in order to help ensure that digitization initiatives are carried out in accordance with best practice (a ten-year chronology of guidelines is provided by Puglia and Rhodes, 2007). Adhering to best practice standards may indeed add to the initial costs of setting up a project, but will help ensure consistency and sustainability, thus making sure that project investment is fully realized. Archives New Zealand has developed a standard specifically for government records,[5] which is being used as the basis for ISO 13028 *Information and Documentation – implementation guidelines for digitization of records*, an international standard applicable to the digitization of any records (Archives New Zealand, 2010b).

Increased demand for originals

One entirely unexpected consequence of digitization could jeopardize the benefits envisaged from being able to protect originals from manual handling. By raising awareness of the existence of archival records, there may be increased demand to see and touch the originals. Because access to archival records, and use of archival repositories, has traditionally been the province of academic or professional researchers, making a record series available digitally may be a revelation to non-users. Returning to Shauna Hicks and the PROV digitization project, the wills, probates and inquest files from 1841 to 1925 were selected for digitization because they were the most heavily used, and their retrieval and use was impacting on staff time and on the records themselves (Hicks, 2008). However, staff at PROV were surprised to find that requests to view specific wills or probates were still being made in the reading room. Once the digitized copies of these documents were made available via the internet, family historians became aware of the existence of particular records that represented a rich source of information about family members. Although this information could be gleaned from the digital surrogates, a significant number of people also wanted to connect on an emotional level with ancestors by physically handling the document itself.[6]

The act of digitization is likely to increase awareness of particular records exponentially, and given that one of the motivators for digitization may be to make information more available to a very large group of users, archivists need to be aware of the potential of a corresponding increase in requests to consult originals. It is ironic that a preservation tool may in fact pose additional risks to the artefact, but awareness of this potential should be factored into digitization strategies.

There are undoubtedly emotional dimensions associated with a physical object that cannot be provided by a digital surrogate. Logically, making information available might be perceived as being sufficient, but once again the significance of the context of a document's creation and use, and the emotional bond it represents, should not be ignored. If seeing the handwriting of a long-dead family member can be very moving, actually handling something that they have also touched would be a powerful incentive to visit an archives institution and negotiate the procedural maze surrounding physical access.

The impact of digitization on traditional archival functions and services

The ability to digitize has been a factor influencing tremendous change in the archives world. Collections have the potential to be opened up, and made available to numbers of users unimaginable when access was limited by the ability to physically access records. Appraisal, archival description and access services are the three core areas that are impacted, and concerns centre on change being driven by digitization capabilities.

Appraisal is the methodology used by archivists to select that tiny percentage of the overall quantity of records created that have archival value, in other words, that merit preservation in perpetuity. Decision making is complex and de-accessioning occurs rarely if ever. The costs involved in long-term preservation are great, so there is a significant burden of responsibility to make sure the right decisions are made. Appraisal requires the impossible – the ability to look into the future and make judgements as to what information will be of value to researchers.

The ability to digitize is undoubtedly a factor that may influence appraisal decision making. Will the archival records of the future be solely those that are most suitable for digitization, those that will be most popular with the greatest proportion of users, the family historians? The implications of these choices for the dimensions of our future memory are significant, and it is essential that digitization is clearly identified as just a single component in appraisal, appropriately weighted against other considerations.

As discussed above, digitization is already influencing approaches to archival description (cataloguing). Wendy Duff and Catherine Johnson describe how studying user behaviour, particularly information seeking, was not a priority for archivists until the 1990s. Once again, it is family historians who have prompted this new awareness and highlight the inadequacy of current archival finding aids (Duff and Johnson, 2003). Greater awareness and readiness to use tools that will facilitate the addition of user-generated content to enhance existing archival description is needed in the sector as a whole, as this must be the principal means by which archival institutions can accommodate such diverse needs.

I have already mentioned the phenomenon of increasing demand for originals after digital copies have been made available. More generally, though, the holdings of archival institutions have become much more visible to a broader community of users as a direct result of digitization, and this has impacted on access services. The numbers of potential users has increased enormously, and expectations have been introduced that all records will be digitally available. The challenges faced by reference archivists in serving a global population of users are great, and can only be met by developing responsive retrieval systems. The traditional workflows supporting access services centre on receiving written requests to consult specific records and the manual collection of those records for use in the reading room at given times. It is essential that these workflows are reconfigured to be appropriate for today's digital expectations.

Service provision to those users who do come to the repository to consult records may be reassessed if resources need to be redirected to supporting digitization activities. This has provoked controversy where it has resulted in reduced opening hours. In 2007, for instance, Library and Archives Canada proposed to reduce the hours when their main reading room was open in order to support the increased digitization of records. The Canadian Historical Association reacted strongly to this proposal because of the prioritization of digitization activities at the expense of on-site consultation of paper records, and three years later the debate continues still (Canadian Historical Association, 2010).

The emergence of new organizational forms in archives

The family history boom has been capitalized on by some archival institutions as an opportunity to provide revenue to support ongoing service provision. This has led to new business models distinguished by joint venture partnerships. The partnerships between archival institutions and LDS FamilySearch activities do not have any cost implications for end-users. In contrast, partnership with a private, for-profit organization does have significant implications for users. For example, Britain's National Archives is proactive in seeking commercial partners to make digitized copies of its records available, and has 'successfully digitised millions of our most popular records, in partnership with commercial publishers' (National Archives, n.d.). This means that to access the information in certain record series such as census returns, users must use a fee-based service such as Ancestry.com or Find My Past.

Digitization has also provided a means by which archives can work together with other memory institutions on collaborative projects. For example, in New Zealand, Matapihi (www.matapihi.org.nz) provides a single interface to facilitate online access to selected digitized objects from a number of different cultural heritage institutions, including archives. In order to participate, institutions have to assign metadata elements to items from a common schema, in this case simplified Dublin Core. To participate in such ventures, archives have to negotiate the risks inherent in making items available out of context, and balance these against not collaborating at all and becoming organizationally invisible. In this age of collaboration and convergence, not being as publicly visible as their library and museum colleagues could present a real threat to the ongoing survival of archival institutions. Funding decisions may be influenced by perceived public profiles – the greater the visibility, the easier it may be to make a case for ongoing support.

Conclusion

The impact of the ability to digitize on archival services has been profound. The growth of the family history phenomenon coupled with the ability to make digital copies of records available and accessible via the internet has significantly changed major facets of the archival endeavour. It remains to be seen whether the extent of influence is recognized as being a powerful force in terms of shaping future direction, and whether archival institutions will succeed in achieving an appropriate balance between the pressure to digitize without alienating or disenfranchising their core, traditional users.

Digitization does present enormous opportunities for archives, particularly in terms of enhancing information retrieval. The change this represents for archival practice is greater than it is for libraries with their accepted, traditional focus on subject access. The consequence of this is that this new approach for archives may be resisted as it could be perceived as a threat to established ways of doing things. The challenge will be to develop models that incorporate the features that best serve the needs of users, without losing sight of the imperative to describe and therefore preserve the context of archival creation and use. Educators also carry a significant burden of responsibility to ensure that future archivists are equipped with the knowledge and skills necessary to engage with digitization initiatives. In other words, we must produce graduates with both specialized knowledge relating to record keeping and an understanding of the broader information environment (Upward and McKemmish, 2006).

The investment required for successful digitization is immense. There is a need for 'warts and all' case studies from those institutions that have undertaken large-scale digitization projects. It is only by reflecting and analysing these experiences that smaller, less well resourced institutions can benefit and use this knowledge to develop their own digitization programmes. Otherwise archivists may simply be contributing to the digital landfill, digitizing in response to user requests but not gaining any real benefit from doing so.

Notes

1 See https://indexing.familysearch.org/.

2 Available at http://warart.archives.govt.nz.

3 *At Island Command*, http://warart.archives.govt.nz/node/411.

4 Transcribe Bentham: Welcome to the Transcription Desk, www.transcribe-bentham.da.ulcc.ac.uk/td/Transcribe_Bentham.

5 The standard can be viewed at http://continuum.archives.govt.nz/files/file/standards/s6/index.html.

6 Although Shauna Hicks spoke about this in her presentation, the written version of her paper does not include these details.

Part 2
Understanding and measuring the use, impact and value of digital collections

5

A strategic approach to the understanding and evaluation of impact

Ben Showers

Introduction

For almost two decades the UK has enjoyed significant amounts of spending on the digitization of scholarly and cultural material. It has been estimated that, since the mid-1990s, £130 million has been spent on the creation of digital content in the UK (JISC, 2005). However, it is now evident that we are experiencing a time of unprecedented challenges and changes within the UK. This is the case with both the information ecosystem that we now inhabit and the new economic climate that exists. This convergence of circumstances has led to concepts such as impact and value re-establishing themselves as important factors for academic institutions and the resources they develop and for the bodies and organizations that fund this important work.

We should avoid the assumption that the desire to better understand the impact and value of digital resources and the uses to which these resources are being put is something new, and the result of this 'perfect storm' of circumstances. Most funding bodies have long expressed the need for the projects they fund to address issues of impact. As an example, the National Science Foundation in the USA has been asking its projects to consider the impact of its work since the early 1990s. There have also been a number of studies and guides that have attempted to address the needs of projects and resources in assessing the usage and impact of digital resources, for example: user analysis (Warwick et al., 2006; Harley et al., 2006); libraries and the impact of digital resources (Spiro and Segal, 2007); and understanding your audience (Quirk et al., 2009).The result of this growing body of research is an increased understanding of the different impacts that digital resources are having within the scholarly community, and the potential benefits they could bring to, and value they could have for, this community.

However, while it is undoubtedly a cliché, there is some truth in the argument that until relatively recently digital resources have often been created with a 'build it and they will come' mentality (Warwick et al., 2008). There has been little understanding of what happens to these digital resources once the project funding or initial creation phase has completed, nor 'any concrete way for collection managers, developers, and funding bodies to attempt to understand and collect data for measuring impact from the onset of a project and throughout the life-cycle of a digitisation effort' (Meyer et al., 2009). Furthermore, it has been noted that while there is an 'impressive accumulation of a body of digital material' there is an associated 'fragmentation in all components of the digitisation infrastructure' (JISC, 2005). This fragmentation is keenly felt in the lack of any systematic and strategic focus on supporting digital resources in measuring impact and capturing value.

As a response to the unprecedented amount of digital scholarly resources, and the renewed need for better strategic support for the measurement and understanding of the impact of these resources, this chapter will explore some the problems faced when attempting to adopt a strategic approach to impact in scholarly digital projects. Specifically the work of the JISC Digitization and e-Content programme will be highlighted to help demonstrate an ongoing attempt to develop a strategic approach to supporting digital scholarly resources in the measuring, analysis and understanding of impact. By examining a number of case studies it will be possible to discern some of the emerging issues that those responsible for digital projects and resources face as they measure and analyse impact and capture the value of digital collections. The first stumbling block to being able to strategically approach impact is in our understanding of the term, and the problems in trying to identify the very thing that we wish to address.

Understanding impact

In attempting to address the notion of impact it is easy to assume that we are trying to identify and define a distinct concept that, if only we could comprehend it, would help resolve the problems that the creators and custodians of digital resources must address in order to understand and communicate the value of their content. Yet impact as a concept is problematic, as developing an understanding of 'impact' is often entwined with the need to address several other key concepts are inherent in digital resources. These include, for example, sustainability, usage, access and discoverability, as well as impact. In attempting to adopt a more strategic approach to the understanding of impact it is essential that the institution, organization or funding body is able to untangle some of these interwoven issues, or at least provide resources with the tools to begin this work themselves. There is a need to identify or unpick this thread of impact; to make it visible, measurable and analysable.

It is also essential that we understand there is no single path to impact. Scholarly resources exemplify this, where a small niche audience can still have a huge impact through citations and the effect on the trajectory of subsequent research. Similarly, beyond research, the impact of digital resources on the student learning experience can be huge, as well as for the tutor and their experience of teaching. If there is a need for support and tools for online collections to utilize in building an understanding of a resources impact, then it is essential that these are taken into account.

Given the problems that confront the creators and managers of digital resources as they attempt to evaluate and measure impact it is understandable that there has been a paucity of support and guidance in this area in the past. Indeed, despite the efforts of institutions and funding bodies, the lack of support for the evaluation of impact and use was in no small part due to the lack of systematic engagement in this area for a number of years. Yet, as the current financial implications of university and academic funding make clear, there are compelling reasons why it makes sense for the impact of scholarly digital resources to be measured and understood. It is no longer possible to take the impact and benefits of these resources for granted. In developing a more strategic and policy-based approach to impact, there are a number of clear reasons why understanding the impact of resources is critical. These include:

- capturing and articulating compelling arguments for continued funding of projects and resources
- building a body of evidence for the impact and value of digital resources on teaching, learning, research and beyond
- the responsibility to everyone to ensure that public funds are being responsibly spent and create value
- stimulating further innovation, new forms of research and the discovery of questions that could not have been posed before.

This is not an exhaustive list, nor are these necessarily the main drivers for developing a resource itself, nor indeed for the (academic) staff who might be involved in these projects. Rather, these staff may argue that impact is a means to sustainability, or the rates of citation have more impact and importance. However, it is also the possibility of publication that results from involvement in a digital humanities project or similar that counts as impact within the scholarly community. A brief but convincing picture of this is painted by Melissa Terras in her plenary at the Digital Humanities conference 2010 where she makes it clear that 'it's not enough to make something that is successful and interesting and well used: you have to write a paper about it that gets published' (Terras, 2010). However, there are clear benefits in being able to deliver a more systematic and embedded approach to understanding impact and moving toward capturing the value of digital resources.

Capturing impact

Since 2004 JISC (whose role is to inspire UK colleges and universities in the innovative use of digital technologies) has, as part of its ground-breaking digitization and e-Content programme, funded the creation of scholarly academic content. The digitization programme, with an initial funding call of £10 million, funded six mass-digitization projects that delivered new digital resources for teaching, learning and research. Since 2004 JISC has invested almost £30 million and funded more than 60 projects, which have ranged from the large-scale digitization of content such as the British Library Newspapers and Pre-Raphaelite resource, through to smaller community and crowdsourcing projects, which have helped engaged a wider audience in the creation and curation of online content (www.jisc.ac.uk/digitisation).

Building on and learning from the work of the original phase one digitization programme, it was the second phase of this programme, running from 2007 to 2009, that cemented the focus on understanding impact as an essential factor in the planning of digitization projects. Along with growing attention on areas such as sustainability and marketing, there was a recognition that more needed to be done on both user analysis and supporting resources in understanding how users engaged with their projects. It is worth noting the evolution of the digitization programme, from an era of large-scale mass digitization, to one that is much more tactical in its approach. This can be seen in the focus on areas such as community engagement, developing digitization infrastructure, capacity and skills, and in a programme of work that began in 2008, looking at enriching existing digital resources to help them take advantage of new technologies (immersive virtual environments, social media, 3D) and thereby improve both their relevance and usage. (More information about the 25 projects that made up the Enriching programme can be found on the programme website, www.jisc.ac.uk/whatwedo/programmes/digitisation/enrichingdigi.aspx.)

In 2008 the digitization programme funded a usage and impact study of five original phase one projects (19th-century British Library Newspapers; Wellcome Medical Journals Backfile; Archival Sound Recordings; Online Historical Population Records; and 18th-Century Parliamentary Papers). The *Usage and Impact Study of JISC-funded Phase 1 Digitisation Projects and the Toolkit for the Impact of Digitised Scholarly Resources* (TIDSR) (Meyer et al., 2009) aimed to measure the impact of the specific projects and to assemble a toolkit to enable other resources to carry out similar work (the toolkit can be found on the Oxford Internet Institute's webpage, http://microsites.oii.ox.ac.uk/tidsr). The two aspects of the study combined, so that the complex and multifaceted nature of the impact analysis could help inform a robust and in-depth toolkit. The toolkit was able to bring together a broad variety of techniques, both qualitative and quantitative, that were often used as distinct methodologies in their own right. The study didn't create any new methods, rather it was the combination of methods and their use within humanities research that proved unique.

A key recommendation that came as a result of the impact study was that 'follow on funding that included funds for the analysis of impact data should be sought by projects and provided by funders, particularly since many impacts have a lag time and won't happen immediately at the end of the project' (Meyer et al., 2009). Indeed, while a strategic approach to impact was embedded with the conception and creation of digital resources, it has been far harder to ensure that the legacy of impact was being addressed. The very methodology that institutions and funding bodies adopt, the management of a short-term digitization project, is itself a threat to the ongoing examination and evaluation of impact. As monies are spent and staff reallocated, a resource can easily lose what impact and value it once had as the content becomes neglected and inertia ensues.

This inherent danger within existing project methodology has again recently emerged in a recent JISC digitization funding call to explore the impact and embedding of digitized resources. As one of the funded project's impact analysis report made clear, 'The problem here is partly one of funding: the project has oscillated between large scale funding and having so little funding that we struggle to stay in existence at all' (Aucott et al., 2011).

Embedding impact

The Impact and Embedding of Digitised Resources Programme (details of the seven projects can be found at www.jisc.ac.uk/whatwedo/programmes/digitisation/impactembedding.aspx) was funded in late 2010 with the explicit aim of evaluating the usage and impact of digitized resources and unearthing practical solutions for how these resources can be embedded within teaching, learning and research. This funding has enabled the managers and creators of these important resources to gain a better understanding of their audiences when developing online collections, be aware of the usage and impact of the resource, and understand how to respond to user requirements in a rapidly changing environment.

Focusing on existing resources (in existence for a minimum of one year), this funding is addressing the recommendation of the TIDSR study that funding bodies (like JISC) provide funding for resources to explore impact beyond the project life cycle. Furthermore, the work has also helped raise awareness of the toolkit and its guidance, while also updating and reinvigorating this important tool for the wider digital scholarly community.

As part of the Impact and Embedding project, resources are expected to undertake an analysis of their current impact and usage, and then develop strategies for addressing these requirements and making the resource more relevant for their specific audience(s).

It is worth noting that the funding call did not attempt to define 'impact'. Rather the focus of the call was to give managers of digital resources an opportunity to explore methods and best practice in analysing and understanding the requirements of their audience(s). With the analysis in place the projects were also expected to explore how their resource could be further embedded in academic practice and the teaching, learning and research of users. This process of embedding acts as a metric for the success of the impact analysis and practices that will be established by the projects, and can be used as a reference point for the ongoing analysis that resources will undertake.

A number of critical issues have been emerging as a result of the analyses the projects have undertaken. The implications of the project methodology have been discussed, but the analysis itself is an important issue that often gets overlooked. Far too often support and guidance is provided in the collection of data, espousing different ways to collect the usage data and various analytics, often with a bias toward the more quantitative methods. However, analysis is not the aggregation of data, rather it is the interpretation and exploitation of that data, and it is this that allows an understanding of the impact of a resource, and this is often the very thing around which there is a distinct lack of support. Furthermore, online collections are often limited by a lack of resources in undertaking this type of analysis, and in addressing the issues that do come to light. While the issue of analysis was inherent in a number of the reports that have come out of the projects in this programme, it is the analysis undertaken by the Vision of Britain through Time project that reveals something particularly interesting about the analysis of data. Their realization is that, despite having an enviable audience size, they are lacking an impact within the group of users their resource should really be attracting. Indeed, this case demonstrates the need to be able to analyse non-users, rather than current users.

Case study: The problem of non-users

The website A Vision of Britain through Time (www.visionofbritain.org.uk) brings together geographical surveys of Great Britain, including every census from 1801 to 2001, as well as a large library of historic maps. Originally launched in 2004 with National Lottery funding as part of the Great Britain Historical Geographical Information System (GIS) project by researchers at the University of Portsmouth, it received further funding from JISC in 2007 to 2009 for additional content and redesign.

The resource is in the enviable position that it has a relatively large audience, and a sizeable number of local and family historians using the site. This popularity seems to be continuing, with analysis showing a continuous upward trend in visitor numbers. Not only that, but the site is also able to utilize this broad audience base to generate revenue through the use of Google Ads and licensing agreements. The income that is generated is sufficient to allow the project to cover its not insubstantial running costs of c. £10,000 per annum. Yet, for its unusual success among academic digitization projects in reaching a mass audience, and generating its own income, it has, by its own analysis, failed to meet the needs of what might be expected to be its core constituency: researchers in historical geography and GIS.

As part of the impact analysis report it was noted that the site lacks certain functionality that users from a historical geography and GIS background require. The analysis of current users, however useful, cannot hope to address the issues that the site faces with regard to the non-users. Indeed, it was the lack of academic users within these fields, uncovered during the analysis, that alerted the project to the need to engage in a qualitative analysis 'offline' with this group. It was clear that while the website resource is probably never going to be a central resource for these geographers, due to its inherent structure and ontology, nonetheless there is functionality that would allow this group of users to engage with the resource. This functionality includes download facilities for the large amounts of geographical data held by the site, as well as statistical mapping.

The Vision of Britain through Time resource explicitly utilizes academic research and complex geographic data in delivering a resource yet, paradoxically, the website itself is of limited importance to those researchers for which such data and research would be useful. The analysis of current usage confirmed the project's suspicions that its usage was limited within the historical geography and GIS domains, despite the richness of data the resource held. By refocusing their analysis on more qualitative research the team are beginning to be able to address their lack of impact within, what might be called, their primary academic audience. The analysis of users led to an analysis of non-users and the academic potential impact of the resource on this audience. It seems now that the Vision of Britain website may be able to both reach a mainstream audience and generate substantial income, while at the same time offering facilities to academics that will help improve the quality and impact of their own research.

The academic nature of the projects contributing to the Impact and Embedding programme mean that often the focus of their analysis is toward traditional (academic) definitions of impact, most obviously citation rates. In the analysis undertaken for the Old Bailey Proceedings Online (OBPO) project, which can be found at www.oldbaileyonline.org, there was a strong focus on bibliometrics using tools such as Scopus (www.scopus.com), complemented with analysis of resources such as Google Books and Scholar, to measure the number of references to the site. It was clear that in subjects such as history there is still a bias toward the 'hard copy' version of a resource. In the specific case of OBPO, references were made to the printed version in articles, with no way of knowing whether there was unacknowledged consultation with the online version. Indeed, the case studies point to some of the broader issues that surround citation as a measure of impact. For example, importing the scholarly notion of citation ranking into digital resources is particularly problematic, because while having an inevitable academic focus, these collections inherently reach out to a far broader audience with a variety of motivations for accessing and utilizing the resources. The focus on citation rankings is problematic in both its narrow understanding of impact, while also attempting to use a traditional (paper-focused) measure on resources that, as digitally based, challenge the assumptions inherent in previous approaches to impact and its evaluation.

Despite the radical different in the content and audience of the resource, the report on the impact analysis of the Siobhan Davies Dance Archive by the Dance Teaching Resource and Collaborative Engagement Spaces (D-TRACES) project found a number of similar issues with citation and linking to their resource. Indeed, despite speaking to researchers who had referenced the site in their research, it became clear that actually locating these citations was problematic, and hampered by the site's change of identity. Clear lessons that emerge are the need for consistent citation formats (if a resource changes name, the ability to track citations is severely restricted). The need for a consistent identity and, maybe more importantly, a consistent citation format that can be copied and pasted by users, can have a huge affect on a resource's impact.

Case study: Impact and digital literacy

The D-TRACES project at Coventry University undertook an analysis of the Siobhan Davies replay archive that forms part of the AHRC-funded Siobhan Davies Dance Archive (www.siobhandaviesreplay.com). The archive brings together all of the materials and documentation associated with Davies' choreographies, including moving and still image, audio and text. This collaboration between Siobhan Davies Dance and Coventry University was officially launched in June 2009. The archive contains approximately 3000 items relating to 36 works and eight projects.

As part of its analysis for the JISC-funded impact programme the resource undertook a user analysis, utilizing best practice from the TIDSR toolkit. The project explored link analysis, Google analytics and online surveys for qualitative data. It was clear that, like other projects within this funding programme, the archive had issues that arose around the changing of the resource's uniform resource locator (URL), the problem of citation and the need for a standardized citation format on the website, as well as user confusion around this archive and a similarly named, but separate, website. Overall it was clear that the resource was well used and valued within the dance community, both for research as well as for teaching and learning.

However, what makes the D-TRACES project approach to both the understanding of the impact and the resource's continued value is in its relationship to students' experience of working with online resources. The project is utilizing the personal development programme (PDP) that undergraduates across the UK are required to undertake as a way to 'encourage more imaginative approaches to developing digital literacy, and for application and transfer to other learning situations' (Whatley, 2010). By embedding the resource in the PDP component of undergraduate dance courses the archive has connected its ongoing impact to the academic development of dance (and other creative arts) students and the growth in information literacy.

And in developing an understanding of the interconnectedness of impact with other complex issues the D-TRACES project has been able to turn this complexity to its advantage; by aligning impact to digital literacy and student academic development the resource is able to both embed itself within the teaching and learning of universities while maintaining its value to researchers and practitioners.

The case studies that have emerged from the Impact and Embedding programme have demonstrated both the myriad ways to approach the issue of impact and the various strategies used to evaluate that impact and improve the resources for their respective audiences. But they are also demonstrating the implications that the growing number of media-rich and innovative resources face when attempting to understand and evaluate their impact. These small and diverse projects are helping to refine, test and implement a growing body of knowledge and practice that is assisting in bringing together a strategic framework to help digital resources, both within and outside academia, measure and evaluate their impact and value. The individual value of the case studies is being enhanced by their contribution to TIDSR, ensuring that it is able to remain relevant and reflects the varied practice and resource types that exist.

Conclusion: towards an impact framework

This chapter has sought to identify the reasons why understanding and capturing impact is such an important aspect of the funding and creation of digital resources. In highlighting some of the work that has been taking place to analyse impact at a project level, it is clear how this 'local' effort is helping to establish a more coherent and strategic approach to the measurement and evaluation of impact in scholarly digital resources.

The TIDSR has helped establish a space where digital resources can find best practice and guidelines for undertaking analysis, as well as being able to learn from and contribute experiences of impact measures and evaluation. This initial work has been built on through the funding of seven impact projects that are helping to test and refine the toolkit, while exploring innovative ways of ensuring that they are able to better understand the needs of their audiences and provide a sustainable and valuable scholarly resource.

It is essential that institutional and public funding bodies they are able to demonstrate the impact of their work. By addressing issues of impact at the project level, developing supporting tools and addressing impact throughout the project life cycle it is possible to lay the foundations for something that begins to resemble a coherent framework for the understanding and evaluation of impact.

While not ideal, the notion of a framework serves as a metaphor to enable an appreciation of what is required to better understand the needs and requirements of users. This understanding of a resource's audience is at first glance a seemingly trivial one, and yet it is arguably the fulcrum of impact, without which scholarly resources' ability to impact on teaching and learning, let alone research, would be all but lost.

It is undoubtedly true that the term impact is becoming more pervasive, bleeding into more and more of the activities that public bodies and institutions undertake. In times of crisis and financial uncertainty, such a measure is useful for demonstrating the transformative and essential work that is being undertaken. Such a measure also provides an opportunity to examine the collective benefits and value of digital resources at a national level, leveraging the wealth of digitized content to demonstrate the impact and benefits of this transformative digitization work and providing arguments for the contribution made to the UK's knowledge economy by the academics, teachers and users who create and exploit them.

Ensuring that we see impact as a route to better understanding the needs and requirements of our audiences prevents us from defining impact too narrowly. Impact thus understood has the potential to transform the possibilities of research, as well as helping create a sustainable national content collection of rich and accessible digital content to foster excellence in research, learning and teaching.

6
User needs in digitization

Milena Dobreva, Andy O'Dwyer and Leo Konstantelos

Introduction

Impact and *value* of digitized collections are concepts that are both being brought to real life through users. Any metrics and criteria that would try to capture impact and value have to factor in first how individual users (or user communities)[1] benefit from the digitized resources in question.

Thus, one specific difficulty in measuring impact and value is the subjective and quickly changing user-related component of the valorization process. How exactly could we find out whether a digital resource had an impact on users? What value propositions have resource creators intended to convey to their target audiences? How well did these target audiences understand the message – is the value they see in the resource and surrounding services identical to what its producers had in mind? This chapter presents a description of user evaluation methodologies, and discusses how user considerations can be factored into the digitization process. It presents a case study describing user involvement in projects on digitization of audiovisual materials.

The user paradox: users are valuable in digitization policies but not sufficiently involved

As the volume of digitized resources grows, so does the number of studies and publications on user studies within the digital library domain, although these have been limited in scope, as noted recently by Michael Khoo and colleagues: 'In the case of digital library researchers, the focus of research is often on technical issues (e.g., information retrieval methods, software architecture, etc.) rather than on user-centered issues' (Khoo, Buchanan and Cunningham, 2009).

In fact, we are currently witnessing a paradox: major institutions from the cultural heritage sector clearly emphasize the place of user evaluation and feedback in digitization-related policies. But in reality, decisions about aspects of digitization that impact users are frequently taken without direct user involvement.

For example, the *National Library of Australia Collection Digitisation Policy* (National Library of Australia, 2008) states that: 'The Library's digitisation activities take account of user evaluation and feedback. Users are encouraged to provide feedback and make suggestions through the Digital Collections user feedback form or other ways.'

Similarly, the *National Library of Wales: digitisation policy and strategy* (National Library of Wales, 2005) says that selection will be made according to 'An appreciation of user requirements which will drive the selection and delivery of digitised material . . . the Library will seek user feedback, including that of current and potential users, by means of online surveys, structured evaluation, web metrics (collecting and interpreting data) [which] will include quantitative and qualitative data.'

The National Library of Scotland states in its 2008–2010 strategy document, 'We will maintain awareness of the needs of our various user (and potential user) communities through market research, consultation and involvement, in order to develop our services in the most appropriate way' (National Library of Scotland, 2008).

JISC in its *Digitisation Strategy* (JISC, 2008) seeks to clearly define its terms of selection in relation to users *before* the actual digitization, wishing to 'continue to fund the digitisation of high quality collections of core relevance to learning, teaching and research in the UK' while also 'understand[ing] both more about the condition and potential of new collections to be digitised (particularly those held within the JISC community) and also to understand where areas of the highest demand for new collections may exist'. Marchionni (2010) has presented a range of user involvement mechanisms as a synthesis of experiences from the JISC digitization programme, including users' feedback, establishing relationships with the users and determining impact.

The examples illustrate a multi-scale view on users: including the current but also the future ones; inviting their participation in different stages of the digitization process – at the planning stages of the digitization, or within the use of the digitized product; and identifying methods that could be used to engage the users – e.g. online surveys, structured evaluation, web metrics.

However, meta-analysis shows that there is evidence of insufficient involvement of users, indicating that users need to be engaged more actively in digitization projects.

Within the context of digital resources for archives, Sundqvist noted that 'the general knowledge of user behaviour is a mixture of common sense, presumptions and prejudices' (2007, 624). The Institute of Museum and Library Services (IMLS) reported that 'The most frequently-used needs assessment methods do not directly involve the users' (2003, 2).

In this chapter we will first outline how and when users could take part in digitization, and will give some examples of user engagement from the audiovisual heritage domain. We also summarize how user studies can be helpful at all stages of digitization projects including front end, summative, normative evaluation, as well as direct engagement in contributing content.

The context of digitization
Digitization as the enabler to access

Digitization may serve many functions, but its primary focus is on enabling and enhancing access to a diverse array of material. Digitized artefacts – of text documents, images or audiovisual material – inherit the flexibility that digital information provides in terms of storage, dissemination and management. The motivation to utilize the benefits of digital surrogates ranges from increasing access to collections in high demand; promoting interinstitutional collaboration, and simultaneous access to resources through networked digital repositories; to enhancing the educational value of analogue resources, capitalizing on the opportunities that increased access offers and safeguarding the integrity of fragile, rare or heavily used analogue material (UNESCO, IFLA and ICA, 2002).

The role of digitization as a mechanism to facilitate and promote access to cultural heritage resources can be evidenced in a number of international efforts. For instance, Smith (2006) provides an extensive account of the British Library's digitization programme, emphasizing the benefits derived from digital access for both on-site and remote library users. It is precisely these benefits – more than other incentives – that have attracted funding and investment in this domain. Digitization *is* primarily 'access – lots of it' (Smith and Council on Library and Information Resources, 1999, 7), which is reflected in the many strategies for building digitized collections (Smith and Digital Library Federation, 2001). Although motivation to digitize material can significantly vary from commercial purposes to high quality artistic reproduction, the results of the process are perceived in this chapter as a research and educational asset for library and archive collections (Lynch, 1998). Within this context, many digital library projects have produced remarkable results and offer access to large-scale collections, such as the Library of Congress Prints & Photographs Online[2] (Natanson, 2007), which currently provides access to over 1.2 million digitized objects; Google Books,[3] which currently includes 130 million unique digitized books; and Europeana,[4] which provides access to Europe's heritage in digital format and currently includes over 14 million objects. This activity is underpinned by a growing demand worldwide for libraries, museums, archives and historical societies to make their assets electronically available (Kaufman, 2004).

The requirements of digitization

Despite the many benefits, digitization remains a costly, complex and time-consuming process. Precisely because these issues can be perceived by institutions as hindrances to digitization, a number of good practice guides provide the fundamental requirements for successfully engaging in and completing digitization projects – maximizing at the same time their impact on the targeted user audience. *The NINCH Guide to Good Practice in the Digital Representation and Management of Cultural Heritage Materials* (HATII and NINCH, 2002) and the UNESCO *Guidelines for Digitization Projects* (UNESCO, IFLA and ICA., 2002) suggest that digitization activities should start with a definition of a selection policy that will specify what (types of) material will be included and for what purpose. Although digitization is by its very nature content-based, selection should reflect (1) the value of the material in cultural terms, (2) the demand for access from user communities and (3) any urgency to digitize due to the physical condition of an artefact (UNESCO, IFLA and ICA, 2002, 13–14).

Between selection of analogue material and delivery of the final digitized product, there is an array of processes, decisions and elements that need to be considered. First, capturing mechanisms must be defined that align with the affordances of the institution for digitization (HATII and NINCH, 2002). Quality control ensures the integrity of the digitized artefacts and establishes that they satisfy the requirements of the project – matching the needs of users and stakeholders (UNESCO, IFLA and ICA , 2002, 21–5). The usability of the digitized artefacts greatly depends on effective digital asset management policies – from the manner that files are hierarchically stored and file naming conventions (file management), to the all important employment of administrative, descriptive and structural metadata to contextualize both the collections and the individual items within each collection (HATII and NINCH, 2002).

Inevitably, different types of material present different digitization challenges, and different user needs. Depending on the type of primary collections that an institution holds, policies should be in place for accessing text documents, images, audio sources and moving images (video). Furthermore, different projected uses and expectations dictate different approaches to the digitization process. The identification of these 'projected uses and expectations' cannot be based on armchair speculation – particularly when the high costs of digitization often demand an equally high expectation for 'return on investment'.

The success of digitization efforts – specifically within libraries, museums and archives – can only be established when *institutional objectives* have been established and when *user needs* for the digitized material have been covered. It is argued here that user involvement in digitization should not be perceived as a mere justification that 'we did things well', but as a guide and sustained roadmap to the design, development and conduct of digitization projects. Our aim is to provide practical information on how to support decision-making processes and how to situate digitization needs for targeted communities of users.

The first challenge in work related to users is to understand who they are and what the best possible ways to involve them are. The following sections describe ways in which digitization projects in the audiovisual sector illustrate the challenges faced in providing information and audiovisual resources that address the needs of a multitude of different users and uses of digital content.

When to involve users
Users can be involved in a range of activities related to digitization. This involvement serves very different purposes, which are summarized in Table 6.1.

How to study users
A variety of methods are used in user studies. We cannot present all of them in detail[5] but provide a brief introduction to the various types of methods.

User study methods based on direct user involvement
A large group of user study methods are based on direct user involvement. They include:

- quantitative methods, such as questionnaires and experiments involving users (most typically studying user behaviour aspects – e.g. search within an existing resource, or eye tracking – studying the gaze fixation during the use of a resource in order to analyse the quality of its interface)

Table 6.1 *Types of user involvement in digitization*

Type of involvement	What is it used for?	Relation to value and impact
Front-end involvement	Users can take part in assessment of a variety of issues in digitization (technical requirements, e.g. resolution, dimensions of digital objects, preferred formats for use). At this stage users can also take part in exploratory research, e.g. needs in new resources and defining requirements, as well as rationale for selection, appraisal and prioritization of material to be digitized.	This type of user involvement aims to identify in advance what the users see as a valuable future resource. It helps to focus digitization on outputs of expected value and impact. A major warning that needs to be made is that the opinions of current users may not be identical to those of future users.
Normative evaluation	This type of evaluation usually takes the form of iterative circles of process and evaluation when implementing digitization of collections. Most typically, such evaluation will focus on usability, e.g. interfaces and presentation of digitized resources; coverage of identified needs for specific audiences.	This type of evaluation helps to potentially increase the value and impact of a resource in development. Iterative circles of evaluation can be really helpful to improve resource discovery tools and interfaces, and to apply corrective measures to the digitization process.
Summative evaluation	Here the focus is the final output and accordance to the expectations and requirements of target communities, organization structures and the wider disciplinary domain.	This type of user involvement may help to valorize the digital resource and to establish its reputation.
Direct engagement in the digital resource creation	Direct user engagement can utilize social media tools that allow users to contribute their own digital objects or to take part in the enrichment of digitized resources – e.g. supplying full texts or metadata. Typical examples are crowdsourcing, e.g. users contribute to create full text versions from images, and the use of Flickr to share digitized resources more widely and invite users to contribute metadata.	This is a specific type of contribution that potentially could increase the value of digital resources for users or communities that appreciate the wider involvement. However, it might also have the opposite effect if there is a danger of compromising the quality and trustworthiness of digital resources.

- qualitative methods, such as focus groups, interviews, expert evaluations and user panels (groups of users who regularly discuss the digital resource that is being studied).

Mixed methods can also be used, blending quantitative and qualitative elements, e.g. longer time experiments where users have to keep a diary of their use of a resource.

Ethnographic studies are another method employing direct user involvement; in this case researchers make observations directly in the environment of creation or use of the digital resource. This method helps to see the larger picture and dependencies of digitization work with other processes in the organization.

User study methods based on indirect observation

A rapidly developing group of methods for user studies is based on indirect observation. A typical method in this category is deep log analysis, which studies the traces of user activities in the use of web resources – e.g. duration of visit, search terms used, websites visited after the use of the research studied. If the users involved in the study have to generate documents (e.g. produce a poster or a presentation), these documents could also be analysed to discover typical patterns of behaviour.

In real-life practice, most current studies are based on hybrid methodologies, e.g. focus groups (a qualitative method) could be used in combination with deep log analysis (a quantitative method) in order to see how user behaviour evidence from the deep logs supports statements made by real users during focus groups.

The knowledge gathered by different methods can be used to build a synthesized profile of a typical user (such unified user descriptions are called *personae*). It also could be used to summarize typical *user scenarios* that show how the digital resources are used in real life.

Table 6.2 summarizes some typical questions and recommended methods in order to demonstrate the suitability of different approaches.

Users and their engagement: examples from the audiovisual heritage sector

Digitization and audiovisual sector

In the broadcasting and audiovisual sector, digitization is now a crucial mechanism for both preservation and access. Storage costs have dramatically reduced and high-quality digital files are suitable for broadcast and archiving. Digital files are rapidly replacing traditional audio and video tape storage cassette formats, which are now unsuitable for modern delivery methods. Digital files offer expedient access, while tapes are expensive by comparison as they require the maintenance of associated replay machines to support obsolete formats, and the associated expenditure to the host organization of maintaining row upon row of shelving in regulated climatic conditions.

Digitization also offers benefits for users, as remote online access makes content more accessible and less dependent on paper-based records and legacy information technology (IT) storage systems. To complement this whole process, enriching the metadata and catalogue can greatly assist in providing user access to this newly preserved content. Once audiovisual media resides in a digital environment, long-term preservation can be achieved through periodic reviews and a strategy to migrate content at the appropriate time to avoid

Table 6.2 *User-related questions and methods*

Question	Method
Who are the potential users of a resource that is planned to be digitized?	A web questionnaire can be used to address a potentially large community of future users. Their responses could be helpful in defining typical users. Depending on the available knowledge about these groups of users, a next step could be to use the method of personae.
How do we evaluate the usability of an existing digital resource?	This could be achieved through an expert group study. Direct user involvement could be accomplished through focus groups.
How do we identify possible steps for extending the user community?	A web questionnaire and deep log analysis could help to build a picture of the current user community. For fine-tuning the measures that could be used to expand the user base, expert evaluation could be helpful. This might be connected to finding possible reuse scenarios.
What are the stumbling blocks for the users of an existing digital resource?	Best suited are methods with direct user involvement (focus groups or studies involving eye tracking); the deep log analysis could also be of help in tracing how many times the users tries to execute a search, or what happens before the user leaves the resource.
How does my digital resource compare with others?	Comparison in this domain is still difficult because studies are too different; expert evaluation seems the best option here.
How do we make the navigation on the website easier?	Use eye tracking to see what the individual users are doing and how, and deep log analysis to define typical patterns of actions within the digital resource.

the obsolescence trap of having information and other media stored on redundant storage systems with no playback mechanism or method of recovery. Long-term preservation of digital content is still challenging, and digital content has a shorter shelf life than traditional storage media, such as paper and film. This places additional pressures on the traditional roles of archivists and curators with mixed media in their collections, who now have to acquire some knowledge of digital preservation as parts of their holdings move from shelves to servers; their awareness of digitization processes and back-up strategies for their digital items may well be as common as how to care for paintings or pottery. Digitally born assets need care and protection policies as much as physical ones, and resources such as the European Union (EU) funded PrestoPRIME[6] have been established to assist archivists, curators and memory institutions to find best practice in this area.

Overall, however, the benefits of digitization are clear: it offers better access and preservation opportunities. Not digitizing suitable collections will result in a lack of electronic access, reduced usage and ultimately the risk of decay or loss of material.

Many public institutions are therefore embracing the value of digitization, leading to an increase in use of their resources and a new engagement with an expanding community of users, many of whom would never have been able to access this material in analogue form. The BBC[7] is a prominent example of this as it offers multimedia content through its archive website, focusing around special collections and anniversaries. Digitization helps organizations like the BBC fulfil their public service remit, presenting an opportunity to make more archive content available for their audiences online. A step in this direction has been achieved with the plan to place the historic broadcasting schedule information online from the *Radio Times*, the BBC's weekly programme guide for radio and television. Through the Genome project[8] the entire back catalogue is being digitized (scanned) in order to place a web version of these schedules online for public access. Making this information available online detailing past programmes from the BBC's collection is likely to be a driver for demand for opening up other parts of the archive, as the public will identify content they cannot currently see or hear. This digitization project will also have an additional benefit of creating a 'digital preservation' set of the *Radio Times* collection for future generations.

The audience for digitization

Audiences for digital resources are notoriously difficult to categorize, as access can be from virtually anywhere and through a variety of media and devices. This is especially true of audiovisual collections, which appeal to, and are used by, enormous numbers of users. To understand this complexity, it can be helpful to develop a typology of users, in order to identify the similarities and differences among the discrete *user communities* that are most likely to access the resource, categorized by:

- user role (end-users, intermediaries from the memory institutions, cultural and scientific heritage professionals)
- specific use of resources (e.g. teaching, research, learning, increasing awareness)
- information literacy skills of the user (from technical novices to experts)
- preferred modes of interaction (searching and browsing are the most popular distinctions, but different activities such as exploring, locating, comparing, evaluating, analysing and synthesizing require different support from the resource discovery and access interface).

Users can be further segmented into various groups, such as academics, educators and learners, research professionals, cultural and business users. Digital resources can be directly accessed by the end-user, or via an intermediary such as information professional, librarian or media manager. A typology of users should reflect the diversity of audiences for online resources. It comprises researchers, educators, curators, memory institutions, broadcasters and the general public. Online information is inevitably derived from a wealth of sources, some written for specialists and others written for a more general everyday consumer.

Just as the expectations and needs of user groups differ, so too will the impact and value a particular digital resource have for them. Catering for these differing requirements can, for content suppliers and web designers, seem overwhelming, particularly when faced with the sheer volume, and variety, of material to be digitized in the audiovisual sector.

Why involve users when digitizing collections?

Users of online resources are often profiled and categorized, and have interfaces tailored to meet their needs and expectations. While this is good practice, there is inevitably a blurring and lack of clear distinction between user types, such as research users, media professionals or those simply browsing. Users search with different priorities and emphasis, often through the same search engine and interfaces. As they narrow down their searches and hone into sites and select pages, usability comes even more to the fore. Users inevitably invest their time on websites and portals they 'can work with' and this comes down to good usability and relevancy.

To achieve this, time and investment is critical in user studies, observational sessions with focus groups, task-led testing and interviews. An accepted practice is to build around user needs, rather than developing resources in isolation. Collaboration between users and developers is recommended, with iterative design sessions to enhance the functionality, features and subjective values such as colour, design and the general look and feel.

From a commercial perspective, lessons from online sales indicate that a high degree of usability, reliability and accuracy are paramount. Companies that successfully sell information and content expend a great deal of effort in designing the purchasing workflow from preview through to checkout and sale. Their ability to make a profit in online sales is influenced in part by the 'ease of use' of a particular interface.

For the academic institutions or general information provider the emphasis is usually less on 'making a sale' and more on providing a good quality research and learning service. While similar principles of understanding the user apply universally, the resources and skills to do this are often not within the financial or time resources available to a project based in a library, or educational organization. If a project is unable to fund user studies, it may commission evaluations to enhance the usability of online content. However, there are quick, effective and practical steps they can take from feedback forms and surveys, and questionnaires placed online to gather users' perspectives on what the organization currently provides and what the user would like to see.

Providing resources with reuse in mind

As digital information is published into the public sphere, content from a variety of sources is presented together and mashed up in a hit list of results from a user's search string. A prime example of this diversity of content can be seen in the growth of book scanning and republishing freely online by organizations like Google Books. Assisted by the fact that thousands of books are out of copyright, texts that were once written for, say, a medical professional in a specialized field can now be available to anyone online; similarly, journals, magazines and encyclopaedias written for the public are also emerging online, in many cases free. The business model to enable these digitization initiatives is usually based on targeted advertising modelled around the users' search criteria.

Defining a user who could use all these disparate resources, accessing them for different reasons, is difficult to define or profile. Moreover, how could you undertake a user requirements exercise for a portal to access this information with such dynamic users?

Categorizing user groups can be a complex process as needs and expectations merge. Diverse groups of users may want access to the same information or service, but they also may want to see or interact with it in a different way. While user accounts and personalization do help to some extent to overcome the burden of addressing differing individual or group requirements, It can be the case that a conflict may exist for information architects and designers on how to represent these requirements across the same data resource to different user groups.

Often it is impossible for an information provider to adapt their front-end user interfaces to meet the needs of all expected groups. The resources, time and cost would make this impractical for all but the largest information providers. This challenge has been addressed in the EU-sponsored project, VideoActive,[9] where different collections have come together and been made available through a central portal.

Project example: Video Active

The EU-funded project Video Active was part of the eContent*plus* programme of the European Commission. The objective was to place thousands of hours of audiovisual content and texts online for the citizens of Europe. Broadcasters, archives and technical partners came together to enable the digitization, metadata alignment and presentation of content, supported through multilingual access. Involving users was at the forefront of the project processes and continued through the life cycle of the project.

A work package within the project was dedicated to usability and assessment, and its initial task was to carry out a user requirements exercise to identify the type of content, services and features that would be attractive, and the range of services needed and features that would address the needs of target user groups. A key component was how to represent audiovisual content and associated texts through a central interface that would support different user profiles. The target audience for this open portal was defined as:

- the public and cultural heritage sector: the broad spectrum of public requirements and online 'cultural tourism'
- educational and academics: targeted content to enhance topics, courses and research initiatives
- media professionals: requiring access for research in programme making and journalism.

The methodology and approach was based around the usability-related set of standards (ISO 9241, *Ergonomics of Human Systems Interaction*,[10] and addressing the familiar aspects of *usability, effectiveness, efficiency* and *satisfaction* in the context of use. Audiences were understood to have differing IT skills, requirements and expectations. A media professional may require a different layout and functionality from a cultural user who may be more open to going on a voyage of discovery, with more time at their disposal, happy to be offered a range of options and to be distracted along the way. In contrast, in the games, competitions and quiz sectors users usually enjoy being challenged and a sense of difficulty is seen as a positive experience.

Video Active conducted a mixture of online surveys, interviews and questionnaires to gather requirements. These surveyed technical requirements relating to the end-user, such as speed of connection and preferred operating systems, and enabled the project to avoid developing audiovisual content in too high a quality that would therefore be slow to access. The project found notable differences in IT capabilities and access to hardware and bandwidth across European countries, and this influenced decisions about content and usability, averaging out file sizes for access to accommodate as many communities as possible online.

This process also uncovered a preference for a degree of personalization and bookmark functionality within the portal to save and share references to pages and content. Media professionals and academics were keen to mark and export references to colleagues and classes on items they had found. A 'basket' of references was seen as a way of not having to duplicate searches at a later date. Users also advised on aspects of navigation and presentation of supporting data and fields for advanced searching, which helped the project team define how data should be organized, displayed and carried across the pages. Professional media users, for example, are keen to see rights information, with contacts displayed alongside the content, while for an academic or teacher this was less important and this type of information could sit on an accompanying page. This was a useful example of how something that can be a benefit for one user group can be a distraction or unnecessary for another.

The Video Active project showed that there is great value to project developers in discovering the potential of detailed personalization of user preferences for portals and aggregators of content. The expected users are likely to be too diverse to encapsulate the majority of needs in the overall design of the central portal. By attempting to please all groups, a single design may be too generic and lack features that raise overall usability and satisfaction.

However, although individual preferences can be seen as a remedy, this can be complex to maintain and visitors to the website can be reluctant to log in unless they are a frequent visitor to the portal and can see benefits they would miss out on as a casual user.

Recommender software based on search patterns and profiling can be useful. But the balance needs to be struck between something seen as genuinely useful and something delivering a distraction during user interaction. In any case the same user may well search both as a professional (for work) and as an individual, often through the same interfaces. Managing a multitude of passwords for different sites and sessions may be cumbersome to keep track of.

More research is needed to address types of users, and their requirements, in order to realize the full value of digital content. Video Active adopted innovative approaches to understand the users of the resource at the outset, and then built their requirements into the resource, enabling audiences to really utilize and appreciate the full potential of the digitized collections.

Conclusion

User studies are an area of recent rapid development. The following is a summary of some of the current, central research questions in this domain:

- The continuum of *user needs – user expectations – user perceptions* has not been studied systematically yet. Knowing more about the connection between the user understanding of value and impact – as a component of user satisfaction – and the consciously expressed needs combined with expectations is essential to develop resources that sustain a stable user community. The understanding of this continuum would also help to adapt digitization projects to the real users.
- The modes of interaction (searching, browsing) can be further studied. Knowing more about their characteristics can help to provide the best possible support according to the mode followed by the user.
- Methods for user studies. There is a wide range of users, some directly involving users (e.g. focus groups, media labs, questionnaires), as well as methods based on the use of data gathered in the process of digital resource use, e.g. user logs. The selection of the most suitable method according to the question addressed is not a trivial task and the provision of more guidance is essential.
- Measures (objective and subjective). There are different ways to measure user performance. There is still no consensus on measures that can be used for digital libraries' user studies. Having an agreed set could facilitate future comparative studies and benchmarking.

User evaluation is a fascinating and multifaceted area of research. User studies are, however, still not utilized widely and in-depth in digitization projects. This chapter shows that user studies can be practically involved in all stages of digitization projects and this involvement leads to various possibilities in increasing the value and impact of digital resources.

Notes

1 Real people could be named differently in order to convey subtle differences on their level of engagement and role – users (in the computer environment), consumers (when we take a business perspective), visitors (when we speak about a particular type of resources, e.g. internet websites). In this chapter we will use the term users.
2 www.loc.gov/pictures/about.
3 http://books.google.com/.
4 www.europeana.eu/portal/.
5 Facet is due to publish a book on user studies for digital library development in 2012. A good overview of methods for user testing within a particular project was made for Europeana Connect by Gitte Petersen et al. (2011) *D3.2.3.H Recommendations for Conducting User Tests: User involvement – A Toolbox. How to Involve Users in Development Processes in Europeana.*
6 www.prestoprime.org.
7 www.bbc.co.uk/archive/.
8 www.bbc.co.uk/blogs/aboutthebbc/2010/08/bbc-genome-the-complete-broadc.shtml.
9 www.videoactive.eu.
10 www.iso.org/iso/iso_catalogue/catalogue_ics/catlogue_detail_ics.htm?csnumber=55486.

7

Measuring impact and use: scholarly information-seeking behaviour[1]

Claire Ross, Melissa Terras and Vera Motyckova

Introduction

Emergent information technologies offer museum professionals new ways of bringing information about their collections directly to their audiences. There is a strong ethos within museums to widen public access to collections via the ever-growing digital provision of collections data. Over the past decade, the number of online museum collections, and the number of online visitors using those collections, has increased significantly. These changes have posed challenges for museum professionals and academics alike, seeking to understand how digital museum resources feature in the information seeking practices of their online visitors.

There are now vast amounts of digital museum resources available to support scholarship. These resources are changing the ways researchers work, offering convenient quick access to a wide selection of materials, particularly with regard to cultural heritage content. However, finding information in museums, as well as libraries and archives (memory institutions), is not an easy task. Collections database information systems can be overwhelming and daunting to many users. Designing intuitive systems that meet researchers' needs requires a thorough understanding of the information-seeking behaviour of collection database users. A proper understanding of how museum visitors use digital museum resources is critical for the success of museums in the information age. As museums cope with the challenges of 'being digital' (Hamma, 2004), meeting the information needs of online visitors has become an important part of the museum's role (Marty, 2004) and it is now critical for researchers and museum professionals to explore the use of museum digital resources, in-house and online (Booth, 1999; Sarraf, 1999).

The British Museum has a commitment to expanding virtual and physical access to its collections, utilizing different mediums to open up the museum collections to a wider, more diverse audience. In October 2007, it launched an online version of its collections database, British Museum Collection Database Online (COL[2]). By the end of 2009, nearly two million records from the museum collections had been made available to the public worldwide. Despite recent technical advances in collections access and interpretation, very little is known about whether and how this material is used, or if it makes possible new kinds of engagement with museum objects. This chapter presents the results of a study that analyses the use and information-seeking behaviour by scholars of the Collection Database Online, through a survey of academic users.[3] A detailed analysis of user survey data illustrates the perceptions that academic user groups have of the museum collection information environment, as well as understanding the functionality and usability of the Collection Database Online. The methodology described here provides a particularly valuable insight into the use, value and impact of digital museum collections, and could be adapted or modified by other organizations to better understand use of their collections.

Museum visitors and information-seeking behaviour

Unprecedented changes in the provision of museum digital resources have transformed the experience of visiting museums (whether physically or by using the online collection). These changes have affected how users interact with digital museum resources and the museum information environment as a whole. Visitor studies have always been important for museums, and numerous research studies have explored the relationships between museums and their visitors, both online and in-house (Falk, 1998, 2006; Falk and Dierking, 2000; Kravchyna and Hastings, 2002; Haley Goldman and Schaller, 2004; Thomas and Carey, 2005), the results of which require museum professionals to adapt, and develop new information needs and information policies (Besser, 1997; Knell, 2003). However, in the complex area of large digital museum collections, such research is at an early stage. Despite recent research focusing on the use of museum digital resources from a user-centred perspective (see Hertzum, 1998; Jörgensen, 2004; Marty, 2007) there is a need for a greater understanding of the information-seeking behaviour of specific user groups using museum online collections.

Studying the information-seeking behaviour of specific user groups, especially academics, has contributed to the development of numerous library and archival services and there is an extensive body of literature on the information-seeking habits of humanities faculty researchers that has shaped academic library and archival services (Rimmer et al., 2006; Makri, 2006; Warwick, 2008). However, there is little research on the information-seeking behaviour of specific user groups using museum online collections. This chapter will focus on scholarly information-seeking behaviour with digital museum resources. The characteristics of humanities scholars' information-seeking behaviour, in particular, can provide insight and a context within which to understand researcher behaviour in a cultural heritage context.

Digital information-seeking behaviour
The humanities

Criticism that digitization programmes of collections have 'sprung up in piecemeal fashion' that has largely been led by 'supply rather than demand, spurred by opportunity instead of actual need' (JISC, 2005) has played a part in the growth of research to understand the impact and uptake of digital resources (Carson, 2005; Harley, 2007; Atkins, Brown and Hammond, 2007; Zuccala et al., 2007; Warwick et al., 2008) as well as the behaviours and needs of users (Nicholas et al., 2006; Rowlands et al., 2008). Recent research exploring the information needs and information-seeking behaviour of humanities scholars has been undertaken by Green (2000), Herman (2001), Talja and

Maula (2003), Barrett (2005), Ellis and Oldman (2005) and Warwick et al. (2008).

A key aspect of the literature about humanities scholars is that their information needs and seeking behaviours are not like those in the sciences or social sciences, although many designers of digital resources have assumed that they are similar (Bates, 2002). Research completed by Stone (1982) and Watson-Boone (1994) showed that humanities users need a wide range of resources, in terms of their age and type. This remains true in a digital environment (Warwick et al., 2008), where humanities users continue to need printed materials and physical objects, as well as electronic resources, which by their nature may imply a much greater range of materials than those used by scientists (British Academy, 2005). Lönnqvist suggests that 'scholars in the humanities do not have homogenous information seeking behaviour or homogenous information needs' (1990, 29). Wiberley (1983, 1988) showed that humanities scholars constructed searches using well defined terms, but these terms were different from those used by scientists, being more likely, for example, to include names of places or people. A range of more recent studies have shown that humanities scholars who use digital resources tend to be demanding of the quality of resources and are capable of constructing complex search strategies, given appropriate training (Bates, 1996; Whitmire, 2002; Dalton and Charnigo, 2004). Though this material is helpful in informing information-seeking research in specific discipline and user groups, the picture is far from complete. Further research needs to be undertaken to understand the information-seeking behaviour of scholars who use online museum collections.

Museums

Museums are developing online collections of digital resources at a rapid pace, despite a critical lack of data about the needs of the intended users of those resources (Cunliffe, Kritou and Tudhope, 2001). The lack of data about the use of digital museum resources is a serious concern for museums and academic researchers, as not understanding user needs means it is not possible for museum professionals to know whether they are providing access to digital museum resources in a way that satisfies the needs of their intended users (Hertzum, 1998). Users of museum resources are no longer satisfied with limited access to information about museum collections, and many desire 24-hour access to museum data, no matter where these data are located, or how the data are organized (Cameron, 2003; Hamma, 2004). As museum information resources become more technically complex, and the users of those resources become more information literate, the needs and expectations of visitors have become increasingly sophisticated and this needs to be fully understood.

Motivated by this gap in scholarly information-seeking studies in a cultural heritage context, this research aims to draw on information-seeking behaviour research to add to the understanding of the perceptions that scholars have of their information environment. Additionally, we aim to provide an insight into scholarly information-seeking behaviour in the cultural heritage domain, while specifically investigating how the functionality and usability of the British Museum's digital collection via the Collection Database Online aids (or hinders) users' information searching.

Study of the use of the
British Museum's Collection Database Online
Method

Research into information-seeking behaviour and user experience frequently displays a tendency toward quantitative methods, often involving basic statistical analysis and structured surveys. This is suitable for obtaining an overall quantitative picture of information use by a particular group but it is unsuitable for gaining a full picture of the users' perception of their information environments and search behaviours. Quantitative data and deep log analysis can determine which web pages are accessed, but not whether the content was actually read or understood, or if a user was satisfied with what they found (Warwick et al., 2008). Our aim was to develop an awareness of the perceptions that user groups have of their information environment as well as how the functionality and usability of the British Museum Collection Database Online aids or hinders their information searching, by shifting from a macro approach to a micro approach involving a more thorough study of user groups. Our study therefore used a combination of qualitative and quantitative research methods: an online survey was undertaken, followed by an investigation of small focus groups via unstructured interview techniques, as well as the analysis of web traffic data and transaction logs (Motyckova, 2010). This combined approach enabled a deeper understanding of specific user groups' information-seeking behaviour, and whether current structures of information are providing adequate support to scholarly users. This chapter considers the implementation and findings of the online survey.

There are many advantages associated with the use of digital technology to support approaches to evaluation (Watt et al., 2002; Dommeyer et al., 2004; Salmon, Deasy and Garrigan, 2004). Online questionnaires are perhaps the best-known technique for surveying large numbers of people especially due to the internet's ability to reach out to a vast population quickly, easily and with a low cost of delivery (Nicholas and Herman, 2009, 149). The survey used for this study was live for the period of one month from 3 June 2010 to 2 July 2010; in that period 2657 responses were collected. The survey was designed to be answered anonymously, concentrating on gathering data specifically on users of the Collection Database Online, focusing on users' perspectives of their use of the database, search strategies and use of digital resources. The questionnaire was developed with input from members of the British Museum Web Team.[4] The survey was divided into 30 questions, comprising multiple choice open-ended questions and free text comments, with a further four questions focusing on specific search-orientated tasks, in order to gain insights into the individual user's attitudes towards, motivation for and use of the search functionality of the Collection Database Online as well as their information-seeking behaviour and awareness of the information environment. The web-based questionnaire was developed and designed using Survey Monkey[5] as the platform, using the British Museum's account and delivered in the form of a pop-up survey. One of the advantages of pop-up surveys is that they can be used to select a random sample of visitors.

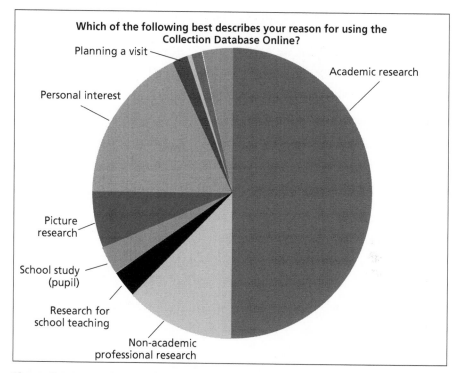

Which of the following best describes your reason for using the Collection Database Online?

Planning a visit

Academic research

Personal interest

Picture research

School study (pupil)

Research for school teaching

Non-academic professional research

Figure 7.1 *Respondents' reasons for using the British Museum Collection Database Online (Ross, Terras and Motyckova, 2011)*

Findings

There was an overwhelming response to the survey, with 2657 completed responses in a one-month period. Respondents were asked to select their reason for using the Collection database from a multiple choice list of reasons for research. The majority (50.2%, 1333 responses (Figure 7.1)) of respondents were self-identified as undertaking academic research, whether as scholars or students. This is perhaps to be expected, as the British Museum Collection Database Online can be found in the Research section of the main British Museum website.[6]

Basic demographic information about the respondents who cited themselves to be academics was gathered to place the subsequent results within context in order to inform analysis and interpretation. Responses were received from users in a total of 57 countries. The most represented countries were the UK (29% of responses), followed by the USA (17.6%). This was followed by Germany (9%) and France (5.7%). Regionally (UK only) there was a strong English representation.

In terms of age (Table 7.1) and gender, 27.7% of the respondents were between 21 and 30, closely followed by the 31–40 age category (22.3%). There was also a strong response rate from respondents aged in the 41–50 age range (19.7%). The preponderance of academic respondents were female (59%) compared with 40.9% male.

Table 7.1 *Respondents using COL by age distribution (Ross, Terras and Motyckova, 2011)*

Age range	Response percentage	Response count
Under 20	1.60	20
21–30	27.70	342
31–40	22.30	275
41–50	19.70	243
51–60	17.20	212
61–70	9.20	114
71+	2.30	28
	answered question	1234
	skipped question	99

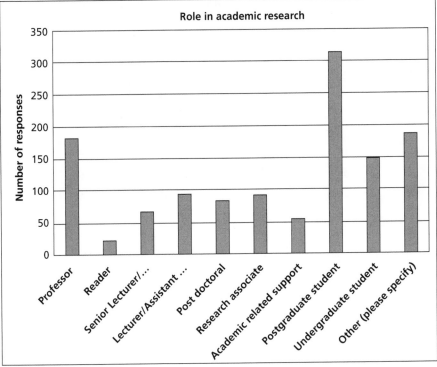

Figure 7.2 *The range of roles in academia held by the respondents (Ross, Terras and Motyckova, 2011)*

In Figure 7.2 we see that the modal group of academic respondents were postgraduate students (25.1%), followed by professors (14.6%) and others (15%).[7] A significant figure in the 'other' category was that of curator or curatorial staff, with 177 responses. Interestingly, the largest user groups were postgraduate students and professors.

Information-seeking and search strategies

Respondents expected to be able to search the Collection Database Online predominately by type of object (47.9%) and by free text search (46.8%). This was followed by date and then in close succession by people, theme, culture and museum number (see Figure 7.3).

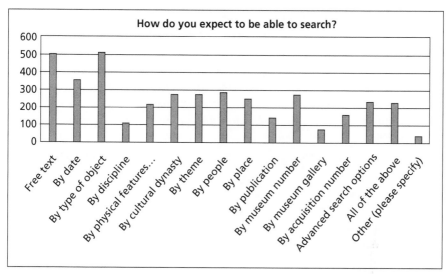

Figure 7.3 *Categories of search in the British Museum Collection Database Online (Ross, Terras and Motyckova, 2011)*

It appears the majority of scholars prefer to search by object type and have the ability to freely create search strings and queries of their own. This suggests that the majority of scholars are already aware of the information environment in which they are searching, and are specifically searching for a known object. This is supported by the fact that the majority of respondents were looking for a specific object (Figure 7.4). Respondents were asked to select all the categories that applied, therefore there could be multiple responses from individual respondents. Nevertheless, the results suggest that scholars have prior knowledge of the information they require and are searching the Collection database with a goal-driven intent. This can be supported by the free text responses

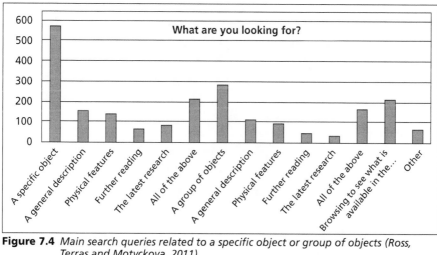

Figure 7.4 *Main search queries related to a specific object or group of objects (Ross, Terras and Motyckova, 2011)*

prompted by the opportunity for respondents to provide a short description of the objects they were looking for. Responses were varied (890 answered), however the majority of people responding carried out exact search strategies refined by date, culture and specific object.

The range of results, excluding free text and type of object categories, suggests that the remaining scholars have very different expectations for searching museum online collections. This suggests that if researchers are not searching for a specific object they are still very information literate, chosing to refine their searching to a specific period, culture or theme. The academic respondents show strong search refinement skills, yet there is a predominance for using free text search. Previous research (Bates, 1996; Wiberley and Jones, 1989) has identified key search query term types that appear in humanities scholars' searches: individual names, geographical terms, chronological terms and discipline specific terms. This appears to also be the case in scholars' preferences of search criteria in the Collection Database Online. It also suggests that academic browsing in a museum environment is somewhat problematic; as users have to be fairly linear in their search strategies. There seems to be little satisfaction when searching broadly or browsing.

Use of the Collection Database Online

The respondents were asked about their Collection Database Online visitation patterns (Figure 7.5). According to the results, the majority of respondents visit and use the database occasionally (33.1%), which suggests that many of the respondents are repeat visitors.

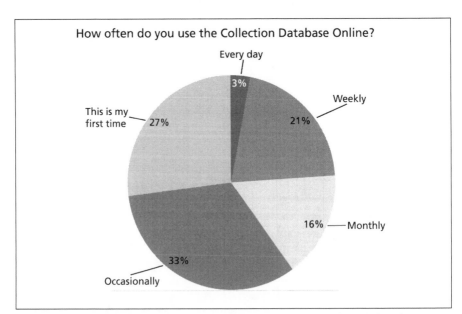

Figure 7.5 *Respondents' visitation patterns to the Collection Database Online (Ross, Terras and Motyckova, 2011)*

Table 7.2 Respondents access points to the Collection Database Online (Ross, Terras and Motyckova, 2011)		
Q. How did you hear about it?		
Answer options	Response percentage	Response count
Friend	2.50	27
Professional environment (colleagues)	29.50	316
Academic environment (website, academic staff, fellow student etc.	27.30	293
School	1.00	11
From a link on the Museum's website	24.60	264
Through a search engine	15.90	170
Other (please specify)	8.40	90
	answered question	1072
	skipped question	261

Respondents were also asked how they had heard about the Collection Database Online (Table 7.2). The highest response rates, perhaps unsurprisingly, were from colleagues in a professional environment (29.5%) and the academic environment (27.3%). Many respondents also utilized the link on the British Museum website (24.6%). A much lower percentage accessed the site from a search engine (15.9%). Responses to 'other' (90 response count) were interesting; the most common answers revolved around the assumption that the British Museum would have an online collections database. This is an interesting response as it suggests that digital resources and online collection databases are so penetrating and pervasive that users have a high level of expectation that big cultural institutions utilize them.

Respondents were asked about their use, and function of the site, and their opinions about the design, layout and functionality of the Collection Database Online. A number of categories were presented to the respondents, with the opportunity to rate their approval or disapproval (see Table 7.3). The majority of responses were positive; this is also reflected in the free text comments: 'I have found it too helpful to name a particular thing. The database has told me new things about areas I myself have been researching for years.' However, some respondents (190 response count) slightly disagreed that the Collection database was easy to use; a small proportion of the free text responses concur, stating that there is 'insufficient hierarchisation of research results' and it is 'hard to refine one search' and 'difficult to navigate'.

Respondents were also asked their views on the content held within the Collection database (see Table 7.4). It was strongly felt that the COL should provide more images. This is also supported by the free text comments: 'lack of pictures make it difficult to tell whether I have found the object I wanted' and 'very few photographs, not enough contextual information'.

The results of this question echo the findings of Ornager, in an earlier study into image databases:

To sum up the requirements, the users want an interface which provide[s] improved access to the images, i.e., a lead-in vocabulary. They also require possibilities to broaden or narrow [sic] their queries, and/or to search from different aspects, i.e., to look for related concepts. One searching need can be met by browsing access to images, which will also support a search for the expressional aspect. (1997, 209)

Table 7.3 *Respondent's opinions on design, layout and functionality of the Collection Database Online (Ross, Terras and Motyckova, 2011)*

Answer options	Strongly agree	Agree	Slightly disagree	Strongly disagree	Don't know	Rating average	Response count
It is easy to find the Collection Database Online within the British Museum website	247	408	167	31	64	2.19	917
The general design and layout of the Collection Database Online is appropriate	199	549	107	13	49	2.09	917
The Collection Database Online is easy to navigate	190	449	190	35	53	2.25	917
I am likely to visit the Collection Database Online again	645	235	11	3	23	1.39	917
It is an effective way to search for objects of interest	418	375	66	13	45	1.79	917
There should be links to physical location of objects	196	417	153	33	118	2.41	917

Table 7.4 *Responses to Collection Database Online potential areas for improvement (Ross, Terras and Motyckova, 2011)*

Answer options	Response percentage	Response count
Improved search facilities	31.90	342
More images	67.60	725
More detailed records	37.10	398
More objects	31.30	336
Audio/video	4.70	50
Other (please specify)	11.80	127

Though a user's search query can be specific, the outcome can still require visually inspecting multiple images in order to find the desired object. Kravchyna and Hastings (2002) point out that there is a lack of studies on the use of online images of museums' collections. They reveal that museum digital resources seldom offer online visitors full access to collection databases and that the descriptive information of the museum collections available to visitors is even more limited. This is not the case with the British Museum COL as information in the object records is made available almost in its entirety.[8]

Developing methods for enhancing images in online collection databases, searching image databases and retrieval is a challenging and ongoing area of research. The digitization

Table 7.5 *Respondents' opinions on content in the Collection Database Online (Ross, Terras and Motyckova, 2011)*							
Answer options	Strongly agree	Agree	Slightly disagree	Strongly disagree	Don't know	Rating average	Response count
I found the content quickly and easily	228	412	110	28	60	2.14	838
The content is easy to understand	298	441	40	1	58	1.9	838
The content is comprehensive	205	408	127	19	79	2.24	838
The content is accurate	209	444	64	5	116	2.25	838
The content is helpful	288	444	36	1	69	1.95	838

of museum objects is a time-consuming and expensive endeavour and it may not always be possible to provide images for all objects in the collections. Retrieval of images in collection databases has traditionally been addressed by two different approaches (Sacco, 2008; Villa et al., 2010): the first one works on low-level multimedia features (such as colour, texture, etc.) and tries to find items that are similar to a specific selected item via Content Based Image Retrieval (CBIR). The second one uses query methods on metadata or on a textual description of each item. Neither of these approaches supports the most common end-user task: the exploration of a collection database in order to find the 'right' object. Given the evidence of demand for images, it may be appropriate for the British Museum to investigate image retrieval more fully in future.

Use of information

The majority of respondents held positive opinions on the content within the Collection Database Online, finding the content easy to understand, comprehensive, accurate and overall helpful to their research (Table 7.5). This indicates that user satisfaction of the Collection Database Online is high. Of particular interest was the number of visitors (64.7%) who intended to reuse the images they had found as a result of searching the database. When asked for what purpose they required the information found, most respondents said they would use it for research, publication, teaching, and for MA and PhD thesis research. A very positive comment from a respondent stated they would 'use the excellent images for study and research, no one else provides such quality of reproduction'. There was also a proportion of responses involved with other museum collections, whether it be comparison, cataloguing or interpretation. It is promising to see that staff from other museums are utilizing the British Museum's Collection Database Online as a case study for cataloguing, interpretation and direct comparison with their own institution.

It is also positive to see that the use of the Collection Database Online encourages a visit to the physical site of the museum (73.9%; Table 7.6). However, there was a strong suggestion that the online visit and the physical visit are for completely different purposes:

> My visit to the museum and my consultation of the database are two completely disconnected events for me.

I am undertaking academic research and need information about collections. I doubt if visiting the museum would give me this.

The two are separate; I go to the museum to autopsy and enjoy. The website is for documentation.

I am a fairly frequent visitor to the museum and plan on going this week although my use of the collections database and visit to the museum are for two entirely separate reasons. My visit to the museum will be for pleasure, whereas my research (although pleasurable) is part of my program of studies.

Table 7.6 *Respondents' opinions on whether the Collection Database Online encourages a visit to the physical museum (Ross, Terras and Motyckova, 2011)*

Does this website encourage you to visit the museum itself?		
Answer options	Response percentage	Response count
Yes	73.9	613
Not sure	17.2	143
No	8.9	74
	answered question	830
	skipped question	503

This conforms to the concept of the physical museum visit to be one of leisure and entertainment (Davis, 1990; Falk and Dierking, 1992; Mintz, 1994; Stephen, 2001) and the online museum visit is for informational value (Kravchyna and Hastings, 2002). Nevertheless, many museum websites have been traditionally designed to supplement the physical museum (Marty, 2004). Future development of museums' websites should reflect that academic users consider the museum website to be a very different information environment from that of the physical museum.

Search outcomes
The survey directly asked respondents if they had found what they were looking for during their visit; the overwhelming response was positive: 66.5% of respondents found what they were looking for. Of these, the majority entered very exact search strings, including period, object name, description and museum number to produce a successful search outcome.

Use of digital resources
It has traditionally been believed that humanities scholars, in particular, prefer undertaking research from physical information resources and have been slow to incorporate digital resources into their research practices (Barrett, 2005; Rimmer et al., 2006). This is no longer the case. Indeed, as a recent British Academy (2005) report found, contrary to some stereotypes, academics in the humanities are not 'luddites', who prefer simply to

use physical libraries, archives and museums in search of resources. This correlates to the findings of Stone (1982) and Watson-Boone (1994), which showed that humanities users need a wide range of resources.

The importance of digital information resources was immediately apparent from the survey results. The academic respondents were enthusiastic about the usefulness of digital resources, with the majority of free text responses using terms including 'extensively' and 'very extensively':

Digital resources are vital to my research. I don't do any research without digital resources.

And

Digital resources can play a major role in my research, but often I still use books and articles.

Social media

There has been a dramatic rise in the number of participatory media technologies that museums have employed to engage people in new ways under the rubric of web 2.0. Blogs, Twitter, wikis, photo and video sharing, and other tools offer users new opportunities to engage with museum content through co-creation and participatory cultural experiences. Therefore it was considered important to ask respondents about the potential of integrating social media applications into the Collection Database Online. Use of social media services is growing exponentially yet, within academia, active use is still centred on the early adopters. The majority of respondents to the survey (69.50%; see Figure 7.6) answered 'no' to wanting social media tools combined with the Collection database. Only 9.1% would like to use social media, while 21.4% of respondents were

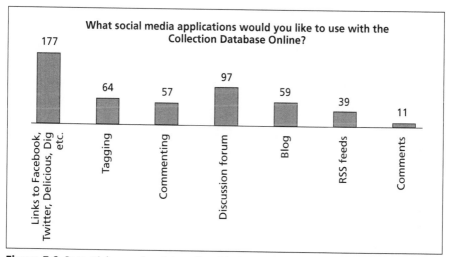

Figure 7.6 *Potential uses of social media with the Collection Database Online (Ross, Terras and Motyckova, 2011)*

unsure. These low figures are interesting given the focus and investment in the use of social media tools around digital collections by cultural heritage organizations.

The respondents who would consider utilizing social media tools would not use all social media applications/services to the same extent. The main service that would be used was that of linking to external social media applications (58.8%) specifically Twitter, Facebook and Delicious, followed by a discussion forum, with 32.2% of the respondents' vote. On the other hand, commenting on objects found in the search results was not considered appropriate, with 18.9% of the respondents' vote. This suggests that many academics are wary of combining social media applications with collection databases because of the perceived inaccuracies that can occur. This supports the notion that many academics are unsure about social media because of trust and authority issues (Williams and Ross, 2010).

Task-based searching scenarios

A key theme in user information-seeking behaviour and retrieval research has been the investigation of the choices users make when searching: what terms they choose and which features (e.g. Boolean logic) they use naturally (Buchanan et al., 2005). An immediate distinction between a user's level of experience can typically be made, in terms of either interactive search or the subject domain. It has previously been found that experienced, trained searchers use more query terms and exploit Boolean logic more frequently (Lucas and Topi, 2002) than other searchers. However, it is now believed that few expert searchers exist, and most seekers use simple two or three term queries (Buchanan et al., 2005). One key information-seeking model is that of Ellis (Ellis, 1989; Ellis and Haugan, 1997), who identifies actions such as *Starting*, where the seeker identifies initial sources of information, and *Chaining*, where references are followed forwards or backwards to extend the scope of the covered area. Previous research suggests that Chaining is used specifically by academics when searching for information in digital libraries (Buchanan et al., 2005); however, it appears that this is not applicable in a digital museum information environment. The majority of respondents utilize more advanced discipline specific search terms: they utilize the museum object number in order to search for a specific object, followed by the name or author of the object and then the content description of the object.

Simulated task-based scenarios were conducted in order to gain knowledge of the respondents' searching behaviour, focusing on the keywords and search queries used. Two simulated search tasks were inspired by the real life information needs of an academic researcher. All the information was provided to the respondent including date, description, museum number and object type, in order to ascertain which type of keyword academics would highlight and use in their search queries. Subsequent to the online survey the search queries entered by the respondents were then tested in the COL search to discover the success rate of the query. The specific objects used for the search-related task were chosen because they proved difficult to find within the database. What is interesting is that, regardless of the search terms the respondents suggested in the hypothetical search section of the survey, the search terms were then

Table 7.7 *Key search terms provided for task-based searching scenario 1 (Ross, Terras and Motyckova, 2011)*

Search term	Number of of users	Search outcome	Number of search results
B 639	48	unsuccessful	14 (all incorrect)
psychostasia	23	unsuccessful	No results matched the search criteria
lekythos psychostasia	9	unsuccessful	No results matched the search criteria
B639	6	successful	6 (all correct)

tested in real time in the Collection database search. The majority of queries returned negative results, implying that the database is not optimized for academic search behaviours.

Task-based search scenario 1: lekythos

In the first task-based search scenario users were asked 'You are searching for a Greek Vase, which you know is in the British Museum as you have seen it in a print catalogue. It is an Attic black-figured lekythos from around 490BC which depicts the myth of "psychostasia" (the Weighing of Souls). The print catalogue gives the reference "B 639". What would you type into the search box to find the object that you are looking for?'

Examining these terms through the online database revealed a clear problem. Out of the total of 174 respondents 48 (Table 7.7) would use the query 'B 639' or 'b 639' (with or without quotation marks). This produces 14 results in the Collection database, none of which is the correct object. The second most popular search query is 'psychostasia', which yields no results, and nor does the next search query 'lekythos psychostasia'. Only six users would search for 'B639' or 'b639' (with no space between the letter and the figures), which would yield a successful search, demonstrating that successful searches required careful selection of search criteria only observed by a few users.

Previous research (Bates, 1996; Wiberley and Jones, 1989) has identified key query term types humanities researchers use when querying digital collections: names of individuals, geographical names, chronological terms and discipline specific terms (the standard terminology within a field – so in this instance museum object numbers). It is argued that these query term types have a specific meaning within a discipline and therefore should be 'good' query terms. However, these term types have not been fully studied from the perspective of user information seeking and information retrieval (Buchanan et al., 2005). It appears there is a gap between the user understanding of a search query or term and the treatment of the query by the computer database. For example, a specific query may carry strong specific keywords, but information retrieval techniques in databases focus most commonly on the rate of occurrence of a word or phrase in the description or metadata of an object. Many of the respondents used one or more of what would be considered a discipline-specific term in their search query in order to demonstrate their search behaviour; yet this produced a negative search result;

for example, combining the correct search term (museum number without spaces) with a more detailed discipline specific keyword search:

B639 Attic black-figured lekythos 490BC depicting psychostasia

This fails to produce a successful search. Is this a suggestion that academics' search strategies are incorrect or that the Collection database, and similar museum databases, require an updated, more user friendly metadata schema, which takes into consideration the information-seeking behaviours of researchers?

Task-based search scenario 2: Hanging Scroll

In the second task-based search scenario respondents were asked 'You are searching for a Hanging Scroll with Mountain Landscape, which you have seen in the British Museum's print catalogue. It is an ink painting on paper from Muromachi period, 16th century and attributed to Zen priest-painter Kei Shokei. The print catalogue gives the reference "Japanese Painting ADD 387". What would you type into the search box to find the object that you are looking for?'

This task proved more successful, with 38 of the 174 (Table 7.8) respondents producing successful searches utilizing the specific keyword 'Kei Shokei'. Again, the use of the museum number with a space produces an unsuccessful search result.

The findings of the simulated task-based scenarios support Bates's (1996) notion that humanities scholars frequently use specific and highly selective query terms. Scholarly searching is shown to be highly precise, focusing on the museum number in order to achieve low but accurate recall. This finding supports the notion that academics are already aware of the museum information environment and are seeking something specific. In general, academics are specifically searching for a known object; there seems to be little satisfaction when searching broadly or browsing. The primary way of finding material in the British Museum Collection Database Online is by object type and use of the free text search facility.

Table 7.8 *Key search terms provided for task-based searching scenario 2 (Ross, Terras and Motyckova, 2011)*

Search term	Number of of users	Search outcome	Number of search results
Kei Shokei	38	successful	2
ADD 387	20	unsuccessful	3 (all incorrect)
Japanese Painting ADD 387	13	unsuccessful	No results matched the search criteria

Conclusion

Our study and analysis of the use and information-seeking behaviour of academics utilizing the British Museum's Collection Database Online has enhanced our understanding and awareness of the scholarly perceptions of their information environment. It presents the usability and functionality of the British Museum's digital collection as an important exemplar of how digital resources effect academic information searching and research processes. The results of this research indicate that analysis of user behaviour through survey can elicit interesting and relevant points that can affect the future development of online collections. Although there are some issues with survey methodologies, highlighted in the paper on this research submitted to the conference Museums and the Web (Ross, Terras and Motyckova, 2011), this is an approach that can easily and fruitfully be adopted by other institutions.

The research suggests that digital resources are used extensively by academics as part of their research process and are considered vital to their research. It became clear in this study that scholars are very aware of digital resources, particular those offered by cultural institutions, as there is a high level of expectation that museums with large collections, like the British Museum, will disseminate their collections online. Collections with a strong visual element are particularly useful: the study shows that academics rely heavily on images, placing a large emphasis on viewing the images to ensure they have found the correct object. However, a clear distinction between a physical visit to the British Museum and an online visit can also be discerned: academics believe that a physical visit is a leisure activity and the online visit is for research and informational value.

It is particularly interesting that the integration of social media applications into the Collection Database Online received a negative response, given the contemporary focus on enhancing collections through the use of social media and community tagging. The users we surveyed showed a willingness to adopt new methods of content dissemination only where the content is audience focused and appropriate for the medium.

Academics display specific information-seeking behaviour and sophisticated search strategies. The majority are seeking a known object, and utilize discipline specific search terms, showing goal-driven intent and a detailed prior knowledge of the museum (and academic) information environment. They have an understanding of their individual search skills and patterning. Our analysis of the information needs of humanities researchers through their use of the British Museum Collection Database Online gives us a better understanding of the search patterns and information-seeking behaviour of a specific user group, and provides a valuable guide for further development and refinement of museum online collections, which should impact on the design and implementation of, and provision of access to, digital museum resources as a whole.

Notes

1   This chapter is a version of a longer research report presented at the conference Museums and the Web 2011: Ross, Terras and Motyckova (2011) *Scholarly Information Seeking Behaviour in the British Museum Online Collection*. Further discussion of results and methodology are available within this research paper, which can be found at
http://conference.archimuse.com/mw2011/
programs/scholarly_information_seeking_behaviour_in_t.

2   www.britishmuseum.org/research/search_the_collection_database.aspx.

3   www.britishmuseum.org/research/search_the_collection_database.aspx.

4 For more information about the study, and for analysis of additional research carried out through online survey and log analysis methods, see Motyckova (2010).

5 Matthew Cock, Head of Web, British Museum, and David Prudames, Senior Content Commissioner, British Museum.

6 Survey Monkey is a web-based, flexible, scalable, secure survey development tool. See www.surveymonkey.com.

7 A separate study (Motyckova, 2010) reported on non-academic use of the British Museum Collection Database Online.

8 Additional responses in the other category included: independent researcher, retired academic, author and art dealer.

9 Taken from About the Collection database, www.britishmuseum.org/research/search_the_collection_database/about_the_database.aspx.

8

The value and impact of digitized resources for learning, teaching, research and enjoyment

Simon Tanner

Introduction

Imagine walking into one of Britain's great cathedrals. As you take in the architectural, cultural and religious ambience, your mobile device automatically engages with content on your behalf.

So, just when you ask for it, the local tour is available in your own language. But there is much more: images and information on the stained glass too high to view, videos of famous ceremonies, 3D walk-throughs showing how the cathedral may have looked in previous centuries, full text of historic and literary references, a list of people buried, baptized or married, choral works performed, oral histories of local residents, news reports through the centuries; this list of opportunities could and will grow even longer.

This is the inherent promise of digitized resources and yet we have not achieved this goal with many of our digital collections. Technology exists to drive forward a vision of intelligent environments that supply the right information to the right person at the right time. Paradoxically, what is missing is the depth of digitized content to make such technical developments more significant than mere mobile playthings. The treasure house of content has to be digitized much more comprehensively.

Much has been achieved, but there are opportunities for much more impact, benefit and a greater return on the investment made in creating digital collections if we continue to invest in the knowledge economy by digitizing our wealth of information resources.

This chapter will consider the opportunities and impacts that digitized resources have made for learning, teaching, research and society. The focus for this chapter comes from the significant impact and value in the UK discovered during the JISC-funded research project, Inspiring Research, Inspiring Scholarship (Tanner and Deegan, 2011). It will conclude with the suggestion that the impacts of digitized resources are being negated by the very modes of measurement and evaluation currently in place, and will posit fresh areas for investigation.

Overview of opportunities, benefits and impacts from digitized resources

What the Bodleian Library is doing now, in digitising large portions of our vast collections, is like the human genome project. Thousands of people can evaluate and use creatively the digital resources to discover new ideas and make innovations. Many hands make light work and those many hands will profoundly touch Britain's future capacity for learning, research and innovation. (Thomas, 2010)

Many countries are aiming to create sustainable national content collections of compelling rich and accessible digital content. The sorts of benefits and impact from digitized resources tend to support the following areas of digital opportunity.

Learning
Educational benefits are gained from a wide variety of activities introducing people to new digitized information and experiences. This might mean using digitized content to teach history at university or biology in a school classroom; an introduction to new activities such as creative writing or renovating a steam train; or visiting museum collections. Education benefits should strive to include all members of society, not just university students or schoolchildren: there is a hunger for learning and for resource discovery at all levels:

> Now I enter the classroom and I think, most of the content that I have to deliver and a whole lot more, is floating around them right now. What I need to do is inspire them and give them the tools to harness that information and harness the skills of other people to do the things they want to get done. And that transforms the way you approach the classroom.
> (Dr Michael Wesch, quoted in Bradwell, 2009))

Research
Research benefits accrue when we invest in deepening our understanding of the world and build upon the intellectual legacy of previous generations. Digitized resources continue to transform the research process. The researcher can now ask questions that were previously not feasible; they can engage in a new process of discovery and focus their intellect on analysis rather than data collation.

Consumption
The most obvious benefit of digitized resources is the value people get from using them. The term consumption is intended to include both the 'entertainment' value of engaging with digitized content and the personal value added from participating in a community of use. Increased consumption will also benefit economic sustainability.

Strengthening communities and regeneration
Digitized resources make it possible for communities to grow more cohesive as common interests and a common vision can be shared. The UK Renaissance in the Regions at www.mla.gov.uk/what/programmes/renaissance has funded museum digitized resources and skills development that engages local communities. Some regeneration projects also include important skills development in the digital domain, although this is sometimes diffuse, for instance, harnessing traditional crafts with web-developed marketing and

services to attract employment and tourism to rural areas that have lost previously established industries. Other programmes aim to use digitized resources to integrate people at risk of exclusion from society.

Building collaboration

Working together in collaboration maximizes impact – whether for research, education or societal benefits. In particular, the digital humanities foster collaboration and best practice between universities nationally and internationally. They enable mutually beneficial links between universities, memory institutions, publishing and media to develop digital content and provide a context for use by a wider community (Zorich, 2008).

Collaboration also has a shown a strong impact on building recognition internationally, leading to new economic and innovation opportunities. Giving access to a high volume of digitized content will confer a high profile to the quality of the institution's work: 'The idea really is that Einsteins live everywhere, but you don't necessarily invite them to your meeting. They might be junior, ex-employees, associates or outside your organisation. But you need to engage them' (Matt Chapman, Imaginatik, quoted in Bradwell, 2009)

Impacts and benefits

In overview, the impacts and benefits of digitized resources can be broadly divided among research, learning, economic and connecting communities. But how does this work in practice? The exemplars in the following sections will illustrate the way benefits are accruing to these broad areas.

Learning, teaching and research benefits

Digitized resources transform the research process

Figure 8.1 shows how digital resources transform research.

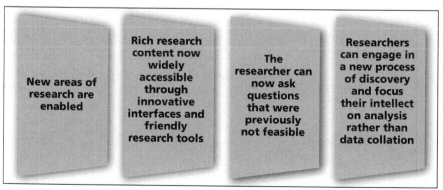

Figure 8.1 *How digital resources transform research*

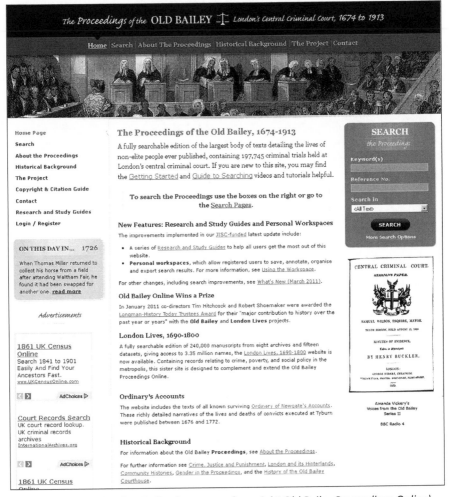

Figure 8.2 *The Old Bailey Online homepage (copyright Old Bailey Proceedings Online)*

Exemplar: the new history from within

The Old Bailey Online at www.oldbaileyonline.org (Figure 8.2) offers a fully searchable database of the largest body of texts detailing the lives of non-elite people ever published, containing 197,745 criminal trials held at London's central criminal court, with over 120 billion words recorded.

Alongside other key projects, such as London Lives 1690 to 1800 at www.londonlives.org, this makes 18th and 19th-century London the most digitized where and when in the history of world:

> Old Bailey Online reaches out to communities, such as family historians, who are keen to find a personal history, reflected in a national story, and in the process re-enforces the

workings of a civil society. Digital resources both create a new audience, and re-configure our analysis to favour the individual (Hitchcock, 2010).

Easier access to scholarly publications

A bedrock of scholarship is the ability to share, discuss and reference thoughts, ideas and discoveries. Scholars require access to the accumulated knowledge of human endeavour to move research and discovery forward rather than in circles.

Improved access to scholarly content makes research and teaching easier, faster and more productive. Hundreds of millions of pages of historic scholarly content are now available, bringing untold thousands of hitherto hidden articles back into circulation, through initiatives including over six million pages accessed almost 600 million times on JSTOR at www.jstor.org and the British Library's Electronic Theses Online Service (EthOS) at http://ethos.bl.uk, which allows instant access to 250,000+ UK theses that have already been digitized, and which will digitize on demand any other thesis produced in the UK. Other examples include the Oxford Journals Archive at www.oxfordjournals.org, providing more than 3.4 million article pages covering content from 1849 to 1995, and Welsh Journals Online at http://welshjournals.llgc.org.uk, which digitized some 400,000 pages of Welsh academic content. These enhance the ability of scholars to cross-search and cross-refer.

New areas of research enabled

Digitized resources enable entirely new areas of research and discovery to be opened up. New research methods can be applied to the digitized resources, which were hitherto unthinkable. New collaborations across disciplines can also be fostered through joint engagement with digitized resources.

The digital projects that have been carried out over the last 20 years by the research community have brought a new spirit of enterprise to the process of scholarship (see Figure 8.3).

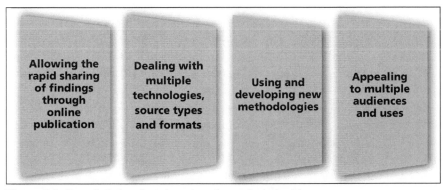

Figure 8.3 *How digital projects have transformed scholarship*

Bringing collections out of the dark

Britain's wealth of information and artefacts underpin the nation's culture. Yet because of the sheer volume, value, fragility, complexity and dispersion of physical assets they can never fully be displayed, accessed or made widely available in that form. The Early English Books Online and Eighteenth Century Collections Online are just two examples of how digital collections transform access: 'Early English Books Online itself has transformed research into early English literature. It has democratised the research process by extending this facility to individuals and institutions without easy access to specialist libraries' (Dr Sarah Carpenter, quoted in Tanner and Deegan, 2011).

Early English Books Online (EEBO) at http://eebo.chadwyck.com provides to scholars and students a digital collection of 22 million pages of early printed text, representing 125,000 books published in England or in English between 1475 and 1700. This is the culmination of more than a century of effort in finding, cataloguing, microfilming, digitizing, rekeying and delivering what is in effect a great virtual library of early books. It is one of the world's greatest digital collections, and its impact on research and teaching is profound. It allows many scholars and students around the world access to what has been in the past only accessible to the very few:

> I would not be able to do my research without the use of EEBO. Moreover, I am looking at lots of medical recipes and need to assess quickly what the ingredients were thought to be useful for. The ability to search full texts to find these ingredients with ease and speed is crucial to my work. It saves me a lot of time not to have to read the whole document to find one herb.
>
> (Jennifer Evans, PhD student, quoted in Tanner and Deegan, 2011)

A similar development to EEBO, Eighteenth Century Collections Online (ECCO) provides more than 30 million pages, representing 180,000 works including every significant English-language and foreign-language title printed in Great Britain during the 18th century, along with thousands of important works from the Americas. ECCO has revolutionized research and teaching in 18th-century studies:

> ECCO is an amazingly rich resource: it puts a magnificent library of eighteenth-century printed material on the desktops of scholars and students. It vastly improves access; it allows the scholar to discover new seams of material; it gives students unprecedented access to masses of primary source material. And of course it supports new kinds of searching.
>
> (Joanna Innes, quoted in Tanner and Deegan, 2011).

What makes these resources even more accessible to scholars is the capacity to search across the metadata of both at the same time: the bibliographic records for ECCO have been loaded into EEBO, which gives EEBO users the possibility of locating additional texts relevant to their research. Digitization brings these materials to a wider public than ever before: either free or at low cost to the consumer and made accessible with a wealth of explanatory context produced by world-class experts.

Virtual reunification

Primary source material is vital to scholarly research but in some cases the source material may have been artificially separated and physically distributed over the whole planet. In the past scholars travelled to libraries around the world if they wanted to compare sources. This was costly, time-consuming and inefficient. In addition to reunifying primary sources, digitized resources enable new tools to facilitate research once the primary resources are brought together again.

Exemplar: Jane Austen

Jane Austen's Fiction Manuscripts Digital Edition at www.janeausten.ac.uk (Figure 8.4) presents all Austen's manuscripts to be viewed side by side for the first time in 150 years. The Digital Edition gathers together in the virtual space of the web some 1100 pages of fiction written in Jane Austen's own hand. Through digital reunification, it is now possible to access, read and compare high-quality images of original manuscripts whose material forms are scattered around the world in libraries and private collections. These manuscripts trace Jane Austen's development as a writer from childhood to the year of her death and provide a unique visual record of her imagination:

> Jane Austen's Fiction Manuscripts Digital Edition offers unprecedented opportunities for new scholarship, particularly in exploring the creative laboratory of her novels, so far an under examined area of Austen studies. It also makes the manuscript sources freely available to the wider public. (Sutherland, 2010).

Teaching benefits

The increasing availability of digitized resources allows educational institutions to provide students with more varied, more accessible and richer teaching materials than ever before.

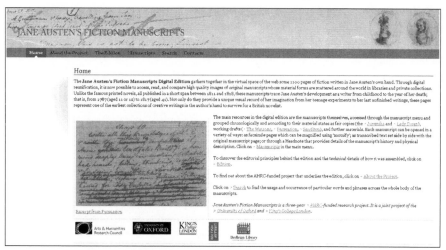

Figure 8.4 *Jane Austen's Fiction Manuscripts Digital Edition (copyright King's College London)*

This encourages a more exploratory, research-based approach to teaching and learning. Entirely new kinds of topics and courses can be studied, new modes of assessment are possible, and students are given a richer educational experience.

Once available digitally, materials produced for one context can be used in many others: advanced research projects can be used by students in a wide range of contexts and backgrounds including in schools and colleges, and by lifelong learners. For instance, Survivors of the Shoah Visual History Foundation identifies on its website at http://libguides.usc.edu/vha that its content would have significant relevance to 42 academic subject areas.

Exemplar: Chopin's First Editions Online

Chopin's First Editions Online unites all of the first impressions of Chopin's first editions in an unprecedented virtual collection, thereby providing direct access for musicians and musicologists to the most important primary source materials relevant to the composer's music:

> This digital resource is the only complete collection of the Chopin first editions, which otherwise are scattered across the globe . . . users have at their fingertips source materials which they otherwise would never have sight of, or only with considerable difficulty and concomitant expense. (Rink, 2010)

> Not only an invaluable resource for studying Chopin's music, but potentially a means of studying music in general – perhaps with application beyond music, too.
> (Professor Nicholas Cook, quoted in Tanner and Deegan, 2011)

Exemplar: using real world data for teaching

The Economic and Social Data Service at www.esds.ac.uk provides real-world economic data that is being used in learning and teaching. Students learn how economics data looks in its raw state and experience first-hand the complexities and difficulties of working with it. Students develop a portfolio of realistic project work to demonstrate their skills and experience to prospective employers:

> It's connected with getting your hands dirty and looking at the real world. Lots of the standard courses have got data that's already in some senses cleaned . . . whereas when you actually start to investigate the world you often find that things aren't straightforward.
> (Nick Weaver, quoted in Tanner and Deegan, 2011).

Availability of new kinds of materials

Digitization takes primary sources beyond the book and the laboratory. Digitized sources bring into the classroom simulated practical experimentation in science as well as rare and fragile artefacts to support teaching:

> The First World War Poetry Archive makes it easier to discuss the creative process in greater

detail with students than was traditionally possible. My teaching is enhanced because there is much more primary source material freely available, especially the full colour images of all the manuscript variants of a poem. This represents a significant benefit to students, teachers and researchers.

(Lee, 2010)

Time-based media

Time-based media can be difficult to access for teaching, though the tape recorder and later the video machine brought about the birth of media studies, a popular and vitally important area of study. Now, digitization allows students and researchers to edit sources into multimedia publications and comment directly on them in ways that were never before possible.

Integrating many different kinds of resources

Students can now participate as genuine researchers and real contributors: online courses and reading lists can link directly to digitized resources – for not only library-type materials but also digitized images for the study of image-rich subjects (art history, for example), 3-D models for chemistry or physics, simulations for teaching medicine, and rich data sets for statistical modelling.

Students are no longer limited by geography: these resources do not even need to be in the student's own institution, they could be on the other side of the world.

Bestowing economic benefits

Widespread access to digitized resources enhances education and research at all levels of attainment. These resources contribute to the vibrant cultural and intellectual life of the UK, promoting education and enjoyment for all while bestowing a range of benefits to local and national economies (see Figure 8.5).

The production and use of digitized resources supports these economic impacts by delivering efficiency, innovation and enhanced skills, by underpinning competitiveness, and by developing a UK brand for universities and higher education worldwide.

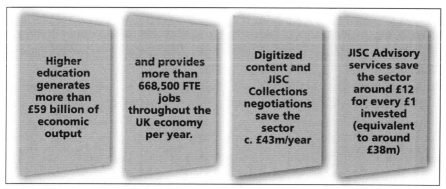

Figure 8.5 *How digitized resources provide economic and educational benefits (Universities UK, 2006, and JISC, 2010a)*

Higher education has a key role in transferring ideas, research results and skills between universities, other research organizations, business and the wider community, conferring a whole range of benefits: economic, social and political. In the modern world, the digital agenda and the digitized resources to support innovation are essential components for higher education investment.

Competitiveness – increasing value while accruing cost savings and efficiency gains

I believe that the economic profile of the acquire, store and access chain suggests that switching to digital has so many cost–benefits that the cost of acquiring through digitization is a solid investment, especially for text-based resources, film and video, or scientific data sets.

Learning, teaching and research are all enhanced by wider, easier and cheaper access to digitized resources. This is being achieved through the large-scale digitization of materials held by educational and cultural establishments worldwide. One result of this is that costly, time-consuming and inefficient travel to visit collections or collate data sets has been radically reduced. Digitization allows multiple resources to be interrogated and compared instantly, making the research process more rapid and facilitating more in-depth study.

Efficiency savings

Significant efficiency savings are being achieved through the use and reuse of data and by reducing the cost of collection and creation.

Reuse is a key economic benefit, with many research and learning uses becoming available to many audiences – many of these uses having not been foreseen by the original creators. The benefits and impact of secondary analysis of digitized resources have been particularly apparent in the sciences.

Dr Amy Irwin, research fellow at the MRC Institute of Hearing Research, has used the British Library's Archival Sound Recordings (ASR) during the course of her work to assess the impact on the human brain of sounds perceived as either pleasant or unpleasant: 'Being able to download clips directly was a great time-saver – the variety of soundscapes available was also useful. Combined with the soundscapes I found from other sources, Archival Sound Recordings provided for all my needs' (Irwin, 2010).

Doing more for less

The cost of creating digitized resources is continuously dropping, and investment in digitization is delivering its benefits and impacts more quickly than previously was possible. As real economies of scale are realized, further benefits accrue through sharing both the direct and indirect costs, while international collaboration is fostered by the ability to share knowledge and resources.

An excellent example of the economic and intellectual leveraging of community engagement through sharing digitized resources is provided by crowdsourcing.

Crowdsourcing is a distributed problem-solving and production model with the community or crowd submitting solutions. It is a very low cost means of engaging with a community, and delivers the benefits of increased skills, enhanced digital resources and improved institutional links with that community.

Exemplars: community engagement with digital collections

- The Australian Newspapers Digitisation Program at www.nla.gov.au/ndp has registered 9000 volunteers who enhance the text in their 8.4 million articles. To date, 12 million lines of text have been corrected, which equates to approximately 70 person years of effort or, assuming an average wage, £1.75 million worth of effort.
- Over three years the BBC asked the public to contribute their memories and artefacts of the Second World War at www.bbc.co.uk/ww2peopleswar. 32,000 people registered and submitted 47,000 stories and 15,000 images.
- FamilySearch Indexing at https://familysearch.org/volunteer/indexing is a volunteer project that aims to create searchable digital indexes for scanned images of historical documents – over 250 million historical records have been transcribed to date (see also Chapter 4 for an archival perspective on this project).

We are now at the point at which the creativity and enthusiasm surrounding user-generated and annotated content can be profitably harnessed to help us sustain and expand our national collections.

Optimizing the research and teaching environment

Digitized resources and the increased sharing of data sets provide opportunities to create a more complete and transparent record of scholarly endeavour (see Figure 8.6).

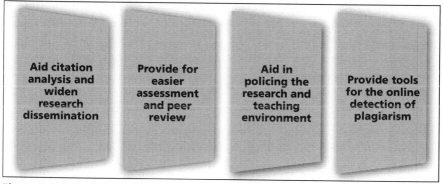

Figure 8.6 *How digitized resources can optimize the research and teaching environment*

Digitized resources can also provide recognition for a wider range of research 'outputs' and contributions than is typical in current programmes based on a monograph and journal model. Art history, for instance, is under extreme economic pressure because the cost of print publication is so high with the need to use colour art images extensively. However, without publication, research dissemination is reduced. Using online modes of publication allows the art historian to link directly to digitized resources, for instance to the JISC-funded Birmingham Museums & Art Gallery Pre-Raphaelite Collection at www.preraphaelites.org or to the Corpus of Medieval Stained Glass at www.cvma.ac.uk, reducing the costs of research dissemination in copyright fees and print publication.

Skills

The growth of digitized resources generates new and improved skills in students, scholars and the wider public (see Figure 8.7). The silver surfer generation has been fostered by the growth in family history resources available online.

Crowdsourcing has raised the skill levels of the wider public by aligning simple online tasks with exciting digital content. The Victoria and Albert Museum has crowdsourced Search the Collections at http://collections.vam.ac.uk/crowdsourcing, asking the public to help manage the 140,000 images in the collection. This brings the users to the content and lifts their information and subject literacy skills.

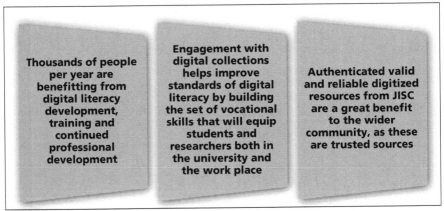

Figure 8.7 *The growth of digitized resources generates new and improved skills in students, scholars and the wider public*

Developing the brand for higher education

Transformational digital content and resources support broader Western government agendas to open up data for the 21st century. Cultural and educational collections are a nation's prize jewels and should be at the heart of the agenda to expose government information to benefit the citizen.

Research and universities are made more visible by digitized resources. Such digitization widens international recognition for the quality of research. In turn this generates revenue by attracting overseas students and by fostering international research collaborations and funding. The establishment of transatlantic digitization collaboration grants between JISC and the US National Endowment for Humanities is recognition that the USA, as the world's biggest research economy, makes a significant contribution to the leading edge performance of collaborating nations. UK–USA collaboration represents more than 30% of the UK's strongest research, with impact factors up to four times higher for papers in biological and physical sciences (see Roberts, 2006).

We also need to consider our position in the digital world and ensure that we can maintain our competitive advantage and make best use of opportunities for cultural diplomacy. Collaboration will be a key feature of future digital economics as the projects become so large as to be unsustainable within an individual institutional context.

Digitized content stimulates the economy, underpins competitiveness and develops a brand for universities and higher education worldwide.

Widespread access to digitized resources contributes to the vibrant cultural and intellectual life of the nation, promoting education and enjoyment for all while bestowing a range of benefits to local and national economies. There is also a social and economic benefit in helping to bridge the digital divide by providing digitized content to the world.

Connecting people and communities

Connecting people and communities with digital content greatly improves life, work and leisure, and ensures that all are included in our digital future.

Access to over one hundred million digitized archival records from archives and libraries transforms local history research and builds expertise in genealogists and local historians. Octogenarians now regularly use complex resources with great facility – the silver surfer generation has been created.

Connecting communities with news

The news, local, national and international, is a vital resource. Now it is put into the hands of everyone, and reveals a wealth of information about our daily lives of the last three centuries:

> Newsfilm Online is a ground-breaking example of a creative partnership between higher education and a leading commercial news archive. It is set to move the agenda forwards in the appreciation of the long-term educational and scholarly value of broadcast news.
>
> (Professor Stewart Purvis, quoted in Tanner and Deegan, 2011)

> Newspapers widen the scope of what historians can explore, bring colour and variety to historical events. The powerful search function available with digitised newspapers is a crucial advantage in exploring in detail and saves a lot of time.
>
> (Dr Peter Rushton, quoted in Tanner and Deegan, 2011)

Community cohesion

Communities (local and distributed) can cohere around digitized resources, sharing common interests and promoting a common vision. This is particularly important in areas of specialized or minority interests, where geographically dispersed communities can be developed and sustained in a way that could never happen around physical resources.

Commenting about Caribbean Histories Revealed, an online exhibition from The National Archives at www.nationalarchives.gov.uk/caribbeanhistory, the award-winning novelist Andrea Levy, best known for *Small Island*, says (in correspondence): 'It is fascinating, and very gratifying, to see the historical records of the Caribbean becoming more accessible to ordinary people. The on-line exhibition makes a great starting point for anyone interested in researching this part of Britain's heritage.'

More effective and usable collections can also be developed by harnessing input from outside higher education. This can be achieved by getting communities to offer their knowledge, donate their objects for digitization and share their histories. Photographic resources from the collections of the Shetland Isles Museum at www.shetland-museum.org.uk have been augmented with comments and tags from a community of technically skilled 'Tele-Crofters'.

A sense of place and time: a deeper engagement with the place and area people live and their personal histories

Digitized resources can offer great support for personal participation in society. They provide information about family and ancestors, educational opportunities, medical and health information, entertainment and a deeper engagement with the places and areas people live in through maps, historical photographs, trade catalogues, etc.

Census data and other digitized resources that can be quarried in-depth for family history or provide a sense of place and time are hugely popular. The UK Government has responded to the growing hunger for social information with a policy to set information free and open up government data sets at http://data.gov.uk. Substantial social and economic gains can be made through this strategy.

Memory institutions are also bringing their collections directly into communities to connect with those disadvantaged or isolated by circumstance from their personal memories or communities. Benefits are shown in Figure 8.8.

Figure 8.8 *Digitized resources offer great support for personal participation in society*

Bringing collections directly into people's homes, especially those of older persons, enables memories to be triggered and allows them to reconnect with their community and their past. It also opens up new opportunities for shared participation and intergenerational interaction. The social benefits of personal memories within a wider context has provided comfort to early stage Alzheimer's sufferers and enabled families to interact with the older generation's memories and social context (see Department of Communities and Local Government, 2008).

Community engagement through revealing content and allowing new content to be discovered

Community projects, in partnership with educational and cultural memory organizations, have helped deliver a wealth of formerly hidden material to a wide and diverse audience, both within and outside the UK: 'Digitised resources allow me to discover the hidden lives of disabled people, who have not traditionally left records of their lives. I have found disability was discussed by many writers in the Eighteenth Century and that disabled men and women played an important role in the social life of the time' (Turner,, 2011).

The wealth of information and artefacts that underpin a nation's culture can never be displayed, accessed or made widely available in analogue form because of the volume, value, fragility, complexity and dispersion of these assets.

Hidden collections exist in libraries, museums, galleries and private collections, sometimes well curated and catalogued and sometimes not. Digitization is bringing these materials to a wider public than ever before; they are either free or low-cost and they are made accessible with a wealth of explanatory context generally produced by world-class experts.

Oral history

Oral histories are an especially powerful means of connecting personal stories with digitized content to create a wider contextual framework. By interconnecting these histories we can better understand or engage with a subject than if they remain uncollected.

The oral history resources of the UK are an enormous and untapped resource, as only a small proportion has been digitized. Layering oral histories with other digitized resources is an effective means of delivering benefit and impact by engaging communities in rich resources.

Lifelong learning and digital communities

The lifelong, voluntary and self-motivated pursuit of knowledge for personal and work gain relies considerably on the availability of digitized resources. This enhances not only social inclusion, active citizenship and personal development, but also competitiveness and employability.

Without digitized resources, many subjects cannot be effectively engaged with and the availability of free to access digital content is addressing issues of digital literacy and the digital divide by democratizing access.

A key characteristic of lifelong learners is that they wish to study outside working hours and in their own homes rather than in libraries or institutions – digitized resources offer them this flexibility.

Digitized resources, especially in areas of very specialist or relatively minority interests, provide the opportunity through the web of developing a sense of belonging and common purpose. It is thus possible to build or sustain a community around an interest in the digitized content that could not easily be done in the physical world. For example, medieval studies is an area energized by the growing availability of digitized resources, which opens up the field to a wider community of lifelong learners and school usage. Resources such as the Digital Image Archive of Medieval Music (DIAMM) at www.diamm.ac.uk have been used in teaching even at primary school level.

As one amateur user of the Fine Rolls of Henry III stated: 'What a treasure trove of information you have here, the simple details that give away the thoughts behind the monarch. I had no idea this was here. . . . It is archives like this that reveal the rich history that this country has' (Hogan, 2009).

Conclusion: the five modes of value for digitized resources

Without doubt the uses to which people in the future will put the outputs of big digitization will be very different from today's uses. All the more reason why we should do our very best to plan today in a way that safeguards the interests of the researchers of tomorrow: 'It is not difficult to imagine how groups of users might respond, given the opportunities and the tools, to the presence of huge quantities of text in digital form: by annotating, translating, citing, discussing, analysing, reusing and repackaging' (Green, 2009).

Measuring and interpreting the broad impact of digitized resources remains a complex undertaking. There is a mass of extant evidence, but attempts to interpret such evidence often tended to rely on commonplace assumptions about the nature of digitization, without fully appreciating the actual way in which end-users interact with such digital content. Digitization projects and programmes need to engage with the core principle of impact assessment – how does this change people's lives?

Very little attempt has been made to provide a deeper analysis that draws evidence from a number of sources and provides a compelling account of the advantages of digitized content. When I looked at value, benefit and impact, statistical measures and evaluations were seen as of primary importance to provide a sense of the scale of use and the penetration of digitization benefits into the community. However, in actuality these were mainly lacking in depth and longitudinal evidence. It is my assessment that many of the evaluations focused on measures of numeric achievement in terms of items digitized. Most evaluations were lacking detail on usage and actual impact.

Narrative accounts and case studies were thus also seen as important factors to personalize the statistics, evaluation and literature synthesis. These narratives add clarity to those benefits and provide a sense of the way digitization actually creates and delivers changes in academic research and teaching practice. This chapter has used such narratives extensively.

It is worth stating clearly that the evidence presented by previous evaluations has either been limited to number-crunching visitor numbers without much segmentation and analysis, or to the use of anecdotal or survey evidence to try to find out about value and benefits.

We remain in a situation where the creative, cultural and academic sectors are not able to adequately demonstrate from a strong enough evidence base that they are changing lives or having a positive impact with regard to digitized content in the way that other sectors have found it possible to do for their services or products.

In short, we need better evidence of impact. How has the digital resource delivered a positive change in a defined group of people's lives? The kinds of changes to be measured are diverse, and are likely to be in the following areas: economic, social, educational, cultural, health, political and environmental, among others. I see this as an important subject for further research especially if such research included a longitudinal element to extend studies beyond the confines of project funding.

Five modes of value for digitized resources

In response to the need to better demonstrate impact I suggest that there are five basic value modes to use as a guide for future digitization impact assessment (Figure 8.9).[1] If these value models for society as a whole are satisfied then many other benefits identified in this chapter will also accrue and can be measured.

Option value
- People value the possibility of enjoying the digitized resources and the resultant research outputs created through the endeavours of academic and higher education (HE) now or sometime in the future.

Prestige value
- People derive utility from knowing that a digitized resource, HE institution or its research is cherished by persons living inside and outside their community.

Education value
- People are aware that digitized resources contribute to their own or to other people's sense of culture, education, knowledge and heritage and therefore value it.

Existence value
- People benefit from knowing that a digital resource exists but do not personally use it.

Bequest value
- People derive satisfaction from the fact that their descendants and other members of the community will in the future be able to enjoy a digitized resource if they choose to.

Figure 8.9 *The five modes of value for digitized resources*

Future modes of evaluation and impact assessment should include some focus on these social factors. Digitization projects and programmes need to engage with the core principle of impact assessment – 'How does this change people's lives?' – in order to succeed in an ever more competitive funding environment.

Note

1 Inspired by the work of Bruno S. Frey and Werner W. Pommerehne (1989) *Muses and Markets: explorations in the economics of the arts*, Blackwell.

Part 3
Enhancing the future impact and value of digital collections

9
Using ICT methods and tools in arts and humanities research[1]

Lorna M. Hughes[2]

Introduction: centralized support for arts and humanities digital scholarship in the UK

In the last two decades, digital resources for the arts and humanities have been developed via a number of initiatives and funding streams, primarily from organizations including JISC, the NEH (National Endowment for the Humanities), the Mellon Foundation, and other national and international initiatives. In the UK, the Arts and Humanities Research Council (AHRC), and its predecessor, the AHRB (Arts and Humanities Research Board) contributed greatly to the expansion in the production and exploitation of digital resources for arts and humanities research, primarily through the Resource Enhancement Scheme, which funded the development of a large number of digital resources during its existence, from 2000 to 2007.

It has recently been estimated that up to 50% of projects funded by the AHRC have some sort of digital output (AHRC, 2007). Thanks to strategic and responsive-mode funding opportunities for digitization, and uptake of these initiatives by libraries, archives and higher education institutions, there is now a critical mass of digital material produced by, and available to, arts and humanities researchers. Given that the source materials for arts and humanities scholarship are varied and complex, their digital surrogates are highly multimedia (Hughes, 2004). This massive expansion of digital resources is comparable, in its complexity if not its volume, to the 'data deluge' experienced by the 'hard' sciences in the same period (Hey and Trefethen, 2005) and has led to an increased adoption of digital scholarship in arts and humanities research and teaching. Digital resources have enabled transformative research projects in the humanities; one of the most significant medieval discoveries of recent years has been the identification of Chaucer's scribe – Adam Pinkhurst, about whom we now know a great deal – by Lynne Mooney of the University of York. This discovery would have been impossible without access to high-quality digital images of manuscripts, which made it possible for Mooney to identify individual hands that worked on different manuscripts (Mooney, 2006). Examples of similar remarkable research using digital collections were the basis of the ACLS report, *Our Cultural Commonwealth: the report of the American Council of Learned Societies Commission on cyberinfrastructure for the humanities and social sciences*, which encouraged the academic community to seize the opportunities of digital collections and integrated research infrastructures for academic research. Similarly, a recent review of the UK's AHRC Resource Enhancement Digitization Scheme acknowledged that 'in a relatively short time, the AHRB/C has enabled a sea change in the production and exploitation of resources, especially digital resources, in the arts and humanities' (AHRC, 2006).

A recognized sea change of this sort requires support and, accordingly, the UK made a considerable investment in centralized support services for advanced ICT in the arts and humanities, mostly directed through the AHRC and the JISC. Centrally funded initiatives included the Arts and Humanities Data Service (AHDS, www.ahds.ac.uk), funded by JISC and the AHRC from 1995 to 2008 to support the creation, management and preservation of digital resources. From 2003 to 2008, the AHRC ran an ICT programme, which supported a number of strategic initiatives, notably the AHRC ICT Methods Network (www.methodsnetwork.ac.uk), based at the Centre for Computing in the Humanities, King's College London. This was the largest project funded by the AHRC ICT programme, and from 2005 to 2008 it received £1,000,000 to support arts and humanities scholars who used advanced ICT methods in their research by demonstrating the value, impact and use of digital collections; developing an understanding of the communities of practice that had evolved around research uses of digital collections; and documenting the ways in which the use of digital collections were becoming embedded in the research lifecycle.

The Methods Network programme and activities

The Network developed a comprehensive programme of over 50 activities, involving 1400 people, demonstrating the ways in which digital collections, tools and methods are used in research practice across the disciplines in the arts and humanities. These are described in the final evaluation report of the Methods Network (Hughes, 2008). While UK based, the Network attracted considerable international participation and attention. The Methods Network was established with one key objective: to understand and demonstrate how the critical mass of digital collections available to arts and humanities researchers could be the basis of transformative and innovative research across the disciplines by allowing greater access to materials, new modes of collaboration and communication; and facilitate the type of research that changes the paradigms of understanding and creates new knowledge, by:

- enabling research that would otherwise be impossible: addressing research questions that would have been impossible to resolve without the use of ICT tools
- asking new research questions, i.e. questions that are driven by insights that were only achievable through the use of new tools and methods
- facilitating and enhancing existing research, by making research processes easier via the use of computational tools and methods.

The lasting legacy of the Methods Network is the documentation of its programmes, publications and activities, which collectively demonstrate the evidence of value and broader impact of digital collections, and the ICT methods, tools and collaborations that underpin their use for research. This chapter outlines some of the key findings of the

AHRC Methods Network, based on a qualitative evaluation carried out at the end of the project. The chapter will also examine the ways in which the Methods Network supported collaboration between arts and humanities researchers and practitioners from other disciplines, fostering a human, collaborative infrastructure, and a methodological commons for digital arts and humanities scholarship.

ICT methods in the arts and humanities

The activities and outputs of the Methods Network are an evidence base for ICT methods in the arts and humanities, demonstrating what scholars actually do with digital resources, and how they are effecting a transformation of research. This usage is a theme in the ACLS report, too: the idea that the use of the e-infrastructure should be underpinned by arts and humanities research methods, and that new developments in technology must be informed by scholarship, and not the other way around.

To formalize what is meant by 'ICT methods', John Unsworth has identified these as the 'scholarly primitives' of the digital humanities: discovering, annotating, comparing, referring, sampling, illustrating, and representing digital content (Unsworth, 2000). Advanced ICT methods include text analysis and mining, image analysis, moving image capture and analysis, and quantitative and qualitative data analysis. They can be found at a key point of intersection between disciplines, collections and researchers: data-rich disciplines (e.g. archaeology, library and information science, and musicology) have refined new ICT methods, and within the data-driven sciences research methods have emerged around data and information processes. The use of advanced ICT methods can effect significant benefits in arts and humanities scholarship: they can enhance existing research methods (for example, by harnessing the processing power of grid technologies to allow large data sets to be searched quickly and efficiently, and in complex or novel ways); and they enable new research methods (for example, developing pattern matching algorithms for image analysis that can be applied to digital images of manuscripts). New approaches can also come about from creative collaboration; for example, the REACH (Researching e-Science Analysis of Census Holdings) workshop series investigated the potential application of grid computing to use of historical census data sets, by applying record linkage research methods developed by researchers in physics working on the AstroGrid project (www.ucl.ac.uk/infostudies/research/reach).

Computational methods demand rigour and precision in their application and, accordingly, research practitioners working in the emerging field of the digital humanities have begun to formalize new theories of the interaction between content, analytical and interpretative tools and technologies, methodological approaches, and disciplinary kinships. Two pieces of work have addressed the need to articulate digital research methods in the arts and humanities, contributing to the need for better documentation and descriptions of ICT methods in the arts and humanities.

The concept was initially expressed as the 'Methodological Commons' in an intellectual and disciplinary map (or 'ecology') of digital arts and humanities in the context of modelling humanities research processes. The map was developed by Harold Short with

Willard McCarty at the Centre for Computing in the Humanities (CCH) at King's College (McCarty, 2005), and initially presented at an Association for Literary and Linguistic Computing (ALLC) 'Roadmap' meeting in Pisa in 2002. The map went through various refinements, and it continues to evolve, although as a matter of presentation rather than the underlying concept.[3] The thinking behind the Methodological Commons also informed the development of the AHRC ICT Methods Network, which was based at CCH and co-directed by Short and Marilyn Deegan.

In Short and McCarty's model, the 'Methodological Commons' has the following core elements:

- technical methods from discipline areas outside the arts and humanities, e.g. engineering and computer science, for mining, visualization and modelling of digital content
- new modes of collaboration across disciplines and communities, particularly in partnership with scientific, engineering and cultural heritage science disciplines
- a combination of data types, technical methods and multiple technologies frequently being needed, for example, combinations of text, database, image, time-based data (video or sound), and geographical information systems (GIS)
- formal methods required for analysis and design of source data and modelling of possible technical approaches
- methods for working with large-scale data sources, as well as aggregating materials from multiple collections or sources.

In a separate yet related initiative, in 2003 Sheila Anderson and Reto Speck of the AHDS (AHDS, 2007) began development of 'The Taxonomy of Computational Methods in the Arts and Humanities' (referred to here as the 'ICT Methods Taxonomy'). This resource classifies ICT method types by behavioural similarity, and was originally developed as part of the AHDS Projects and Method Database project[4] as an extensive taxonomy of computational methods common to the creation, management and sustainability of digital resources in the arts and humanities. The ICT Methods Taxonomy formalizes, and provides a controlled vocabulary for, the way in which we describe the use of ICT in the arts and humanities. In the ICT Methods Taxonomy, 'Method' broadly indicates all the techniques and tools that are used to gain new knowledge in arts and humanities disciplines. A method is a computational one if it is either based on ICT (i.e. database technology) or critically dependent on it (i.e. statistical analysis).

Terms in the methods taxonomy are classified at two levels: 'content type' and 'function type':

- Content types describe the type of digital resource created, for example: narrative text; data set/structured data and text; still image/graphics; moving image; 3D object; spatial; and sound.
- Function types describe the broad functions commonly undertaken in digital

resource creation processes. These include: capture, i.e. the conversion of analogue information into (raw) digital data (via 'digitization'); structuring and enhancement, i.e. the organization and integration of the data captured from one or various sources into a uniform conceptual framework, via, for example, normalization, standardization and enhancement of its data; analysis, i.e. the extraction of information/knowledge/meaning from the resource; and dissemination and presentation, i.e. the presentation and dissemination/communication of the results of the research project.[5]

The taxonomy provides a framework for understanding how ICT methods sit within and enable research practice in the arts and humanities, and how they might be replicated by future research projects.[6] Developing a better understanding and classification of methods in practice shows that ICT Methods do not relate merely to the end-use of digital materials by scholars (for example, applying text analysis to a pre-existing digital corpus). They are a crucial component of the entire digital life cycle. Considerations about the use of advanced digital tools and methods by researchers affects decisions about selection, digitization, curation, preservation and, most importantly, sustainability over the long term. The way that digital resources end up being used may be unanticipated at the outset; or they may have value for different communities and disciplines from those originally intended. Conversely, some digital resources are less 'valuable' to scholarship because their creator did not factor considerations about how the resource would be used (and reused) into the development of the resources.

Digital tools for the arts and humanities

A discussion of ICT methods introduces a need for consideration of the use of digital tools that enable these methods. A digital 'tool' is defined here as any piece of software that can be used to gather, analyse and/or process data. A useful distinction can be drawn between tools that enable existing (i.e. analogue) research processes to be conducted better and/or faster, and tools that enable researchers to ask, and answer, completely new research questions.

A Methods Network workgroup on digital tools development[7] identified a number of specific research challenges, or aspects of the research process, where digital tools and technologies can support scholarly primitives in the arts and humanities, concluding that the following categories of computer-based analytical and interpretative tools required further investigation, investment and development. These are described below, with examples of recent research projects that provide exemplars of their use.

Knowledge mining and organization tools, especially for non-textual data

As data in the humanities are highly multimedia, tools to deep-mine and interpret non-textual materials (moving image, image and sound) are needed to discover patterns, connections and contexts in the same way as we analyse text. Logically, this requires tools to join up and integrate highly distributed small-scale collections of data. An example of this is Purcell Plus,[8] based at Goldsmiths College, University of London, which is investigating information retrieval methodologies and technologies for musicological research, working with digital music corpora.

Grid tools

These are tools that use the computational grid, the data grid and the access grid for processing and interpreting large amounts of data, and in support of collaborative working, have much potential for the arts and humanities. In creative and practice-led research, there has been enthusiastic adoption and use of the Access Grid,[9] which has identified the need for an integrated interface that can link resources in multiple media types to reveal the creative process, especially in relation to 'live' or ephemeral forms such as dance and body-based performance practices. This can enable access to existing performance archives, and allow new possibilities for documentation, analysis and dissemination. This can in turn bring new possibilities for feeding historic performances into live ones, and thus opportunities for creative experimentation with space and time. The e-Dance project at the University of Bedfordshire[10] experimented with grid-based and multicast performances to allow new ways of thinking about distributed creativity, exploring the ways in which the technology (including its limitations) can affect the way musicians and performers approach composition, production and study of performances.

Tools to automate and/or assist with tagging and annotation

A significant barrier to the discovery, analysis and interpretation of digital resources is the need for tools to support the classification of people, places and time-related information, including lexica, authority files and gazetteers: 'reference collections in a digital library environment' (Buckland, 2007). This is the underpinning intellectual infrastructure to digital content, but its development is challenging. The Archaeotools Project (http://ads.ahds.ac.uk/project/archaeotools, concluded in 2009), a collaboration between the University of Sheffield and the University of York, investigated data mining, faceted classification and e-archaeology, and aimed to create a major sustainable resource for archaeological research consisting of metadata records of sites and monuments in the UK, and to develop new digital tools for indexing and classification of this material also incorporating index terms used in older antiquarian literature. It also investigated automation of tagging and annotation of source materials, and mining and organization of the data, using visualization tools to represent search results.

Tools for capturing research processes and workflows, including those for creative practice

Reflecting developments in collaborative workflow research in the 'hard' sciences (such as myExperiment[11]), tools to capture and document the creative and research processes themselves are needed. These should be able to incorporate the interpretive and critical processes that are the essence of research in the arts and humanities, or the process of making a work (e.g. of dance or art). The e-Science and Ancient Documents (e-SAD) project, based at the University of Oxford, is developing tools to assist the reading of damaged texts like the stilus tablets from Vindolanda, and an interpretation support system (ISS) to support and keep track of the day-to-day reading and interpretation of ancient documents. A combination of image processing tools and an ontology-based support system will be developed to support experts by tracking their developing hypotheses, allowing further layers of interpretive scholarship and deliberative concepts, with visualization of outputs.

Visualization tools and tools for temporal and spatial exploration and representation

Visualization tools and tools for the analysis of temporal and spatial data allow the representation of content in many formats. The E-Curator project at UCL[12] used 3D colour scans for remote object identification and assessment, exploring the potential of e-science technologies in documentation, conservation and communication of material heritage. It developed a prototype application for 3D laser scanning of museum artefacts, which has been tested by conservators, curators and museum and heritage researchers. Birmingham University's project, Medieval Warfare on the Grid: the case of Manzikert,[13] used temporal and spatial modelling to illustrate complex historic information – including materials from a variety of conflicting primary sources – to explore the military and logistical research questions posed by the Battle of Manzikert in 1071, using agent-based modelling and distributed simulations.

Capturing practice and experience: supporting communities of practice and embedding interdisciplinary exchange

This survey of research projects shows broad impact in terms of the research challenges addressed, collaborations fostered, and the application of ICT tools and approaches to arts and humanities research challenges. As the digital scholarship field matures, it is also recognized as one in which collaboration is enabled, and in which partnerships between different aspects of research, and between researchers from multiple disciplines, must be supported in order for the digital collections, tools and methods to be fully exploited (Blanke and Dunn, 2006): ICT methods define and formalize the digital humanities. Digital tools facilitate these methods. Both cross-disciplinary boundaries and the communities of practice that engage with them are varied and complex. There are mutual strategic benefits for collaboration: the arts and humanities could benefit from scientific approaches to dealing with large amounts of data; and the scientific and computational disciplines could benefit from a better understanding of arts and humanities approaches to complex and non-standard data. Within current practice in the arts and humanities, however, there is very little opportunity to share experience and expertise across disciplines and to encourage dialogue and experimentation (Hockey and Ross, 2008). Interdisciplinary work of this nature needs to be sustained and supported, and a crucial 'added value' of the Methods Network was its ability to foster collaboration. The AHRC

ICT Methods Network programme of activities identified and brought together cross-disciplinary stakeholders to facilitate collaboration among communities of practice from the arts and humanities as well as scientific disciplines: the computational science community, including both computer and computational scientists; software engineers; technical experts, archivists, librarians and curators; and representatives of the creative industries. Each activity was a practical application of the methodological commons in action, showcasing how ICT tools and methods can add value to digital collections. For example, the Expert Seminar on text editing, organized by Marilyn Deegan of King's College London and Katherine Sutherland, University of Oxford,[14] examined a range of software tools and ICT research methods to extract new knowledge from the following digital collections:[15]

- the Canterbury Tales project
- the Jane Austen Fiction Manuscripts project
- the Nineteenth Century Serials Edition project
- the Inscriptions of Aphrodisias (InsAph) project
- the HyperNietzsche project
- various other projects, especially at the National Library of Norway and the Royal Library of Belgium.

An Expert Seminar on History and Archaeology held in 2006 also exemplified this integration. It examined the ways in which digital and virtual representations of space, time and object were fundamentally shifting the ways in which researchers have critically engaged with primary source materials via their digital interrogation of cultural objects. From advanced handwriting analysis of medieval manuscripts to geospatial computation allowing visualizations of the North Sea floor, the seminar presented advanced ICT methods and e-science tools and approaches that showcased the state of the art research applicable to history, archaeology and classics (Greengrass and Hughes, 2008). The advanced methods examined at this event included those for digital representation of spatial and temporal analysis; ways of recording the various assumptions and circumstances that go into any virtual representation (e.g. the reconstruction of an object or the recreation of a historical event); and those that allow the digital reinterpretation of the past through such cultural objects, including text where advanced markup and data mining have the capacity to reveal intertextualities and historical dependencies that cannot be discovered by other means.

By demonstrating the relationship between digital source, methods and tools, there is, nonetheless, a continuum with the traditional method of scholarship (editing, markup, classification, etc.) and the digital methods. The 'scholarly primitives' are clearly recognizable.

Impact of the Methods Network

The value and impact of this approach can be seen by the outputs of the Methods

Network's activities. Each produced a number of outputs, including detailed rapporteur reports of each activity; videos and audio podcasts of individual presentations at the events; and articles or newsletter pieces for different publication venues. Events often led to the development of plans for follow-up events and grant applications. In some cases, significant outputs were developed to support various communities of practice. For example, the 2006 Workshop 'Making 3D Visual Research Outcomes Transparent',[16] led to the creation of the 'London Charter', a resource supporting the use of paradata to enhance the academic rigour of 3D visualization by making the research processes more transparent.[17] Other outputs included training materials, such as those developed for the workshops on 'Corpus Approaches to the Language of Literature' and 'Using Large Scale XML Corpora', which brought together academics in the fields of corpus linguistics, literary stylistics and literary criticism to discuss the data sets, tools and methods that might be used for studying the language of literature, utilizing electronic versions of literary texts, corpora of literature and language, and tools for text and corpora analysis. The resulting training materials, now freely available online, will provide a recently identified community of researchers with training to use corpus analysis tools and methodologies.[18] Similarly, the workshop 'Digital Restoration for Damaged Documents' produced a valuable guide on digital enhancement of damaged manuscript materials using Photoshop enhancement of high resolution digital images to reveal hidden or lost parts of an original document.[19] This resource demonstrated how the DIAMM project has been able to use new technology to return documents to legibility that had previously been considered unreadable. This has a major impact on research because these documents now become part of the corpus of relevant texts, from which they had previously been omitted. Similarly, older materials containing portions of text that had been unreadable can now be re-appraised for scholarship.

This is changing the way that some scholars are approaching manuscript studies within certain disciplines, and fostering interdisciplinary work, thanks to the increased availability of manuscript images. Those working in manuscript studies, and who understand digital imaging methods, will find their research made easier.

One of the most lasting outputs of the Methods Network events was the volumes in the resulting publication series, Digital Research in the Arts and Humanities. Nine volumes have been produced to date, from a selection of expert seminars and workgroups, presenting the state of the art in the adoption of ICT Methods in a number of disciplines.[20]

However, the most interesting 'outputs' of the Methods Network programme have been intangible: the benefits of networking, of meeting colleagues across the disciplines, and of understanding how new tools and research methods can be applied from other academic disciplines. The true value of the Network was through sharing understanding and experience and building communities of practice around ICT-based research, bringing together practitioners around data sets, tools and methods and developing new ideas in discussion and collaboration. For example, the workshop 'Historical Text Mining', in July 2006, was cross-disciplinary and attended by individuals with various experiences of computing, from introductory to expert. It was designed to facilitate interdisciplinary collaboration, chiefly between the English language studies, literature, linguistics and computer science communities. The idea was to introduce the ideas of text mining to new people, and the event led to a second Methods Network event being organized called 'Text Mining for Historians'.

Other outputs, resulting directly from these collaborations, have included the development of journal articles and further workshops. Another impact was making researchers aware of the potential for research of the full range of digital resources already in existence.[21] Most interestingly a large number of grant applications were developed as a result of the collaborative partnerships developed and nurtured at these workshops. These included successful applications to the JISC–NEH 'Digging into Data' programme, NEH–JISC grant programme, the AHRC–JISC–EPSRC (Engineering and Physical Science Research Council) e-Science in the Arts and Humanities programme, and the ESF COST (European Science Foundation – Cooperation in Science and Technology) programme, as well as individual research grant applications.

Conclusion

The activities and outputs described above were developed under the auspices of a centrally funded national programme in the UK. They comprise a valuable framework for understanding how ICT tools and methods are becoming embedded in research projects and practice in the arts and humanities, and the research life cycle of discovery, analysis, publication and dissemination, while adding the additional layer of collaboration and interdisciplinary exchange that is part of the methodological commons.

This work provides an important evidence base to inform the future agenda for ICT support in the arts and humanities, in the UK and elsewhere: demonstrating the value of this work, which enables the development of new research questions and findings; allowing old kinds of research to be carried out in significant new, and more efficient, ways; extending the evidence base for research; showing the institutional and disciplinary impact; demonstrating the impact of the digital humanities on developments in ICT in other fields (e.g. TEI (Text Encoding Initiative) on EXtensible Markup Language (XML)); and extending the social and economic impact of the arts and humanities (by expanding the communities of users).

Digital resources, while valuable, are also expensive to develop. The academic sector – in the UK and elsewhere – faces an unprecedented period of reduced funding and an uncertain future for centrally provided ICT support in the arts and humanities, so the focus for the research community must be to look to the lessons of what has gone before in order to inform future development, and to ensure that expertise gained is not lost. This will be an important legacy of the UK's centrally funded ICT support services.

The broader digital humanities community must continue to gather and disseminate evidence of the use, value and impact of digital collections, tools and methods in the arts and humanities, and to push the agenda for innovative research and collaboration despite a lack of centralized funding. The work described here shows that there is clear 'value' in investing in digital collections and digital research, in terms of achieving research outcomes that would otherwise have been impossible to accomplish. Arguments for a support infrastructure for digital collections, tools and methods in the arts and humanities are more powerful if based on evidence of its role in enabling new and valuable scholarship that pushes forward the intellectual boundaries across the disciplines.

While an integrated research 'e-infrastructure' for academic research could allow shared access to large-scale data sets, advanced tools for analysis of this data, and fully integrated systems for representing and publishing (ACLS, 2006), this will only have real value in the arts and humanities if it is a collaborative, human infrastructure that that puts scholarship, not just digital scholarship, at its heart.

Notes

1   An earlier draft of this chapter was originally discussed in the context of a proposed submission for an e-science publication edited by my colleagues at King's College London, Tobias Blanke and Stuart Dunn. I am grateful for editorial input from Dr Dunn that helped develop some of this material.

2   Lorna M. Hughes was the Programme Manager of the AHRC Methods Network from 2005 to 2008.

3   It is maintained on the ALLC website (www.allc.org/node/196).

4   The principal aim of the Projects and Method Database project was to establish a register containing detailed information on current and recent arts and humanities research projects using ICT, and on the computational methods employed by such projects. It has subsequently been incorporated into http://arts-humanities.net.

5   These functions are not completely discrete entities but can overlap in significant ways. Therefore, for the purposes of the taxonomy, certain computational methods can be classified under more than one function type heading (i.e. the method 'Record linkages' is classified as both as a structuring/enhancing method and as an analytical one).

6   http://arts-humanities.net has embedded the ICT Methods Taxonomy into its descriptions of ICT UK funded research projects with a digital output, and the ICT methods and tools these projects have adopted, and used it to organize content and to help users categorize content they add to the sites, via an emerging folksonomy providing suggestions for user-generated tags. The Centre for e-Research (CeRch) at King's College London is also hosting further research into the ICT Methods Taxonomy as a widely referenced ontology, in collaboration with the Digital Humanities Observatory (DHO) in Ireland (which has adopted it as the basis of its DRAPIER (Digital Research and Projects in Ireland) project).

7   See Methods Network Tools report, www.methodsnetwork.ac.uk/redist/pdf/wg1report.pdf.

8   See www.purcellplus.org. Tim Crawford, the primary investigator of the project, organized the AHRC ICT Methods Network Expert Seminar on Advanced Methods for Musicology, the proceedings of which have been published (Crawford and Gibson, 2009).

9   See, for example, the work of the work of the Multimedia Art Research Centers and Electronic Laboratories (MARCEL) project, a permanent broadband interactive network and website dedicated to exchange between art and science, and the collaboration between over 60 international member institutions. See www.mmmarcel.org. In the USA, this work has also

been at the forefront of the Internet 2 performance strand; see www.internet2.edu/arts.

10 See http://projects.kmi.open.ac.uk/e-dance.

11 See www.myexperiment.org.

12 See www.museums.ucl.ac.uk/research/ecurator.

13 See www.iaa.bham.ac.uk/research/fieldwork_research_themes/projects/logistics/ Manzikert/Index.htm.

14 The proceedings of this workshop were published (Deegan and Sutherland, 2009).

15 The proceedings of this workshop were published (Archer, 2009).

16 The workshop Making 3D Visual Research Outcomes Transparent was organized by Professor Richard Beachan and Dr Hugh Dunard of the King's Visualisation Lab.

17 See www.londoncharter.org. The Italian Ministry of Culture (which oversees all archaeological sites in Italy) has recently adopted the London Charter as a standard, which it expects adherence to for projects under its guidance. The Charter has been translated into Italian and Japanese. Other languages are forthcoming.

18 See www.arts-humanities.net/eventresources/corpus_approaches_language_literature.

19 The workshop was organized by staff of, and used digital images from, the Digital Image Archive of Medieval Music (DIAMM), a project funded by the AHRC and the Mellon Foundation (www.diamm.ac.uk).

20 For a full list of publications in the series, see www.ashgate.com/digitalresearch.

21 For example, access to the full text EEBO corpus was negotiated with ProQuest via the JISC licence following the workshop on Historical Text Mining.

10
Creating a research data infrastructure: policy and practicalities

Ann Borda and Lyle Winton

Introduction

The recent development of modern and faster computerized infrastructures has enabled researchers to routinely generate research data at an unprecedented level, both quantitatively regarding the amount of data generated from instruments, for example, such as genomic and sensor network data, and qualitatively, producing types of data previously unavailable, such as digital census and health care data. Similarly, an increasing amount of non-born digital research products and source materials are being digitized, such as cultural collections, to facilitate research, management, collaboration and access.

These developments have contributed to a 'data deluge' (Hey and Trefethen, 2004; e-Science Directors' Forum Strategy Working Group, 2009) that gives researchers access to a rich and massive amount of data across disciplinary boundaries. At the same time, the provision of high-capacity networks and improvements in research data capture methods have provided researchers with a means to take data sets produced in one geographical location and aggregate them with data produced elsewhere. Some have described this as the evolution of a new kind of science – 'data-intensive science' or *fourth paradigm* (Hey, Tansley and Tolle, 2009) – that is characterized by three principal activities: data capture, curation and analysis.

For comparison, the *first paradigm* was characterized by observational science that has existed from the time of early civilizations, followed by a *second paradigm* – an empirically based approach, first exemplified by Roger Bacon's descriptions in the 13th century. The *third paradigm*, which evolved in the latter half of the 20th century, is characterized by increasingly complex research challenges based principally on large-scale computational simulation. This has led to the concept of holistic systems; the evolution from wet labs (hands-on scientific research and experimentation) to virtual labs; and an emphasis on modelling, simulation, projection and prediction. The *fourth paradigm* (Hey, Tansley and Tolle, 2009) is largely focused on the evolution of large databases and digital data archives, and research methods focused on data analysis and mining and patterns discovery, among others.

The age of the fourth paradigm is further aligned with the movement towards 'open science', opening up scientific results to the public through the internet, as well as the increased participation of the public ('citizen science' (Bonney et al., 2009; Lyon, 2009; Hand, 2010)) as a contributing part to the scientific process, e.g. the global initiative Galaxy Zoo (www.galaxyzoo.org). These changes in the methods of research are complemented by an equally important potential for transforming scholarly communications processes (Hey and Hey, 2006) enabled by open access publications and pre-prints and the increasing demand to link research papers with provenance data.

The concepts of e-science, cyberinfrastructure and e-research can be considered as encapsulating or enabling activities driving the fourth paradigm. The term *eScience* was first coined by Sir John Taylor, Director General of the UK Research Councils in 1999. Taylor spoke of e-science as a global collaboration in key areas of science and the next generation of infrastructure that will support it (Taylor, 1999). In the USA the term *cyberinfrastructure* is used to describe research environments that support advanced data acquisition, data storage, data management, data integration, data mining, data visualization and computing services over networks and the internet. The term *e-research*, largely used in Australia, denotes the use of advanced information technologies to support existing and new forms of research across disciplines, including the humanities and social sciences.

Each of these terms is characterized by the collaborative and multidisciplinary nature of the research being undertaken at both national and international levels and access to shared resources and common services that transcend institutional, organizational, geographic and political boundaries.

Research infrastructures

> [Research infrastructures are] principally *about* data: how to get it, how to share it, how to store it, and how to leverage it into the major downstream products (knowledge, discoveries, learning, applications, etc.) we want our sciences to produce. At the same time, there is significant variation (both within and across disciplines) as to what *counts* as data. For some, data is first and foremost a question of *things*: samples, specimens, collections. For others, data is what comes out of a model – or perhaps the model itself. Data may be tactile, visual, textual, numeric, tabular, classificatory, or statistical. Data may be an intermediate outcome, a step on the road to higher-order products of science (publications, patents, etc.). Or data may be the product itself. (Jackson et al., 2007)

Large investments over the last decade by governments in Europe, the UK, the USA and Canada, and Australia, in implementing national research data and digitized data infrastructures have been integral to drive national productivity and innovation.

In the USA, the National Science Foundation (NSF) produced a strategic five-year plan to identify and support 'the next generation of major equipment and facilities to enable transformational research' (NSF, 2006). Prior to the NSF plan, a UK government-funded e-infrastructure report published in 2006 (OSI, 2007) underlined the importance of good quality data as essential to maximize investment and innovation. The report indicated that the process of creating data is key to getting good quality data with appropriate metadata. It stressed therefore the importance of automated metadata creation and software to enhance the quality of the data creation process. Enriching the data requires the application of structure, description and attributes to the 'raw' or source data and, if these are done according to commonly agreed standards, the whole data environment can be enriched by any number of common services such as search, discover, access, analysis, visualization, data submission and presentation services, etc.

The UK report included digitization on its digital data creation agenda. It called for 'a strategic approach to digitization and repurposing of data as a means of enabling access and new forms of analysis'. The report *Our Cultural Commonwealth* by the American Council of Learned Societies similarly emphasized the importance of supporting and co-ordinating the digitization of legacy materials particularly in the humanities disciplines. The report concluded that: 'extensive and reusable digital collections are at the core of the humanities and social science cyberinfrastructure' (ACLS, 2006).

In Europe, the European Strategy Forum on Research Infrastructures (ESFRI, 2009) has identified a number of projects that aim to provide major infrastructure directly aligned with research needs across the physical sciences, and in the humanities, arts and social sciences, e.g. the Council of European Social Science Data Archives (CESSDA), and the Digital Research Infrastructure for the Arts and Humanities (DARIAH).

In Australia, the Department of Innovation, Industry, Science and Research (DIISR, 2011) is developing the *2011 Strategic Roadmap for Australian Research Infrastructure*, which will articulate Australia's national research infrastructure priority areas and where it may improve research outcomes over the next five to ten years. Among its aims, the *2011 Roadmap* will consider new or emerging areas of research that may require different types of infrastructure in the future, and will consider priorities in an international context, reflecting the international, collaborative nature of modern research and the important role of collaborative research infrastructure in bringing researchers together.

Under the remit of the Australian Government's National Collaborative Research Infrastructure Strategy initiative, the Australian National Data Service (ANDS) was formed in 2008 and underpinned by two fundamental concepts:

1. with the evolution of new means of data capture and storage, data has become an increasingly important component of the research endeavour, and
2. research collaboration is fundamental to the resolution of the major challenges facing humanity in the 21st century. (Sandland, 2009)

ANDS is currently tasked with building the Research Data Australia (RDA) service (http://services.ands.org.au/home/orca/rda) with the intent to increase both the visibility and discoverability of Australian research data collections. Behind the RDA sits the Australian Research Data Commons (ARDC), which holds meta level records describing shareable Australian research collections, descriptions of those collections including the information required to support their reuse, the relationships between the various elements involved (e.g. the data, the researchers–producers, the instruments from which data has been derived and the institutions), and the infrastructure needed to enable, populate and support the ARDC.

These and other major infrastructure investments have been aligned with and clearly support the outputs of the third and fourth paradigms in particular. What is also evident arising from these nationally funded initiatives, such as ANDS, is that research data and digital collections are integral building blocks of research infrastructure. Digital data collections in general have been identified by the NSF as fundamental to a new research model, stating in its strategic report (NSF, 2006) that:

> It is exceedingly rare that fundamentally new approaches to research and education arise. Information technology has ushered in such a fundamental change. Digital data collections are at the heart of this change. They enable analysis at unprecedented levels of accuracy and sophistication and provide novel insights through innovative information integration. Through their very size and complexity, such digital collections provide new phenomena for study. At the same time, such collections are a powerful force for inclusion, removing barriers to participation at all ages and levels of education.

The role of infrastructure providers

Government investments in research and infrastructure have led to an evolving *ecosystem* of infrastructure and service providers, some focused on information technology, others on expertise and new technologies (NSF, 2007; Lyon, 2007; e-Science Directors' Forum Strategy Working Group, 2009). While digital systems have been critical for service provision for decades, online systems are increasingly part of the access mechanism for researchers.

In Australia, 'e-research service provider' is the term used for organizations focusing on the provision and development of digital research systems (DIISR, 2011). In light of emerging research data retention policies, most service providers place the burden of retention on their end-users, the researchers. Considering operational costs and current funding models for fixed time periods, long-term data retention is not possible for providers. Relying on the storage capability of longer-lived research institutions and discipline repositories can be considered a sensible operational strategy. However, as funded service providers there is an expectation and responsibility to support the needs of researchers in providing systems that facilitate project management, records keeping, data archiving and the transferring of data and information back to virtual research environments or institutional repositories.

Additionally, many infrastructure providers work as close collaborators on research projects and provide expertise to support service use, custom service development, research design and analysis (University of Oxford, NCeSS and JISC, 2011). They may participate in the research project's collaborative environment or help in the design and development of the environment. Such embedded collaboration and development can give providers a unique perspective on the context of the research, an external perspective that is generally focused on process and outcomes. The usefulness of such a perspective in documenting research context towards retention and longer-term reuse has yet to be proven (Ruusalepp, 2008).

It has been proposed by several initiatives that frameworks be developed for the sharing of such documentation and to help facilitate future development efforts in research infrastructure; for example, the international e-Framework for Education and Research (Olivier, Roberts and Blinco, 2005), the e-Infrastructure Use Cases and Service Usage Models (eIUS) project (http://projects.oucs.ox.ac.uk/eius/), e-Research Community Intelligence System (Voss, 2011), collaborative virtual research frameworks (Borda, 2009), and a cyberinfrastructure framework for virtual organizations (NSF, 2007).

To date no documented frameworks are in extensive use nor have any been considered as supporting records for research activities. This is a cross-disciplinary and iterative activity in the realization of a common purposeful goal of effective outcomes for the community, for wider uptake, for minimizing resource costs and for possible reuse.

Policy and practicality

Research infrastructure is about new ways of organizing the practice of scientific knowledge and scholarship, drawing on new computational resources, enabling new collaborative and organizational forms, and new forms of discovery and learning (Jackson et al., 2007). The development and implementation of research infrastructures have, to some extent, been further shaped by the open access movement, which over the last decade has advocated the open publishing of academic material, including research results and, more recently, provenance data. Not least, the widespread availability of content in digital formats demands an infrastructure to support these and the novel forms of research arising (Lyon, 2009).

Research projects are also continually providing a new context for the creation and emergence of 'data'. Researchers are no longer seen as using pre-existing data but are increasingly constructing new relationships between researchers and the data, particularly in secondary analysis where there is a shift towards the process of recontextualizing and reconstructing data (Moore, 2007). The growth of such 'cyberscholarship' is dependent on content being digitally captured, managed and preserved in ways that are significantly different from conventional methods (Arms and Larsen, 2007).

The key benefits of data preservation and sharing have been articulated in, for example, the Social Sciences and Humanities Research Council of Canada Research Data Archiving Policy. This is an extract:

> Sharing data strengthens our collective capacity to meet academic standards of openness by providing opportunities to further analyse, replicate, verify and refine research findings. Such opportunities enhance progress within fields of research as well as support the expansion of inter-disciplinary research. In addition, greater availability of research data will contribute to improved training for graduate and undergraduate students, and, through the secondary analysis of existing data, make possible significant economies of scale. Finally, researchers whose work is publicly funded have a special obligation to openness and accountability.
>
> (SSHRC, 2009)

Numerous national funding bodies now require that the basic data products of publicly funded research are not merely published but should also be available for further use as outlined in the US National Science Foundation's data sharing policy (NSF, 2010), the UK Medical Research Council's policy on data sharing and preservation (MRC, 2011) and the UK Biotechnology and Biological Sciences Research Council's data sharing policy (BBSRC, 2011). In the UK, the Arts and Humanities Research Council will soon launch a data management plan following a project to develop detailed guidelines for data management in the arts and humanities in consultation with the UK's Network of Expert Centres (www.arts-humanities.net/noc).

Quite apart from publication, organizations are specifically required to retain records of research, through funding requirements and legislation (e.g. records acts, freedom of information). Within Australia, researchers are required by the Australian Code for the Responsible Conduct of Research (NHMRC and ARC, 2007) to retain data beyond the end of projects, a recommended minimum of five years from the date of publication or longer depending on the type of data. Australian universities generally have institutional policies conforming to this code and legislation, specifically for the retention of research data and records. Data management planning is an integral part of this responsible conduct of research and is recognized by numerous international funding bodies. In order to facilitate both digital publication and policy compliance, many institutions have established digital storage capability and repositories for research.

A data management plan (DMP) is a document that explicitly describes a research data collection to aid in maintaining the integrity, future access, interoperability and appropriate use and reuse of the data. Australian universities, such as Monash University, University of Queensland and the University of Melbourne, have proactively engaged with their researcher communities in data management planning and in providing checklists to more easily enable compliancy. Organizations, such as the Digital Curation Centre in the UK (www.dcc.ac.uk), provide guidelines to researchers based on UK research funders' requirements for data management and sharing plans. Many of the research councils and government funding bodies mentioned above mandate documented data management plans as a condition of funding.

Table 10.1 can be considered a guide to a selection of research data outputs and corresponding data management plan areas.

Retention of both physical and digital records and data is an issue of concern for

Table 10.1 *Research data output types and data management planning areas*	
Research data (output types)	Data management plan
Multiple data collection locations	Collection process, quality control
Sensitive or high-value or non-repeatable data	Policies and responsibilities, traceability, access protocols, security
Large volumes of data	Collection process, maintenance, infrastructure requirements
Longitudinal studies	Data maintenance, persistence, archival practice
Staged data collection	Infrastructure requirements and planning
Distributed collaboration	Interoperability, availability, identifiers and attribution

finitely funded research activities. However, due to the continuously growing capacity and decreasing cost of technology, the cost of digital storage can be projected into the near future. The cost for storing a fixed quantity of data exponentially decreases over time. (Moore's Law is often used to predict growth in ICT – doubling capacity every 18 months; however, technology developments predict even greater increases in capacity (Walter, 2005).) Practically, analysis of commodity storage disks can suggest a slowing from Moore's Law, for example a doubling of capacity every 22 months (Blok, 2010). Taking into account periodic refreshes of technology, and fractional maintenance costs shared across many data sets, it is possible to calculate a finite cost of retaining data essentially forever. However, this cost would not include the enterprise operation of a digital repository or digital archive service (Winton, 2010), specifically ensuring long-term preservation, accessibility and usability of data sets. Practical cost issues remain if reuse is of ongoing concern.

There is another issue of practicality that must be addressed when considering longer-term reuse of retained data. Many data sets have broad research applicability and remain valuable over time, for example government, education, health, humanities and cultural data sets. However, many research data sets (particularly scientific data sets) are collected under complex circumstances, at the limits of academic understanding, or with the help of 'bleeding-edge' technologies. A great deal of research effort is spent on exploring and intimately understanding these circumstances and the impact they have on the data, analysis methods and outcomes (Lyon, 2007; Hey, Tansley and Tolle, 2009).

In some scenarios data sets can be made more accessible to others by 'cleaning' the data, accounting for bias, accurately expressing quality and uncertainty, and by providing more accessible packaging and formats. Such effort and cost is rarely accounted for within project and data management planning. In other circumstances it is not possible or desirable to clean the data. Great effort and attention is then needed to accurately represent the research context: methods, assumptions, conditions, equipment, processing and limitations around the data. Simply downloading the data for reuse may require the equivalent in expertise of the original researchers. Even with a well articulated context, specialist knowledge is often required to grasp fundamental concepts that do not transcend disciplines, specializations, collaborations or even projects.

Policies alone may similarly not result in a higher use of research data in the longer term. Optimum accessibility and usability of data importantly presupposes a trajectory of proper organization and curation of data, with access services and analysis tools that can provide researchers with added value (Ruusalepp, 2008).

Infrastructure approaches

Accurately documenting the practice of research, and therefore the context of research data (often referred to as metadata), serves several aspirational goals: policy compliance, professional research conduct and record keeping, a knowledge base facilitating collaboration, and easy discovery of appropriate data in the future. So an immediate goal for research projects is to record the research process, deliberation and decisions as efficiently as possible, with minimal effort and cost. The modern infrastructure and tools of researchers and collaboration, both digital and physical, should support this goal.

Increasingly, research institutions are providing enterprise-grade research support systems that facilitate researchers in managing and collaborating on projects and communities. These online working environments are occasionally called virtual research environments (VREs) or collaboration environments, and are flexible enough to support a range of activities. As a broad definition, VREs are platforms for enabling collaborative research activities beyond geographical barriers that are enhanced through the systematic use of web applications, online tools, systems and processes interoperating within and without institutional boundaries (NSF, 2008; Carusi and Torsten, 2010).

Such environments can organically grow with knowledge bases and documentation of research, and can be themselves considered repositories of research records and data. Sharing and reusing data are also a form of collaboration and it is through collaboration that the examples of effective enablers to data sharing can be established (Ruusalepp 2008).

Figure 10.1 is a generalized view of research infrastructure, aspects of which can typically be found in any collaborative research environment boundaries (NSF, 2008; Carusi and Torsten, 2010).

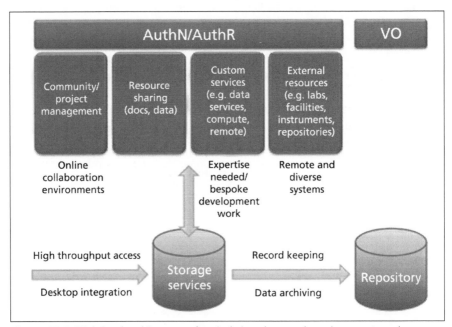

Figure 10.1 *High-level architecture of typical virtual research environments and supporting infrastructure (copyright VERSI)*

Digital research environments may provide a range of capabilities or functions:

- community/project management
- resource sharing

- custom services
- external resources.

These capabilities are potentially protected by authentication, authorization (AuthN/AuthR) for secure and role-based access to resources, and by virtual organization (VO) management systems. The latter, for instance, can support a group of researchers whose members and resources are distributed geographically, but which function as a coherent unit through the use of end-to-end research infrastructure (NSF, 2007, 2008).

The research infrastructure modules in general are underpinned by specific data workflows, outputs and inputs.

Online collaboration environments allow for free form development of processes and knowledge supporting either projects or communities. Examples of collaboration platforms include SharePoint®, Confluence, Basecamp® and Sakai. Both project documentation and research data can be shared using repository technologies, sometimes built into collaboration environments, sometimes separate. Examples include FedoraCommons™, Storage Resource Broker (SRB) and iRODS™ (Integrated Rule-Oriented Data System), Dropbox, data grid technologies and traditional file shares. Given enough resources, available ICT and research skills, custom portals and databases can be developed for specific projects and contexts. These often store a wealth of structured data and information, and can be designed to collect, disseminate, process and/or generate data. Many research activities also rely on external laboratories, facilities or resources for part of their work, some of which have systems for remote access.

All of these capabilities (see Figure 10.1, rectangular panels) will produce research records, context and metadata, and raw and derivative research data, ideally stored on reliable and accessible storage. These research products need to be retained beyond the end of project funding and activities. The current practice is to extract a subset of records and data for archiving in institutional or discipline repositories, or to continue operation of the project's digital environment until infrastructure support is no longer possible, or shelve the digital environment for possible later extraction of data (Ruusalepp 2008).

Costs and risks are associated with each as shown in Table 10.2.

Table 10.2 *Retention strategies, costs and risks*

Strategy	Costs	Risks
Extract a subset of records and data for archiving	Time to prepare archival records and metadata (researcher cost) Ongoing archive management, preservation and access (institutional cost)	Potential loss of context information and data
Continued operation of a project's digital environment	Ongoing operation and infrastructure costs (researcher cost)	Software and data format obsolescence Security of sensitive data
Shelving of the environment	Storage costs only Potentially large cost to un-shelve the environment for data extraction (researcher cost)	Software and data format obsolescence

The benefits of the first two strategies are the potential for reuse. The first, archiving in institutional and discipline repositories, allows for easy discovery of research data. The second, continued operation, allows subsequent researchers to explore the detailed context in which the data was collected, and the potential for collaboration with the original researchers (Lyon, 2007; e-Science Directors' Forum Strategy Working Group, 2009).

Case studies

Case studies can provide a framework for understanding how researchers are currently and may in the future engage with research data infrastructures, and how these support virtual research collaborations (e.g. NSF, 2008). Of particular note, the eIUS project in the UK had the primary aim of gathering and documenting concrete evidence of how e-infrastructure is, or is planned to be, used as a facilitator of the research process across major disciplines, with the further intention to broaden participation in the use and future development of e-infrastructure services (University of Oxford, NCeSS and JISC, 2009).

Several of the other research infrastructure reports cited in this paper are illustrated with supporting use case scenarios and exemplars of research collaboration and data sharing that describe environments not dissimilar to the generalized architecture described in Figure 10.1 (e.g. Lyon, 2007; NSF, 2007; e-Science Directors' Forum Strategy Working Group, 2009; Hey, Tansley and Tolle, 2009; Lyon, 2009).

The recent Australian government research infrastructure roadmap (DIISR, 2011) is similarly descriptive of essential data infrastructure investments, their research use and scenarios of use. Two examples are provided below with a description of their high level architectures in reference to Figure 10.1 and Table 10.2.

Case study: Histopathology and Organ Pathology service – case management system

The Histopathology and Organ Pathology service located at the University of Melbourne is one of the 12 facilities that constitute the Australian Phenomics Network (APN), with the wider APN goal of providing researchers with mouse models for the study of human and animal disease. A recent collaboration between the service, the University of Melbourne eScholarship Research Centre (www.esrc.unimelb.edu.au), the ANDS and the Victorian eResearch Strategic Initiative (www.versi.edu.au) has led to the development of digital infrastructure to facilitate operating procedures, manage context metadata and manage the resulting research data and materials. The service produces and retains digital images, including high resolution microscopy, reports and observations (digital) and preserved tissue samples (physical). The developed infrastructure can be viewed as three components:

- a case management system (CMS), a custom system supporting local workflow and information architecture

- integration with a national discipline repository, the APN's Phenomics Ontology Data Driven (PODD) repository, for partial retention and publication of results (still in development at this time)
- digital storage supported by the institutional research storage capability.

Effectively the infrastructure covers two of the general capabilities outlined in the previous section, custom services and external resources, as well as storage services. While the university is providing enterprise-grade research storage, services supporting long-term preservation of data and records are still in planning. So the existing preservation strategy is to continue operating their digital environment, the CMS. However, the APN PODD repository will support a secondary preservation strategy, with eventual extraction of research records and data for longer term archiving.

Case study: The Australian Social Science Data Archive

The Australian Social Science Data Archive (ASSDA, www.assda.edu.au) is a consortium of national Australian universities, managed by the Australian National University (ANU). ASSDA was established at the ANU in 1981 with a brief to provide a national service for the collection and preservation of computer readable data relating to social, political and economic affairs and to make these data available for sharing, further analysis and reuse.

ASSDA is the most comprehensive social science data collection in Australia to date, with a catalogue of around 3000 data sets, including Australian surveys, opinion polls and censuses, and includes data from other countries within the Asia Pacific region. As well as the central management at the ANU, distributed archive nodes have been progressively established across the country. These include the University of Queensland, the University of Western Australia, the University of Technology, Sydney, and the University of Melbourne. These nodes provide a national coverage of specialist services and thematic archives with particular foci. The ANU Supercomputer Facility provides the online data services and supporting enterprise infrastructure as the central 'hub'.

In response to its community, ASSDA has been extending its holdings to include qualitative data, and it has established the Australian Qualitative Archive (AQuA) based at the University of Queensland to administer this specialist research data. The development of AQuA has occurred alongside the establishment of other archival services operating as part of a distributed ASSDA network. Recently, the ASSDA Services for eSocial Science (ASeSS) project was funded to improve the curation and archiving of social science data, and to develop a VO component; this was in order to provide integrated web-based access to data held by ASSDA, and other similarly curated data, both as a customized service and in support of community managed data.

Conclusion

It is clear that advances in technology have provided unprecedented opportunities for data collection and generation, unprecedented access to research data, and challenges and opportunities to analyse more data than ever before as characterized by the fourth paradigm (Hey, Tansley and Tolle, 2009). Additionally, researchers are under greater obligation to retain, share and publish research data, due to emerging scholarly practice and as a critical outcome of research funding.

As a result governments worldwide have been investing in research data infrastructures to drive productivity and innovation. However, practical issues of research data retention and reuse still remain. Mature research infrastructure supporting both data and collaboration is being established at all levels – nationally, regionally and within research institutions.

Current infrastructure approaches support many of the capabilities needed by research projects, but further support is needed for efficient documentation of the research context (metadata), retention of research data and records, and facilitation of data reuse. Mature tools to automate and semi-automate metadata recording are needed. Existing tools often introduce barriers such as complex information models or are not easily integrated into existing systems or day-to-day practice. Research institutions, facilities and infrastructure providers need to work together on strategies for record keeping and data retention.

Notwithstanding, the creation of larger scale national and international facilities for data access and sharing are seen to have the potential to create 'a high quality research infrastructure' (RIN, 2008); (see also Ruusalepp, 2008; UKRDS, 2009; e-Science Directors' Forum Strategy Working Group, 2009), which can bring great benefits to individuals and society as a whole.

As the UKRDS states: 'Research data have become a valuable resource that needs to be maintained for future access and re-use if we are to reap the full benefits of [UK] investment in research. . . . The rewards of managing this resource effectively include . . . the ability to share research data, minimising the need to repeat work in the laboratory, field or library, thus saving time and effort' (UKRDS, 2009).

Economic investment and cost-effectiveness of valuable resources can be enhanced by appropriately considered research data infrastructures. There is already a concerted drive toward this on an international scale and across institutional boundaries, in which data sharing and better exploitation of large amounts of data and the preservation of this data are understood to add value and to increase the returns from public investment.

11
Improving sustainability of publicly funded digital resources

David Robey

Introduction

In the course of its relatively brief life, the UK Arts and Humanities Research Council (AHRC) has funded a considerable number of digital resources in the arts and humanities (A&H), far more than any other UK public funder or charity. Established in place of the previous Arts and Humanities Research Board (AHRB) in 2005, alongside the other, existing UK research councils, each of which has its specific subject domain, the AHRC is easily the most important source of research project funding for the UK A&H (for more information about the AHRC, see www.ahrc.ac.uk). Most of this funding, from both the AHRC and its predecessor, AHRB, has gone to projects that have produced outputs in the form of conventional print publications; what is not always realized is how many of the funded projects have also produced digital research resources, either alongside print publications or as their sole or main output. This chapter starts with a review of almost all the digital resources produced by these projects for the ten years from 1999 to 2009, in order to give an idea of their nature, and then discusses the sustainability and related issues to which they give rise. Virtually all of them are data or content resources rather than digital tools; the AHRC has funded the production of digital tools, but only to a very limited extent.

Review of resources with digital outputs

The data that follows was collected in the course of a survey I led in 2009–10, in collaboration with the King's College London Centre for e-Research and the UK Network of Expert Centres in the digital A&H (see www.arts-humanities.net/noc), and funded by the AHRC. Our information was incomplete for the earlier part of 1999, and did not go beyond the early part of 2009, but otherwise was sufficient for us to identify with reasonable confidence all the projects whose outputs included digital research resources. This was possible because during the period covered all project grant applications with planned digital outputs were required to complete a technical appendix (which we shall return to later); starting from the projects thus identified, we were able through a process of desk research and direct enquiry to separate out all the projects where the digital output constituted a research resource, as opposed, for instance, to a project information web page. Through this process we arrived at a list of 474 projects that produced digital research resources; these are listed, with further information about each one, at www.arts-humanities.net/ahrc, where access may also be had to the detailed report, by Anna Winterbottom and me, from which some of the information that follows is drawn.

The projects in question cover all the main subject areas for which the AHRC is responsible. The largest number were in history (88, e.g. 'The Court of Chivalry and the Defence of Honour in England, 1633–1641'), followed by visual arts (66, e.g. 'Weaving communities of practice. Textiles, culture and identity in the Andes: a semiotic and ontological approach'), English language and literature (50, e.g. 'Integrating prosody, pragmatics and syntax in a corpus-based linguistic description of Irish standard'), archaeology (43, e.g. 'The development of the Celtic Coin Index') and modern languages (41, e.g. 'Out of the Wings (Spanish and Spanish American Theatres in Translation: a Virtual Environment for Research and Practice)'). Almost half (219) are concentrated in 14 institutions, each with ten or more digital resources to its credit. Oxford has easily the largest number (34), followed by Cambridge (26). The resources vary considerably in design and scope. The largest group is made up of digital archives, in the sense of collections of texts and/or images; the next largest groups are registers (bibliographies, relational databases of names, etc.), catalogues and digital editions. The majority are available online, but some are downloadable, and a very few available on CD-ROM. Most are highly specialist in their scope, as the examples given indicate – a point of some importance, to which we shall return.

The majority of projects were funded by two of the many schemes run by the AHRB/C: Standard Research Grants, which has run almost from the beginning of the AHRB up to the present day, and Resource Enhancement, which ran from 2000 to 2007. The first was concerned mainly with the production of research findings, the second, as its name implies, with the development of research resources. After the end of the Resource Enhancement scheme the AHRC ceased largely to fund the development of resources as a self-standing activity, but continued to fund it extensively through standard research grants in projects that also aimed to produce research findings. Both schemes belonged to the responsive-mode category: open to applications in any area of any of the subjects that the AHRB/C covered, with no policy preference for or against the use of digital technologies. Thus the number of projects producing digital resources, and their distribution by institution, subject and type, can serve as a rough index of the interest in digital technologies in the research communities in question.

Altogether the 473 projects that produced digital research resources represent almost one fifth (19.07%) of all the awards made in the schemes in question. Given the very varied nature of these schemes, we have taken the largest one, that for standard research grants, as the best illustration of this proportion, and to limit ourselves to the years 2000–2008, for which we have full information; here the proportion of projects producing digital resources rises to over one quarter (26.53%). In the case of the Resource Enhancement scheme the proportion of digital resource projects is very much higher, indeed the production of digital resources is the main or only purpose of the great majority of the scheme's projects: of a total of 205 awards made by the scheme, 171 funded the production of digital resources. All these digital resource projects also represent a significant public investment of money, to a total cost of approximately £121.5 million across all the years and schemes covered. Taking, once again, standard research grants for the years 2000–2008 as the more reliable basis for illustration, we can see that the average cost of digital resource projects is significantly higher than that of all projects in this group taken together: £309,110 as against £232,948. The average cost increased substantially from 2006 because of the move to full-cost funding: in 2008 the respective figures for standard research grants were £413,838 and £324,703.

Sustainability issues

Given the substantial cost both of individual projects and overall, the question of the sustainability of these digital resources is obviously a critical one. It is made all the more critical by the highly specialist nature of the resources. As with all specialist resources in the A&H, indeed as with the vast majority of A&H scholarly outputs, their value lies in the longer term. In the great majority of cases they will have little in the way of immediate numerical impact, but will be used, and continue to be used, by small numbers of scholars over a large number of years. Yet problems of sustainability necessarily increase with the passage of time.

We need to introduce a central distinction here between the two aspects of sustainability, which we might call academic and technical. Academic sustainability means keeping the content of the resource up to date. This may not be a problem with certain types of resource, for instance digital editions, which can retain their value for a very long period without any updating of their content. At the other extreme online bibliographies may lose their value quite quickly if their content is not kept up to date. But the problem of academic sustainability is necessarily less serious than that of technical sustainability, because resources will always retain at least some value whether or not their academic content is kept up to date, whereas if they are not updated technically they will sooner or later cease to be usable. Here too the seriousness of the problem varies from case to case: a downloadable text resource might not need technical updating for a very long time, whereas an online, interactive, multimedia database will cease to work within a few years if it is not updated as its technical environment changes. At least one resource distributed on CD-ROM no longer works because of the superannuated CD-ROM type. Technical sustainability also depends on the quality of the resource's technology: the right kind of technical preparation, and following the appropriate standards, can increase a resource's sustainability considerably.

We need to make a further distinction between technical sustainability and preservation. Sustainability means keeping a digital resource accessible and usable; simply preserving digital objects, for instance in a so-called 'dark' archive, usually means that they remain potentially usable, but varying degrees of effort may be required to make them actually usable. An extreme case is the superannuated CD-ROM cited earlier: it would no doubt be possible to retrieve the data from it, but to make it usable would probably be rather expensive. The large category of online multimedia archives present a less acute version of the same problem, but it is a serious one nonetheless. The data in question (the 'back end') can be preserved separately from the online resource, and if preserved in the right way could remain retrievable and usable for a long time without further updating. But the online interface that facilitates access to the data, and in which much of the intellectual content of the resource resides, is likely to stop working in a matter of years if not updated.

Sustainability and the AHDS

This distinction is an important one when we come to consider the, generally admirable, facilities for the support of data creation and preservation that were provided in the UK for a number years up to 2008 by the AHDS. Funded by the UK JISC jointly with the AHRB/C, the AHDS was in its time a groundbreaking institution that provided not only open-access archiving for publicly funded digital resources, but advice and training materials on data creation and curation; it also gave visibility to the resources through its catalogue, and helped the AHRB/C by vetting the technical appendix referred to above, which all grant applications were required to complete if they were planning digital outputs. It thus played an important part in helping to ensure both the technical quality of digital resources funded by the AHRB/C and their preservation and sustainability, though within significant limitations. The AHDS's role in relation to projects operated typically up to the point of the grant award, and then at the end of the project period when data outputs had to be offered to it for archiving; there tended to be little or no contact during the funding period, and thus little or no involvement by the AHDS in the actual work of technical development. Partly as a result of this, many digital resources were developed in a form that made it unfeasible for the AHDS to sustain them in their entirety: in the case of the large number of online resources, the AHDS was able to preserve the underlying data, but not, with a few model exceptions, to sustain the user interface or front-end, which was usually left to the institution that hosted the development work. Even while the AHDS existed, therefore, there were serious sustainability problems for AHRB/C-funded data outputs.

The AHDS closed because the AHRC withdrew its funding contribution, and as a result the service became unviable. The funding was withdrawn on cost-benefit grounds: the AHRC judged that the relatively little use made of the objects preserved by the AHDS did not justify the cost of its contribution, which for external reasons was set to increase substantially. At a time of financial stringency the decision to save costs was understandable, but the AHRC was rightly criticized for terminating funding, and therefore the service, without a satisfactory exit strategy. Nor was there any open discussion about the possibility of maintaining a scaled-down service, which might for instance have maintained the AHDS's advisory role and knowledge base, and dispensed with the archiving role, especially since, as we have seen, this did not ensure the full sustainability of many digital resources. For there should be little doubt that the advisory role and knowledge base were needed, indeed needed to be strengthened. When it took its funding decision, the AHRC argued that the digital humanities community had reached a stage of maturity that made the services of the AHDS unnecessary. That this was not the case was shown by two studies commissioned by the AHRC ICT in its Arts and Humanities Programme, which I directed;

they were made public in 2007, and are available at www.ahrcict.reading.ac.uk/activities/strategy_projects/reports.

In her project 'LAIRAH: Log Analysis of Internet Resources in the Arts and Humanities', Claire Warwick conducted a user questionnaire, interviews and workshops focusing on a selection of arts and humanities data projects, including projects funded by the AHRB (Warwick, 2006). While this constituted a fairly limited evidence base, a number of the findings merit serious attention.

- Their evidence suggests that 30–35% of arts and humanities digital resources remain unused.
- The title of the resource affects whether it is used or neglected, and should therefore be as unambiguous as possible.
- Users require high quality resources, both in terms of interface and content. If in any doubt about a resource's quality or authority they tend to abandon it.
- Barriers to access deter many users. These may include having to download data, copyright permissions forms or an interface that is not easy to use.
- Non-expert users found it difficult to understand the purpose of several resources. As well as an unambiguous project title, they required information about the contents, scope and how it was selected; the purpose of the resource; and advice about how it might be used.
- Few projects kept formal documentation or made it easily available.
- Few projects carried out formal user testing, and thus had little idea of the needs of their user community. Those projects that had carried out user tests were among the best used in the survey.
- Staff who are knowledgeable both about humanities research and ICT techniques were key to successful projects. However, a lack of appropriate training meant that they were difficult to find, and scarce funding made them difficult to retain from one project to another.
- Few projects realized the importance of ensuring their resource remained sustainable and that both content and interfaces must be maintained and updated. They did not appear to realize that archiving a resource with the AHDS did not guarantee its future accessibility.

Even while the AHDS existed, therefore, the evidence of this survey was that of data creation projects not sufficiently informed by the expertise required to ensure sustainability, usability and technical quality. This failure should not be laid at the door of the AHDS, whose advisory role, as we have seen, generally ended at the point of award. Rather it shows that many projects lacked the necessary infrastructure of expertise within their host institutions. This is borne out by a second study commissioned by the ICT Programme at the same time, Lesly Huxley's 'Gathering Evidence: Current ICT Use and Future Needs for Arts and Humanities Research' (Huxley, Mullings, Hodos and Jones, 2006). A number of its finding are relevant to the present topic:

- Fifty-seven per cent of respondents (out of 449) reported that ICT had brought significant change to their research.
- Most reported changes related to facilitating research: speed of finding resources, improved access to existing resources and access to a wider range of resources. Less change was reported for research productivity, quality of research or collaboration, or new ways of thinking.
- There was low awareness of national support and advice services; but when these services were known and used they were much appreciated.
- Overall, little research output appeared to be deposited in local or national archives, electronic or otherwise.
- Most-used sources of informal information or advice were dominated by web search engines like Google, colleagues and contacts both within and without each respondent's department.
- Exactly half of the respondents cited the quality and reliability of resources as the source of most difficulty in their use of ICT in research.
- Sustainability of research resources was identified as a problem, particularly when material was deposited or published locally rather than nationally.
- Many respondents commented on support for ICT in teaching at institutional level, in some cases to the perceived detriment to research support. ICT training and technical assistance at both institutional and department or faculty levels appeared good. Subject-specific advice and support was perceived to be low.
- Just over half of the respondents (52%) felt there were gaps in current ICT provision in their discipline. This was mainly in the availability of specialized tools or resources for their specific research area, but also in 'basic' ICT resources such as hardware, software and network provision.
- Scholars seemed very keen to become more ICT active, learn more ICT skills and collaborate more in their research.

Survey of sustainability of digital resources

These findings helped to inform a detailed survey, which the ICT programme then conducted on the sustainability of the digital resources funded from November 2000 until May 2006 through the AHRB/C's Resource Enhancement Scheme, its leading initiative in the area of digital resource creation. The survey was completed in December 2008, after the closure of the AHDS, and part of its purpose was to ascertain the impact of the closure on the projects; it is available at www.ahrcict.reading.ac.uk/activities/review/sustainability.htm. Questionnaires were sent to all 173 grant holders that had completed the technical appendix to elicit views on the sustainability of their data outputs and related matters; 115 replies were received. Of these resources the greatest number were websites with online searchable databases (83), followed by online catalogues (23). All but 23 of the total were hosted on university websites, including specialist centres or libraries and the former AHDS archive, which has continued to be maintained, at least for the time being, by the host universities.

Views on technical sustainability varied considerably according to the type of host. Projects had the most confidence in their university library to maintain the digital resource, followed closely by external 2specialist centres. Specialist centres internal to the university and other university hosts enjoyed less confidence. Those managing all projects hosted at the AHDS expressed grave concerns for their project's sustainability in the light of the AHDS closure. Concerns about sustainability also varied according to type of resource. The great majority of those managing online catalogue projects had no concerns; about half of the 80 online searchable projects did. Our impression was that many project managers in the last category did not plan in detail from the beginning how to sustain their outputs. Concerns expressed included: the short-term nature of hosting contracts with external providers; absence of funding for technical support; payment of future licence fees for images and other material; and staffing issues, especially loss of technical staff. Means used for keeping resources technically up to date included voluntary work by project leads and the use of funds (and sometimes staff) allocated to later projects, an approach to sustainability resembling a 'Ponzi scheme'. A few universities provide dedicated support for technical sustainability.

Academic updating of the content of resources was required by the vast majority of projects (92/115), of which about half envisaged difficulty in carrying this out, mostly because of the non-availability of funding. Many projects carried it out on a voluntary basis, some with the help of funding from new projects; in a few cases users helped.

On related matters, over half the respondents to the questionnaire (65/115) said they were collecting usage statistics for their web resource, or had plans to do so once the site went live. When considering publicity and promotion respondents ranged from those who had received national media interest, to those who did not advertise their resource at all, due to lack of funds. Most project leaders publicized their work to their subject communities, at conferences and so forth. Comments on the technical support provided by the home institution for digital projects were categorized from excellent to none (i.e. no support). Of the 109 who answered this question 34 were categorized as excellent, 23 good, 28 acceptable, 19 minimal, 5 none. About two thirds of the respondents in the first three categories of answer hosted their resource at their own institutions; rather fewer in the last two categories did so.

Our conclusion, based largely on the responses relating to technical sustainability, was that there was a significant threat to the sustainability of a substantial though as yet unquantifiable proportion of the resource enhancement outputs, and that the AHRC would be wise to address this. There were also lessons to be learnt about the funding of future data creation projects: steps could and should be taken to increase their prospects of sustainability, by firming up the technical appendix and through greater involvement of expert centres as project partners.

What these studies also show, taken together, is that the issue of sustainability is closely linked to two others, the first of which is visibility. If digital resources are to be sustained, they need to be used as much as possible by the relevant communities, and therefore these communities need to be aware of them. As we have seen, this is by no means always the case, and with the closure of the AHDS, and the prospective demise, sooner or later, of its integrated catalogue, the problem is likely to get worse. As we have also seen, there are steps that projects can take to make themselves more visible, but there must be a continuing need for centralized finding services of the kind provided by the AHDS catalogue. Some help is provided by the www.arts-humanities.net site, with the list of AHRC-funded digital resources that we referred to at the start. More help could be provided by including digital resources in university online library catalogues, and thus also in the combined catalogue at http://copac.ac.uk. The Intute website provides an excellent finding system for digital research resources (www.intute.ac.uk/humanities), but regrettably funding for that has also been terminated.

The second sustainability-related issue is that of optimization. Given the stiff competition and the rigorous academic vetting process for the grant awards, it can be more or less taken for granted that the quality of their data outputs' academic content is high; unfortunately the same cannot always be taken for granted with regard to technical quality, as Claire Warwick's study has shown. Resources are by no means always optimized for technical sustainability, usability and reusability. Often user tests have not been conducted, technical and user documentation is inadequate, and insufficient thought seems to have been given to realizing the full methodological potential of the data: the uses to which it could be put beyond those that interest its creators. All of this is for very understandable reasons: many digital resources have been created in relative technological isolation, with little in the way of underpinning expertise in the institutions in which they have been created. The result is that while virtually all the resources funded by the AHRC are good and valuable in their fields, many of them could have been better.

Conclusion: sustainability and technical quality

To conclude this discussion, let me consider some measures that could be taken in the present context to try to ensure better sustainability and technical quality (I have no further suggestions about visibility) in publicly funded digital resources, focusing on measures that could be implemented both at the grant application stage and after the data creation process. To begin with the latter, I would like to cite a further study commissioned by the AHRC ICT Programme alongside the two that have been adduced above: David Bates, 'Peer Review and Evaluation of Digital Resources for the Arts and Humanities', available with the other two at www.ahrcict.reading.ac.uk/activities/strategy_projects/reports (Bates et al., 2006).

Academic research literature, in print or online, generally undergoes a rigorous quality assurance process, through peer review and editorial control; why should something similar not be applied to the publication of digital resources, indeed why do we not think in terms of publishing digital resources, rather than simply making them available? Working with the Institute of Historical Research and the Royal Historical Society, the project explored ways of answering this question based on an online survey (777 responses), focus groups, interviews and benchmarking reviews by specialists of a range of web-based digital resources for history, archaeology and classics, with the following results:

- Seventy-one per cent of respondents considered peer evaluation and recommendation to be either important or extremely important in their selection of digital resources for use in their personal research.
- A kite marking system should not be adopted for research projects with digital outputs for the arts and humanities. Any system of evaluation or review should not adopt a simple 'pass/fail' approach when considering a digital resource in its entirety.
- Instead, a multi-staged assessment process should be adopted after the completion of a resource but before its 'publication'. There is a role for learned societies and subject organizations in such a process. Exchanges between reviewers and resource creators should be made publicly available.
- A strong need for adequate project documentation was identified by many of those consulted by the project, both to assist the user and to inform the assessment process.
- Common and widely publicized citation standards for digital resources should be established.
- The proposed system of peer review and evaluation was one means of ensuring that digital resources are properly assessed and receive due credit in research evaluation exercises.

Whether or not one adopts the specific process recommended by this project, the institution of one kind or another of formal evaluation would be a major aid to ensuring the quality, and therefore the sustainability, of digital resources. Public funders would do well to insist on this as a standard condition of the relevant grants.

At the application stage, the model of the AHRC technical appendix needs further developing in line with changing circumstances and changing technologies. A review of the technical appendix was recently carried out by the UK Network of Expert Centres, led by me and working closely with the Humanities Research Institute of the University of Sheffield, whose report is available at www.shef.ac.uk/hri/projects/projectpages/technicalappendix.html.

The overall recommendation of this review was that the technical appendix should be replaced by a technical plan that covers most of the issues its predecessor covered, but with some significant changes of detail and emphasis. The technical plan should include information about:

- technical methodology: standards and formats; hardware and software; and data acquisition, processing, analysis and use
- preservation and sustainability
- technical support and relevant experience.

The last two points merit some further explanation. The distinction between preservation and sustainability has been made above, and is an important one that grant holders are often not fully aware of. Applicants should be required to explicitly confront both issues: as a matter of good practice they should always preserve digital outputs essential to their project's research outcomes after the end of the project period; and where appropriate they should make them sustainable in the sense of easily accessible to the research community and beyond. The great majority of data outputs are probably worth preserving, if only to allow research results based on them to be checked; not all outputs are worth sustaining, and the resource devoted to sustaining them should be proportionate to the data's value to the research community and beyond. Grant applicants should be required to specify a minimum period for which digital outputs would be preserved and sustained, again in proportion to the value of the outputs to the research community. They should also state how the future costs of preservation and sustainability would be provided for. In the absence of a national service like the AHDS, it is not unreasonable to expect grant holders or their institution to meet these costs; with proper preparation, they are unlikely to be excessive.

The point about technical support and relevant experience also raises important issues. I have already suggested that such deficiencies as can be found in the resources we surveyed seem often to have resulted from the limitations of the technical expertise employed. It is important that grant applications should not only provide evidence of the expertise of proposed project staff, but also show how this expertise would be underpinned by that available in the institution to which they belong. There must be many projects whose sustainability depends on a single individual who could at any moment depart from the institution that hosts them. The problem is that while there is a great deal of relevant digital expertise in UK universities, it is concentrated in a relatively few institutions – as we have seen in the reports of inadequate institutional support from some of the respondents to our surveys. The solution to this problem is not that data resource creation should be confined to a small number of centres of technical excellence, but that prospective grant holders whose institutions lack the necessary technical support should make collaborative arrangements with those that have it.

This last proposal may seem to run counter to the inclusiveness and egalitarianism that has up to now characterized the AHRC's approach to applicants. But it is not an argument for exclusiveness in relation to the whole A&H academic community, for concentrating on academic centres of excellence. The important point is that, given the very considerable cost of funding digital resources, and the great difficulty of delivering them properly, they should be produced through a serious and equal collaboration between academics on the one hand, wherever they may be located, and centres of technology expertise on the other – not, as often happens, by hiring technical help locally simply for reasons of convenience.

References and further reading

ACLS (2006) *Our Cultural Commonwealth: the report of the American Council of Learned Societies Commission on cyberinfrastructure for the humanities and social sciences,* www.acls.org/cyberinfrastructure/ourculturalcommonwealth.pdf.

AHDS (2007) *AHDS: the AHDS Taxonomy of Computational Methods,* http://ahds.ac.uk/about/projects/pmdb_taxonomy_v1_3_1.rtf.

AHRC (2005) *Resource Enhancement Scheme,* www.ahrc.ac.uk/FundedResearch/Pages/ResourceEnhancementSchemeReview.aspx.

AHRC (2006) *AHRC Changes to AHRC Research Funding in Responsive-mode,* www.ahrc.ac.uk/ahrb/FundedResearch/Pages/ResourceEnhancementSchemeReview.aspx.

AHRC (2007) *AHRC Annual Report 2006–2007,* www.ahrc.ac.uk/About/Policy/Documents/AR2006-07.pdf.

AHRC (2009) *Leading the World: the economic impact of UK arts and humanities research,* www.ahrc.ac.uk/news/latest/pages/leadingtheworld.aspx.

AHRC (2010) *AHRC Delivery Plan, 2010,* www.ahrc.ac.uk/About/Policy/Pages/DeliveryPlan.aspx.

Alston, R. (1993) The Battle of the Books, *Humanist Discussion Group,* **7** (0176), www.digitalhumanities.org/humanist/Archives/Virginia/v07/0175.html.

Anderson, K. (2008) *The Archives Industry Perspectives on Significance as a Collections Management Tool,* www.collectionscouncil.com.au/articles.aspx?articleType=ArticleView&articleId=79.

Anderson, P. (2007) *What is Web 2.0? Ideas, technologies and implications for education,* JISC Technology and Standards Watch (TSW0701), www.jisc.ac.uk/media/documents/techwatch/tsw0701b.pdf.

Anderson, S. (2007) *The Arts and Humanities e-Science Scoping Survey,* AHeSSC, www.ahessc.ac.uk/scoping-survey.

Archer, D. (ed.) (2009) *What's in a Word-list?: investigating word frequency and keyword extraction,* Ashgate.

Archives New Zealand (2009) *New Zealand Shipping Lists Digitised,* http://archives.govt.nz/about/news/2009/12/new-zealand-shipping-lists-digitised.

Archives New Zealand (2010a) *Ship Comes in for Genealogist,* www.archives.govt.nz/about/news/2010/11/ship-comes-genealogist.

Archives New Zealand (2010b) *Archives New Zealand's Framework to Support Digitisation in the Public Sector,* http://archives.govt.nz/advice/training-and-events/previous-forum-papers-html/archives-new-zealand-s-framework-support-digit.

Arms, W. Y. and Larsen, R. L. (2007) *The Future of Scholarly Communication: building the infrastructure for cyberscholarship*. Report of a workshop held in Phoenix, Arizona, 17–19 April 2007, www.sis.pitt.edu/~repwkshop/SIS-NSFReport2.pdf.

Atkins, D. E., Brown, J. S. and Hammond, A. L. (2007) *A Review of the Open Educational Resources (OER) Movement: achievements, challenges, and new opportunities: a report to the William and Flora Hewlett Foundation*, www.hewlett.org/uploads/files/ReviewoftheOERMovement.pdf.

Atkinson, J. and Kensler E. (2004) With a Little Help from my Friends: developments in Welsh academic library collaboration, *SCONUL Focus,* **33**, 51–4.

Atkinson, J. and Riley P. (2009) Building on Collaboration: the WHELF e-book deal, *SCONUL Focus,* **45**, 11316.

Atkinson, M., Crowcroft, J., Goble, C., Gurd, J., Rodden, T., Shadbolt, N., Saloman, M., Sommerville, I. and Storey, T. (2004) *Computer Challenges to Emerge from e-Science*, www.nesc.ac.uk/talks/opening/agenda_talk.pdf.

Aucott, P. et al. (2011) *Impact Report on 'A Vision of Britain through Time' 2004 –2010*, www.jisc.ac.uk/whatwedo/programmes/digitisation/impactembedding/vobimpact.aspx.

Baggs, C. (1997) The National Library of Wales Book Box Scheme and the South Wales Coalfield, *National Library of Wales Journal,* **30** (2), 207–9.

Barrett, A. (2005) The Information Seeking Habits of Graduate Student Researchers in the Humanities, *Journal of Academic Librarianship,* **31** (4), 324–31.

Bate, J. (2010) *The Public Value of the Humanities*, Bloomsbury.

Bates, D., Nelson, J. L., Roueche, C. and Waites, J. (2006), *Peer Review and Evaluation of Digital Resources for the Arts and Humanities: final report*, www.ahrcicf.reading.ac.uk/activities/strategy-projects/reports.

Bates, M. J. (1996) The Getty End-user Online Searching Project in the Humanities: report no. 6: overview and conclusions, *College and Research Libraries,* **57** (6), 514–23.

Bates, M. J. (2002) The Cascade of Interactions in the Digital Library Interface, *Information Processing & Management,* **38** (3), 381–400.

Batt, C. (2009) *Digitisation, Curation and Two-way Engagement, final report*, www.jisc.ac.uk/media/documents/programmes/digitisation/dcatwefinalreport_final.pdf.

BBSRC (2011) *BBSRC Data Sharing Policy*, www.bbsrc.ac.uk.

Bearman, D. (2006) Moments of Risk: identifying threats to electronic records, *Archivaria,* **62** (Fall), 15–46.

Bentham Project (n.d.) *Who was Jeremy Bentham?*, www.ucl.ac.uk/Bentham-Project/who.

Besser, H. (1997) The Transformation of the Museum and the Way it's Perceived. In Jones-Garmil, K. (ed.), *The Wired Museum: emerging technology and changing paradigms*, American Association of Museums, 153–70.

Bevan, P. and Robson, G. (2008) *Implementing an Integrated DAMS: FEDORA/VITAL at the National Library of Wales*, http://dev.llgc.org.uk/wiki/index.php?title=Presentations&printable=yes.

Big Lottery Fund (2006) Digitisation of Learning Materials and Community Grids for Learning: final evaluation findings, *Big Lottery Fund Research,* **26**.

Bignell, J. and Fickers, A. (eds) (2008) *A European Television History*, Wiley-Blackwell.

Blanke, T. and Dunn, S. (2006) The Arts and Humanities e-Science Initiative in the UK, *IEEE Proceedings*, http://ieeexplore.ieee.org.

Blok, R. (2010) *Trends in Computing*, www.zoology.ubc.ca/~rikblok/ComputingTrends.

Bonney et al. (2009) Citizen Science: a developing tool for expanding science knowledge and scientific literacy, *BioScience*, **59** (11), 977–84.

Booth, B. (1999) Understanding the Information Needs of Visitors to Museums, *Museum Management and Curatorship*, **17** (2), 139–57.

Borda, A. (2009) A Framework for Virtual Collaboration. In Whitworth, B. and De Moor, A. (eds), *Handbook of Research on Socio-Technical Design and Social Networking Systems*, IGI Global.

Borda, A. (2011) *Collaborative e-Research Framework to Enable Efficient Resource Sharing and Use*, VeRSI, https://www.versi.edu.au.

Borgman, C. (2007) *Scholarship in the Digital Age: information, infrastructure and the internet*, MIT Press.

Booth, B. (1999) Understanding the Information Needs of Visitors to Museums, *Museum Management and Curatorship*, **17** (2), 139–57.

Bradwell, P. (2009) *The Edgeless University: why higher education must embrace technology*, Demos, www.demos.co.uk/publications/the-edgeless-university.

British Academy (2005) *E-resources for Research in the Humanities and Social Sciences: a British Academy policy review*, www.britac.ac.uk/policy/erousources/e-resources.cfm.

British Library (1979–2010) *Annual Reports*, The British Library.

British Library (2010) *2020 Vision Project: Trends in the Library Environment*, www.bl.uk/aboutus/stratpolprog/2020vision/trendsinlibrarynviron.pdf.

Brown, S. and Greengrass, M. (2010) Research Portals in the Arts and Humanities, *Literary and Linguistic Computing*, **25** (1), 1–21.

Browne, J. (2010) *Independent Review of Higher Education Funding and Student Finance*, http://hereview.independent.gov.uk/hereview.

Buchanan et al. (2005) Information Seeking by Humanities Scholars: proceedings of European Digital Library Conference, *Lecture Notes in Computer Science*, **3652**, 218–29.

Buckland, M. K. (2007) The Digital Difference in Reference Collections, *Journal of Library Administration*, **46** (2).

Burns, M. (2008) *Significance and Libraries*, www.collectionscouncil.com.au/articles.aspx?articleType=ArticleView&articleId=80.

Cameron, F. (2003) Digital Futures I: museum collections, digital technologies, and the cultural construction of knowledge, *Curator*, **46**, 325–40.

Canadian Historical Association (2010) *The Canadian Historical Association Comments on New Directions for Library and Archives Canada*, www.h-net.org/announce/show.cgi?ID=174610.

Carpenter, L., Prescott, A. and Shaw, S. (eds) (1998) *Towards the Digital Library: the British Library's Initiatives for Access Programme*, British Library.

Carson, S. (2005) *MITOpenCourseware 2004 Program Evaluation Findings Report*, MIT.

Carusi, A. and Torsten, R. (2010) *Virtual Research Environment Collaborative Landscape Study*, Joint Information Systems Committee.

Chrisbatt Consulting (2009) *Digitisation, Curation and Two-way Engagement, final report*, Joint

Information Systems Committee, www.jisc.ac.uk/media/documents/programmes/digitisation/dcatwefinalreport_final.pdf.

Comité des Sages (2011) *The New Renaissance: report of the Comité des Sages; reflection group on bringing Europe's cultural heritage online*, http://ec.europa.eu/information_society/activities/digital_libraries/doc/reflection_group/final-report-cdS3.pdf.

Crawford, T. and Gibson, L. (eds) (2009) *Modern Methods for Musicology*, Ashgate.

Cunliffe, D., Kritou, E. and Tudhope, D. (2001) Usability Evaluation for Museum Web Sites, *Museum Management and Curatorship*, **19**, 229–52.

Dalton, M. S. and Charnigo, L. (2004) Historians and their Information Sources, *College & Research Libraries*, **65** (5), 400–25.

Darnton, R. (2009a) Google and the Future of Books, *New York Review of Books*, 12 February.

Darnton, R. (2009b) Google and the New Digital Future, *New York Review of Books*, 17 December.

Darnton, R. (2010a) Can We Create a National Digital Library?, *New York Review of Books*, 28 October.

Darnton, R. (2010b) The Library: three jeremiads, *New York Review of Books*, 23 December.

Davies, S. (1994) Attendance Records, *Leisure Management*, **15** (2), 41–4.

Davis, D. (1990) *The Museum Transformed: design and culture in the post-Pompidou age*, Abbeville.

Deegan, M. and Sutherland, K. (eds) (2009) *Text Editing, Print and the Digital World*, Ashgate.

Deegan, M. and Tanner, S. (2001) *Digital Futures: strategies for the information age*, Facet Publishing.

Dempsey, L. (1999) Library Places and Digital Information Spaces: reflections on emerging network services, *Alexandria*, **11** (1), 51–8.

Dempster, S. (2010) *A Guide to the Strategic Content Alliance*, JISC Strategic Content Alliance, www.jisc.ac.uk/whatwedo/themes/content/contentalliance/vision.aspx.

Denbo, S., Haskins, H. and Robey, D. (2008) *Sustainability of Digital Outputs from AHRC Resource Enhancement Projects*, Arts and Humanities Research Council (AHRC).

Department for Culture, Media and Sport and Department for Business Innovation and Skills (2009) *Digital Britain*, Cm 7650, www.official-documents.gov.uk/document/cm76/7650/7650.pdf.

Department of Communities and Local Government (2008) *Delivering Digital Inclusion Annex: public sector use of information and communications technologies to support social equality*, www.communities.gov.uk/publications/communities/digitalinclusionannex.

Department of Innovation, Industry, Science and Research (2011) *2011 Strategic Roadmap for Australian Research Infrastructure*, discussion paper, DIISR, Research Infrastructure and Science Policy Branch.

Designing Libraries (2011) www.designinglibraries.org.uk.

Digital Library Initiative (2005) *Letter from Six Heads of State to the President of the European Commission, Jose Manuel Barosso*, http://ec.europa.eu/information_society/activities/digital_libraries/doc/letter_1/index_en.htm.

Dommeyer, C. J. et al. (2004) Gathering Faculty Teaching Evaluations by In-class and Online Surveys: their effects on response rates and evaluations, *Assessment & Evaluation in Higher Education*, **29** (5), 611–23.

Duff, W. and Johnson, C. (2003) Where is the List with all the Names? *American Archivist*, **66**, 79–95.

Dunn, S. (2007) Humanities, e-Science and Visualization, paper presented at *Methods Network Workshop on Visualization*, 19 June, www.viznet.ac.uk/cross_domain/abstract3D.html.

Ellis, D. (1989) A Behavioural Model for Information Retrieval System Design, *Journal of Information Science*, **15** (4/5), 237–47.

Ellis, D. and Haugan, M. (1997) Modelling the Information Seeking Patterns of Engineers and Research Scientists in an Industrial Environment, *Journal of Documentation*, **53** (4), 384–403.

Ellis, D. and Oldman, H. (2005) The English Literature Researcher in the Age of the Internet, *Journal of Information Science*, **31** (1), 29–36.

e-Science Directors' Forum Strategy Working Group (2009) Century of Information Research (CIR): a strategy for research and innovation in the century of information, *Prometheus*, **27**, 27–45, http://wikis.nesc.ac.uk/escienvoy/Century_of_Information_Research_Strategy.

ESFRI (2009) *European Roadmap for Research Infrastructures, Implementation Report*, http://ec.europa.eu/research/infrastructures/pdf/esfri/home/implementation_report_2009_en.pdf

Etherton, J. (2006) The Role of Archives in the Perception of Self, *Journal of the Society of Archivists*, **27** (2), 227–46.

Falk, J. H. (1998) Visitors: who does, who doesn't and why, *Museum News*, **77** (2), 38–43.

Falk, J. H. (2006) The Impact of Visit Motivation on Learning: using identity as a construct to understand the visitor experience, *Curator*, **49** (2), 151–66.

Falk, J. H. and Dierking, L. (1992) *The Museum Experience*, Whalesback Books.

Falk, J. H. and Dierking, L.D. (2000) *Learning from Museums: visitor experiences and the making of meaning*, AltaMira Press.

FamilySearch (n.d.) *About FamilySearch*, www.familysearch.org/eng/default.asp?page=/eng/Policy/about_us.asp.

Frey, B. S. and Pommerehne, W. W. (1989) *Muses and Markets: explorations in the economics of the arts*, Blackwell.

Fuhr, N. et al. (2007) Evaluation of Digital Libraries, *International Journal on Digital Libraries*, **8** (1), 21–38.

Green, A. (2007a) *The Theatre of Memory*, www.llgc.org.uk/fileadmin/documents/pdf/SCONUL2007.pdf.

Green, A. (2007b) The Future of National Libraries and Archives. In Osmond, J. (ed.), *Myths, Memories and Futures: the National Library and National Museum in the story of Wales*, www.llgc.org.uk/fileadmin/documents/pdf/future_national_libraries_archives.pdf.

Green, A. (2009) Big Digitisation: where next?, www.llgc.org.uk/fileadmin/documents/pdf/darlith_big_digitisation_where_next.pdf.

Green, R. (2000) Locating Sources in Humanities Scholarship: the efficacy of following bibliographic references, *Library Quarterly*, **70** (2), 201–29.

Greengrass, M. and Hughes, L. (2008) *Virtual Representations of the Past*, Ashgate.

Guthrie, K., Griffiths, R. and Maron, N. (2008) *Sustainability and Revenue Models for Online Academic Resources*, http://sca.jiscinvolve.org/files/2008/06/sca_ithaka_sustainability_report-final.pdf.

Hainsworth, P. and Robey, D. (2002) *The Oxford Companion to Italian Literature*, Oxford University Press.

Hainsworth, P. and Robey, D. (forthcoming) *Very Short Introduction to Italian Literature*, Oxford University Press.

Haley Goldman, K. and Schaller, D. (2004) Exploring Motivational Factors and Visitor Satisfaction in On-line Museum Visits. In Bearman, D. and Trant J. (eds), *Museums and the Web 2004*, Archives and Museum Informatics, 223–35, www.archimuse.com/mw2004/papers/haleyGoldman/haleyGoldman.html.

Hallam, E. and Prescott, A. (1999) *The British Inheritance*, British Library and Public Record Office.

Hamma, K. (2004) Becoming Digital, *Bulletin of the American Society for Information Science and Technology*, **30** (5), 11–13.

Hand, E. (2010) Citizen Science: people power, *Nature*, **466**, 685–7, www.nature.com/news/2010/100804/full/466685a.html.

Hannay, T. (2007) Web 2.0 in Science. In Dirks, L. and Hey, T. (eds), *CTWatch Quarterly: the coming revolution in scholarly communications and cyberinfrastructure*, www.ctwatch.org/quarterly/articles/2007/08.

Hargreaves, I. (2011) *Hargreaves Review of IP and Growth*, www.openrightsgroup.org/ourwork/reports/hargreaves-review-of-ip-and-growth.

Harley, D. (2007) Use and Users of Digital Resources: a survey exploring scholar's attitudes about educational technology environments in the humanities, *EDUCAUSE Quarterly*, **4**.

Harley, D. et al. (2006) *Use and Users of Digital Resources: a focus on undergraduate education in the humanities and social sciences*, Centre for Studies in Higher Education, University of California.

HATII and NINCH (2002) *The NINCH Guide to Good Practice in the Digital Representation and Management of Cultural Heritage Materials*, National Initiative for a Networked Cultural Heritage.

Hedges, M., Hasan, A. and Blanke, T. (2007) Management and Preservation of Research Data with iRODS, *Proceedings of the ACM First Workshop on CyberInfrastructure: Information Management in eScience*, ACM, 17–22.

Herman, E. (2001) End-users in Academia: meeting the information needs of university researchers in an electronic age. Part 2: Innovative information-accessing opportunities and the researcher: user acceptance of IT-based information resources in academia, *Aslib Proceedings*, **53** (10), 431–57.

Hertzum, M. (1998) A Review of Museum Websites: in search of user-centered design, *Archives and Museum Informatics*, **12**, 127–38.

Hey, T. (2006) *Foreword*. In Hine, C. M. (ed.), *New Infrastructures for Knowledge Production: understanding e-science*, Information Science Publishing.

Hey, T. and Hey, J. (2006) e-Science and its Implications for the Library Community, *Library Hi Tech*, **24** (4), 515–28.

Hey, T. and Trefethen, A. (2004) The Data Deluge: an e-science perspective. In Berman, F., Fox, G. and Hey, T. (eds), *Grid-Computing: making the global infrastructure a reality*, Wiley, 809–24.

Hey, T. and Trefethen, A. E. (2005) Cyberinfrastructure for e-Science, *Science*, 817–21.

Hey, T., Tansley, S. and Tolle, K. (eds) (2009) *The Fourth Paradigm: data-intensive scientific discovery*, http://research.microsoft.com/en-us/collaboration/fourthparadigm.

Hicks, S. (2008) Collaborative Digital Access Projects: free online access to Victorian will, probates and inquest files – making researchers happy. Paper presented at *Archives – Collaborating Towards a Networked Future*, ARANZ conference, Dunedin.

Hill, F. (1953) Thomas Watts 1811–69, *British Museum Quarterly*, **18** (2), 32–9.

Hitchcock, T. (2010) Interview for Inspiring Scholarship, Inspiring Research, University of Hertfordshire.

Hockey, S. and Ross, S. (2008) Conclusion. In Hughes, L. (ed.), *The AHRC ICT Methods Network: an evaluation*, OHC.

Hogan, E. (2009) E-mail to Harold Short at the Centre for Computing in the Humanities, King's College London.

Howard, J. (2011) University of California Tries Just Saying No to Rising Journal Costs, *Chronicle of Higher Education*, 27 October.

Hughes, L. (2004) *Digitizing Collections: strategic issues for the information manager*, Facet Publishing.

Hughes, L. (2008) *The AHRC ICT Methods Network: an evaluation*, OHC.

Huxley, L., Mullings, C., Hodos, T. and Jones, D. (2006) *Gathering Evidence: current ICT use and future needs for arts and humanities researchers*, AHRC.

IJDDiP project plan, JISC, www.jisc.ac.uk/media/documents/programmes/digitisation/intutefinal.pdf.

IMLS (2003) *Assessment of End-User Needs in IMLS-Funded Digitization Projects*, www.imls.gov/pdf/userneedsassessment.pdf.

Irwin, A. (2010) *Case Studies and Testimonial at the British Library Archival Sounds Recordings*, http://sounds.bl.uk/CaseStudies.aspx.

Jackson, S. J., Edwards, P. N., Bowker, G. C. and Knobel, C. P. (2007) Understanding Infrastructure: history, heuristics, and cyberinfrastructure policy, *First Monday*, **12** (6), http://firstmonday.org/htbin/cgiwrap/bin/ojs/index.php/fm/article/view/1904/1786.

Jansen, B., Spink, A. and Taksa, I. (2009) *Handbook of Research on Web Log Analysis*, Information Science Reference.

JewishGen (n.d.) *The Issue of the Mormon Baptisms of Jewish Holocaust Victims and Other Jewish Dead*, www.jewishgen.org/InfoFiles/ldsagree.html.

JISC (2005) *Digitisation in the UK: the case for a UK framework*, JISC.

JISC (2008) *JISC Digitisation Strategy, February 2008*, www.jisc.ac.uk/media/documents/programmes/digitisation/jisc_digitisation_strategy_2008.doc.

JISC (2009) *Formative Evaluation of the JISC Digitisation Programme Phase 2, Final Report*, www.jisc.ac.uk/media/documents/programmes/digitisation/digevalfinalreportf2_final_002.pdf.

JISC (2010a) *Transformation Through Technology: illustrating JISC's impact across two decades*, www.jisc.ac.uk/publications/generalpublications/2010/jiscimpact2010.aspx.

JISC (2010b) DiSCmap: digitisation in special collections: mapping, assessment, prioritisation; report and appendices, www.jisc.ac.uk/whatwedo/programmes/digitisation/reports/discmap.aspx.

JISC (2011) *RLUK One to Many; Many to One: the Resource Discovery Taskforce vision*, http://discovery.ac.uk/files/pdf/jisc-rluk-vision-final-june2010.pdf.

JISC Strategic Content Alliance (2010) *Developing Digipedia: a guide to the digital content lifecycle*, http://sca.jiscinvolve.org/wp/files/2010/06/Digipedia_Booklet_A5_v1-04.pdf.

Jörgensen, C. (2004) Unlocking the Museum: a manifesto, *Journal of the American Society for Information Science and Technology*, **55**, 462–4.

Kaufman, P. (2009) *On Building a New Market for Culture*, www.jisc.ac.uk/contentalliance.

Kaufman, P. B. (2004) Digitization, Economics, and Humanities – Peter Kaufman of Innodata Isogen discusses how digitization has changed libraries forever, *Information Outlook: the Monthly Magazine of the Special Libraries Association*, **8** (7), 17.

Khoo, M., Buchanan, G. and Cunningham, S. J. (2009) Lightweight User-friendly Evaluation Knowledge for Digital Libraries, *D-Lib Magazine*, **15**, July/August, www.dlib.org/dlib/july09/khoo/07khoo.html.

Knell, S. (2003) The Shape of Things to Come: museums in the technological landscape, *Museum and Society*, **1** (3), 132–46.

Knowles, J. (2010) Collaboration Nation: the building of the Welsh Repository Network, *Program: electronic library and information systems*, **44** (2), 98–108.

Kravchyna, V. and Hastings, S. (2002) Informational Value of Museum Web Sites, *First Monday*, **7** (2), www.firstmonday.org/issues/issue7_2/kravchyna.

Lee, S. (2010) *Interview for Inspiring Scholarship*, Inspiring Research, University of Oxford.

Lehmann, S. and Renfro, P. (1991) Humanists and Electronic Information Services: acceptance and resistance, *College and Research Libraries*, **52**, 403–13.

Lewis, M. (2010) The University of Sheffield Library Information Commons: a case study, *Journal of Library Administration*, **50** (2), 161–78.

Locock, M. (2009) *Cylchgronau Cymru, Welsh Journals Online*, JISC Capital Programme Final Report, www.jisc.ac.uk/media/documents/programmes/digitisation/welshjournalsfinal.pdf.

Lonnqvist, H. (1990) Scholars Seek Information: information-seeking behaviour and information needs of humanities scholars, *International Journal of Information & Library Research*, **2** (1), 195–203.

Losh, E. (2004) Reading Room(s): building a national archive in digital spaces and physical places, *Literary and Linguistic Computing*, **19** (3), 373–84.

Lucas, W. T., Topi, H. (2002) Form and Function: the impact of query term and operator usage on web search results, *JASIST*, **53** (2), 95–108.

Lynch, C. A. (1998) The Role of Digitization in Building Electronic Collections: economic and programmatic Choices, *Collection Management*, **22**, 133–41.

Lyon, L. (2007) Dealing with Data: roles, rights, responsibilities and relationships, consultancy report, JISC, www.ukoln.ac.uk/ukoln/staff/e.j.lyon/reports/dealing_with_data_report-final.pdf.

Lyon, L. (2009) Open Science at Web-Scale: optimising participation and predictive potential. consultative report, JISC, www.jisc.ac.uk/publications/documents/opensciencerpt.aspx.

MacDonald, L. (ed.) (2006) *Digital Heritage: applying digital imaging to cultural heritage*, Butterworth-Heinemann.

MacMahon, G. (2009) *The Institutional Repository and the Return of the University Press?*, www.slideshare.net/gmcmahon/the-institutional-repository-and-the-return-of-the-university-press.

McCarthy, F. (2008) A House for the Mind, *Guardian*, 23 February.

McCarty, W. (2005) *Humanities Computing*, Princeton.

McGann, J. (2010) Sustainability: the elephant in the room. In McGann, J. (ed.), *Online Humanities Scholarship: the shape of things to come*, Rice University Press.

McHugh, A., Konstantelos, L. and Barr, M. (2009) *Report on Emerging Digital Art Characterisation Techniques*. Preservation and Long-term Access through NETworked Services (Planets) Report PC/5-D5, www.planets-project.eu/docs/reports/digital_Art_Characterisation_Techniques.pdf.

Makri, S. (2006) Studying Academic Lawyers' Information Seeking to Inform the Design of Digital Law Libraries, *IEEE Computer Society Bulletin of the Technical Committee on Digital Libraries*, **3** (3).

Malhotra, N. K. (1999) *Marketing Research: an applied orientation,* 3rd edn, Prentice Hall.

Malpas, C. (2011) *Cloud-sourcing Research Collections: managing print in the mass-digitized library environment*, OCLC Research, www.oclc.org/research/publications/library/2011/2011-01.pdf.

Manguel, A. (2008) *The Library at Night*, Yale University Press.

Marchionni, P. (2010) Why are Users so Useful?: user engagement and the experience of the JISC Digitisation Programme, *Ariadne*, **61**, www.ariadne.ac.uk/issue61/marchionni/.

Marty, P. F. (2004) The Evolving Roles of Information Professionals in Museums, *Bulletin of the American Society for Information Science and Technology*, **30** (5), 20–3.

Marty, P. F. (2007) The Changing Nature of Information Work in Museums, *Journal of the American Society for Information Science and Technology*, **58** (1), 97–107.

Meredith, C. (2008) *The National Library's Digits – Books Next?*, www.academi.org/copyright-debate/i/132168.

Meyer, E. et al. (2009) *Usage and Impact Study of JISC-funded Phase 1 Digitisation Projects and the Toolkit for the Impact of Digitised Scholarly Resources*, University of Oxford, Oxford Internet Institute.

MINERVA EC (2008) *Handbook on Cultural Web User Interaction*, www.minervaeurope.org/publications/Handbookwebuserinteraction.pdf.

Mintz, A. (1994) That's Edutainment!, *Museum News*, November/December.

Mooney, L. R. (2006) Chaucer's Scribe, *Speculum*, **81**, 97–138.

Moore, N. (2007) (Re)using Qualitative Data, *Sociological Research Online*, **12** (3), www.socresonline.org.uk/12/3/1.html.

Mortimer, I. (2002) Discriminating Between Readers: the case for a policy of flexibility, *Journal of the Society of Archivists*, **23** (1) 59–67.

Motyckova, V. (2010) *The British Museum's Collection Database Online: information seeking behaviour of the general public*, unpublished dissertation, UCL.

MRC (2011) *MRC Policy on Data Sharing and Preservation*, UK Medical Research Council, www.mrc.ac.uk/.

Natanson, B. O. (2007) Round Table – American Faces: twentieth-century photographs – worth a billion words? Library of Congress Pictures Online, *The Journal of American History*, **94** (1), 99–111.

National Archives (2009) *3.4 Million Searches on www.1911census.co.uk in Family History Frenzy*, www.nationalarchives.gov.uk/documents/14jan2009.pdf.

National Archives (n.d.) *Licensing our Records*, www.nationalarchives.gov.uk/business/licensing.htm.

National Audit Office (2003) *Unlocking the Past: the 1901 census online*, report by the Comptroller and Auditor General, HC 1259, Session 2002–2003, 14 November, www.nao.org.uk/publications/0203/unlocking_the_past_the_1901_c.aspx.

National Library of Australia (2008) *National Library of Australia Collection Digitisation Policy*, 4th edn, www.nla.gov.au/policy/digitisation.html.

National Library of Scotland (2008) *Expanding Our Horizons: National Library of Scotland strategy 2008–2011*, www.nls.uk/about/policy/strategy2008#relations.

National Library of Wales (2005) National Library of Wales: digitisation policy and strategy, www.webarchive.org.uk/wayback/archive/20080823000824/http://www.llgc.org.uk/fileadmin/documents/pdf/digitisationpolicyandstrategy2005_S.pdf.

National Museum Directors' Conference (1999) *A Netful of Jewels: new museums in the learning age*, www.nationalmuseums.org.uk/media/documents/publications/netful_of_jewels.pdf.

National Museum Directors' Conference (2010) *Museums Deliver*, www.nationalmuseums.org.uk/media/documents/what_we_do_documents/museums_deliver_full.pdf.

National Science Foundation (2006) *Investing America's Future Strategic Plan FY 2006–2011*, www.nsf.gov/pubs/2006/nsf0648/nsf0648.jsp.

National Science Foundation (2007) *Cyberinfrastructure Vision for 21st Century Discovery*, www.nsf.gov/pubs/2007/nsf0728/index.jsp.

National Science Foundation (2008) *Beyond Being There: a blueprint for advancing the design, development and evaluation of virtual organizations, final report*: Workshops on Building Effective Virtual Organisations, www.ci.uchicago.edu/events/VirtOrg2008/VO_report.pdf.

National Science Foundation (2010) *Dissemination and Sharing of Research Results*, www.nsf.gov/bfa/dias/policy/dmp.jsp.

NHMRC and ARC (2007) *Australian Code for the Responsible Conduct of Research*, National Health and Medical Research Council, Australian Research Council and Universities Australia, www.nhmrc.gov.au/publications/synopses/r39syn.htm.

Nicholas, D. and Herman, E. (2009) *Assessing Information Needs in the Age of the Digital Consumer*, Routledge.

Nicholas, D. et al. (2006) The Information Seeking Behaviour of the Users of Digital Scholarly Journals, *Information Processing and Management*, **42** (5), 134565.

Oblinger, D. (2006) Space as a Change Agent. In Oblinger, D. (ed.), *Learning Spaces*, Educause.

Old Weather (n.d.) *Old Weather: our weather's past, the climate's future*, www.oldweather.org.

Olivier, B., Roberts, T. and Blinco, K. (2005) *The e-Framework for Education and Research: an overview*, www.e-framework.org/.

Ornager, S. (1997) Image Retrieval: theoretical analysis and information seeking studies on accessing information in images, *Proceedings of the 60th Annual Meeting of the American Society for Information Science*, **34**, 202–11.

OSI (2007) *Developing the UK's e-Infrastructure for Science and Innovation*, report by the OSI e-Infrastructure Working Group, www.nesc.ac.uk/documents/OSI/.

Osterwalder, A. and Pigneur, Y. (2009) *Business Model Generation*, Wiley.

Petersen, G. et al. (2011) *D 3.2.3 – Recommendations for Conducting User Tests. User involvement – a toolbox. How to involve users in development processes in Europeana*, www.europeanaconnect.eu/documents/D3.2.3_eConnect_usability_guidelines_v1.0_KB-DK.pdf.

Poole, N. (2010) *Implementation of the Commission Recommendation on Digitisation and Online Accessibility of Cultural Material and Digital Preservation: UK progress report 2008–10*, Collections Trust, www.collectionstrust.org.uk/collectionstrust/assets/File/001378.doc.

Prescott, A. (1988) *English Historical Documents*, British Library.

Prescott, A. (2002) *The Benedictional of St Aethelwold: a masterpiece of Anglo-Saxon art: a facsimile*, British Library.

Proffitt, M. and Schaffner, J. (2008) *The Impact of Digitizing Special Collections on Teaching and Scholarship: reflections on a symposium about digitization and the humanities*, OCLC, www.oclc.org/programs/publications/reports/2008-04.pdf.

Puglia, S. and Rhodes, E. (2007) Digital Imaging – how far have we come and what still needs to be done?, *RLG DigiNews*, **11** (1), http://worldcat.org/arcviewer/1/OCC/2007/08/08/0000070519/viewer/file137.html.

Quirk, R. et al. (2009) *The Guide to Researching Audiences*, Strategic Content Alliance.

Raban, J. (2007) Tenure, Promotion and Digital Publication, *Digital Humanities Quarterly*, Spring, **1** (1).

Research Information Network (2011) *E-Journals: their use, value and impact*, www.rin.ac.uk/our-work/communicating-and-disseminating-research/e-journals-their-use-value-and-impact.

Rimmer, J., Warwick, C., Blandford, A., Gow, J. and Buchanan, G. (2006) Humanities Scholars' Information-seeking Behaviour and Use of Digital Resources, *Workshop on Digital Libraries in the Context of Users' Broader Activities, DL-CUBA at The Joint Conference on Digital Libraries*.

RIN (2008) Data Sharing Review: consultation on the use and sharing of personal information in the public and private sectors, response from the Research Information Network, www.justice.gov.uk/docs/Research-Information-Network-Data-Sharing-Response.pdf.

Rink, J. (2010) *Interview for Inspiring Scholarship*, Inspiring Research, University of Cambridge.

Roberts, G. (2006) *International Partnerships of Research Excellence: UK–USA academic cooperation*, Wolfson College, Oxford, www.wolfson.ox.ac.uk/archive/uk-us-academic-collaboration/GarethRobertsIPoREx.pdf

Robey, D (2000) *Sound and Structure in the Divine Comedy*, Open University Press.

Robson, G. (2009) *Vital at the National Library of Wales*, http://dev.llgc.org.uk/wiki/index.php?title=Presentations&printable=yes.

Robson, G. (2010) *Harvesting and DAMS*, http://dev.llgc.org.uk/wiki/index.php?title=Presentations&printable=yes.

Rosenzweig, R. (2011) *Clio Wired: the future of the past in the digital age*, Columbia University Press.

Ross, C., Terras, M. and Motyckova, V. (2011) Scholarly Information Seeking Behaviour in the

British Museum Online Collection, paper given at *Museums and the Web 2011*, http://conference.archimuse.com/ mw2011/programs/scholarly_information_seeking_behaviour_in_t.

Rowlands, I. et al. (2008) The Google Generation: the information behaviour of the researcher of the future, *Perspectives*, **60** (4), 290–310.

Ruusalepp, R. (2008) *A Comparative Study of International Approaches to Enabling the Sharing of Research Data: a Digital Curation Centre and JISC Report*, UK, www.jisc.ac.uk/publications/reports/2008/nationaldatafinalreport.aspx.

Sabbagh, D. (2010) James Murdoch v the British Library, *Guardian*, 7 June, www.guardian.co.uk/media/2010/jun/07/james-murdoch-british-library.

Sacco, G. M. (2008) Rosso Tiziano: a system for user-centered exploration and discovery in large image information bases, *Database and Expert Systems Applications Lecture Notes in Computer Science*, **5181**, 297–311.

Salmon, P., Deasy, T. and Garrigan, B. (2004) What Escapes the Net? A statistical comparison of responses from paper and web survey, paper presented at the 2004 Evaluation Forum *Communicating Evaluation Outcomes: Issues and Approaches*, Melbourne, Australia.

Sandland, R. (2009) Introduction to ANDS, *Share: Newsletter of the Australian National Data Service*, **1** (1), http://ands.org.au/newsletters/newsletter-2009-07.pdf

Sarraf, S. (1999) A Survey of Museums on the Web: who uses museum websites? *Curator*, **42**, 231–43.

Sassoon, J. (2007) Beyond Chip Monks and Paper Tigers: towards a new culture of archival format specialists, *Archival Science*, **7**, 133–45.

Schnapp, J. and Presner, T. (2009) *Digital Humanities Manifesto 2.0*, www.humanitiesblast.com/manifesto_V2.pdf.

Shepherd, E. (2009) *Archives and Archivists in 20th Century England*, Ashgate.

Smith, A. and Council on Library and Information Resources (1999) *Why Digitize?*, CLIR.

Smith, A. and Digital Library Federation (2001) *Strategies for Building Digitized Collections: strategies and tools for the digital library*, Digital Library Federation, Council on Library and Information Resources.

Smith, N. (2006) Digitising Documents for Public Access. In MacDonald, L.W. (ed.), *Digital Heritage: applying digital imaging to cultural heritage*, Elsevier, 3–31.

Spiro, L. (2009) Collaborative Authorship in the Humanities, on the Collaborative Scholarship in the Humanities Blog, http://digitalscholarship.wordpress.com/2009/04/21/collaborative-authorship-in-the-humanities.

Spiro, L. and Segal, J. (2007) *The Impact of Digital Resources on Humanities Research*, Fondren Library, Rice University.

Sporton, G. (2007) *Real-time Collaborative Art Making*, AHRC ICT Methods Network, www.methodsnetwork.ac.uk/activities/act23.html.

SSHRC (2009) *Research Data Archiving Policy*, Social Sciences and Humanities Research Council, www.sshrc-crsh.gc.ca/funding-financement/policies-politiques/edata-donnees_electroniques-eng.aspx.

Stein, A. (2009) Trauma and Origins: post-holocaust genealogists and the work of memory.

Qualitative Sociology, **32**, 293–309.

Stephen, A. (2001) The Contemporary Museum and Leisure: recreation as a museum function, *Museum Management and Curatorship*, **19** (3), 297–308.

Stewart, B. (2007) *NEH and Digital Humanities*, position paper presented at NSF/JISC Repositories Workshop, www.sis.pitt.edu/~repwkshop/papers/stewart.html.

Stone, S. (1982) Humanities Scholars – information needs and uses, *Journal of Documentation*, **38** (4), 292–313.

Sundqvist, A. (2007) The Use of Records – a literature review, *Archives & Social Studies: A Journal of Interdisciplinary Research*, **1** (1), 623–53.

Sutherland, K. (2010) Interview for Inspiring Scholarship, Inspiring Research, University of Oxford.

Talja, S. and Maula, H. (2003) Reasons for the Use and Non-use of Electronic Journals and Databases – a domain analytic study in four scholarly disciplines, *Journal of Documentation*, **59** (6), 673–91.

Tanner, S. and Deegan, M. (2011) *Inspiring Scholarship, Inspiring Research*, JISC.

Taylor, J. (1999) *The Definition of e-Science*, www.lesc.ic.ac.uk/admin/escience.html.

Terras, M. (2006) *Image to Interpretation: intelligent systems to aid historians in the reading of the Vindolanda texts*, Oxford Studies in Ancient Documents, Oxford University Press.

Terras, M. (2008) *Digital Images for the Information Professional*, Ashgate.

Terras, M. (2010) *DH2010 Plenary: present, not voting: digital humanities in the Panopticon*, http://melissaterras.blogspot.com/2010/07/dh2010-plenary-present-not-voting.html.

Thomas, S. (2010) Interview for Inspiring Scholarship, Inspiring Research, Bodleian Library.

Thomas, W. A. and Carey, S. (2005) Actual/virtual Visits: what are the links? In Bearman, D. and Trant J. (eds), *Museums and the Web 2005*, Archives and Museum Informatics, www.archimuse.com/mw2005/papers/thomas/thomas.html.

Toolkit for the Impact of Digitised Scholarly Resources, http://microsites.oii.ox.ac.uk/tidsr/.

Trant, J. (2009) Emerging Convergence? Thoughts on museums, archives, libraries, and professional training, *Museum Management and Curatorship*, **24** (4), 369–87

Tucker, S. (2007) Doors Opening Wider: library and archival services to family history, *Archivaria*, **62**, 128–58.

Turner, D. (2011) Interview for Inspiring Scholarship, Inspiring Research, Swansea University.

UKRDS (2009) The Data Imperative: managing the UK's research data for future use, www.ukrds.ac.uk/resources/.

UNESCO (1989) *Unesco Draft Medium Term Plan 1990–1995*, 25 C/4, http://unesdoc.unesco.org/images/0008/000825/082539eb.pdf.

UNESCO, IFLA and ICA (2002) *Guidelines for Digitization Projects: for collections and holdings in the public domain, particularly those held in libraries and archives*, http://archive.ifla.org/VII/s19/pubs/digit-guide.pdf.

Universities UK (2006) *The Economic Impact of UK Higher Education Institutions*, Universities UK, www.universitiesuk.ac.uk/Publications/Pages/Publication-237.aspx.

University of Oxford, NCeSS and JISC (2011) *eIUS, e-Infrastructure Use Case and Service Usage Models Project*, http://projects.oucs.ox.ac.uk/eius.

Unsworth, J. (2000) Scholarly Primitives: what methods do humanities researchers have in common, and how might our tools reflect this?, presented at *Humanities Computing: formal methods, experimental practice*, sponsored by King's College London, http://jefferson.village.virginia.edu/~jmu2m/Kings.5-00/primitives.html.

Unsworth, J. (2003) *Tool-Time, or 'Haven't We Been Here Already?' Ten years in humanities computing*, paper presented at *Transforming Disciplines: The Humanities and Computer Science*, http://www3.isrl.uiuc.edu/~unsworth/carnegie-ninch.03.html.

Upward, F. and McKemmish, S. (2006) Teaching Recordkeeping and Archiving Continuum Style, *Archival Science*, **6**, 219–30.

Villa, R. et al. (2010) Can an Intermediary Collection Help Users Search Image Databases Without Annotations?, *International Conference on Digital Libraries Proceedings of the 10th Annual Joint Conference on Digital Libraries*, 303–12, http://portal.acm.org/citation.cfm?id=1816123&picked=prox&preflayout=flat.

Voss, A. (2011) *e-Research Community Intelligence System*, University of St Andrews, www.researchconnect.org/findings.

Voss, A., Mascord, M., Castelleiro, M.A. et al. (2007) e-Infrastructure Development and Community Engagement, *Proceedings of e-Social Science '07*, www.ncess.ac.uk/events/conference/2007/papers/paper110.pdf.

Voss, A., Mascord, M., Fraser, M. et al. (2007) e-Research Infrastructure Development and Community Engagement, *Proceedings of the UK e-Science All Hands Meeting, Nottingham*, http://www.allhands.org.uk/2007/proceedings/papers/866.pdf.

Voss, A., Procter, R. and Hewitt, T. et al. (2007) Sustainability of e-Infrastructures (for the Social Sciences), *Proceedings of e-Social Science '07*, www.ncess.ac.uk/events/conference/2007/papers/paper127.pdf.

Walter, C. (2005) Insights: Kryder's Law, *Scientific American Magazine*, August.

Warwick, C. (2008) If You Build It….The LAIRAH Project and users of digital resources, *JISC Digitisation Phase Two Programme Meeting: Bath, 14–15 February*.

Warwick, C. and Carty, C. (2001) Only Connect: a study of the problems caused by platform specificity and researcher isolation in humanities computing. In Hubler, A., Linde, P. and Smith, J. W. T. (eds), *Electronic Publishing 01, 2001 in the Digital Publishing Odyssey, Proceedings of an ICCC/IFIP Conference at the University of Kent at Canterbury*, 36–47.

Warwick, C. et al. (2006) *The LAIRAH Project: log analysis of digital resources in the arts and humanities: final report to the Arts and Humanities Research Council*, www.ucl.ac.uk/infostudies/claire-warwick/publications/LAIRAHreport.pdf.

Warwick, C. et al. (2008) If You Build It Will They Come? The LAIRAH Study: quantifying the use of online resources in the arts and humanities through statistical analysis of user log data, *Literary and Linguist Computing*, **23** (1), 85–102.

Waters, D. (2004) The Economics of Digitizing Library and Other Cultural Materials: a perspective from the Mellon Foundation. In Hughes, L. *The Price of Digitization: new cost models for cultural and educational institutions: a report*, www.ninch.org/forum/price.report.html.

Watson-Boone, R. (1994) The Information Needs and Habits of Humanities Scholars, *Reference*

Quarterly, **34** (2), 203–16.

Watt, S. et al. (2002) Electronic Course Surveys: does automating feedback and reporting give better results?, *Assessment & Evaluation in Higher Education*, **27**(4), 325–37.

Whatley, S. (2010) *Dance Teaching Resource and Collaborative Engagement Spaces Project Plan*, www.jisc.ac.uk/media/documents/programmes/digitisation/dtraces_pp.pdf.

Whitmire, E. (2002) Disciplinary Differences and Undergraduates' Information Seeking Behaviour, *Journal of the American Society for Information Science and Technology*, **53** (8), 631–8.

Wiberley, S. E. (1983) Subject Access in the Humanities and the Precision of the Humanist's Vocabulary, *Library Quarterly*, **53** (4), 420–33.

Wiberley, S. E. (1988) Names in Space and Time: the indexing vocabulary of the humanities, *Library Quarterly*, **58** (1), 1–28.

Wiberley, S. E. (2000) Time and Technology, *College and Research Libraries*, **61** (5), 421–31.

Wiberley, S. and Jones, W. (1989) Patterns of Information Seeking in the Humanities, *College and Research Libraries*, **50** (6), 638–45.

Williams, P. and Ross, C. (2010) *Understanding the Value of Social Media for the Dissemination of UCL News*, unpublished research report.

Winton, L. J. (2010) *Research Data and Digital Archives* [white paper], http://versi.edu.au/sites/default/files/VeRSIWhitepaperDigitalArchives.pdf.

Yakel, E. (2004) Seeking Information, Seeking Connections, Seeking Meaning: genealogists and family historians, *Information Research*, **10** (1), paper 205, http://InformationR.net/ir/10-1/paper205.html.

Yakel, E. (2007) Creating the Next Generation of Archival Finding Aids, *D-Lib Magazine*, **13** (5/6), www.dlib.org/dlib/may07/yakel/05yakel.html.

Zorich, D. M. (2008) *A Survey of Digital Humanities Centers in the United States*, Council on Library and Information Resources, www.clir.org/pubs/reports/pub143/pub143.pdf.

Zuccala, A. et al. (2007) Web Intelligence Analyses of Digital Libraries, *Journal of Documentation*, **63** (4), 558–89.

Index

Information Users and Usability in the Digital Age
G G Chowdhury and Sudatta Chowdhury

Information users and usability constitute the main building blocks of today's electronic information world. This important new text is the first to give a holistic overview of all of the necessary issues relating to information users and the usability of information services in the digital world, including user-centred design, and the characteristics and behaviour of information users.

This book helps readers understand why information users and the usability of information services are important and equips them to play a proper role in designing user-centred information systems and services and to properly exploit information services for the maximum benefit of users. It covers all of the major issues, the current situation and what the various research studies from around the world show. The chapters are:

- An introduction to information users and usability
- Information needs and user studies
- Human information behaviour studies and models
- Usability study basics
- Usability study participants
- Usability data analysis
- Web usability
- The usability of digital libraries
- Digital divide, digital natives and usability
- Issues and trends in usability research.

The book is essential reading for researchers and practitioners interested in the design and evaluation of digital information systems and services, as well as for students on library, information, and digital library courses.

G. G. Chowdhury is the Director of the Centre for Information and Knowledge Management, University of Technology, Sydney, and Sudatta Chowdhury is Lecturer in Information and Knowledge Management, University of Technology, Sydney

ISBN 978-1-85604-597-1

E-books in Libraries
A practical guide
Kate Price and Virginia Havergal

Despite the fact that e-books have been in existence for decades in various guises and added to library collections for several years now, there has been a noticeable lack of published manuals on the subject. This is doubtless owing to the rapidly evolving nature of the market. There is now a plethora of different types of digital object that may be termed 'e-books' and a bewildering number of business and access models to match.

Moreover the pace of change shows no sign of abating, but there is an increasing amount of popular interest in e-books, and what is needed is practical information to assist library and information professionals managing collections of e-books and doing their best to inform their users right now.

This timely book, the first of its kind to provide a practical appraisal of e-books, aims to fill that need by addressing the key questions: Where do e-books come from and what are the key business models that support them? What needs to change before e-books become universally and easily used? What will the e-book landscape look like in ten years' time? How can you be sure you are building a good collection that your users can access easily? What about money and budgets?

The book is divided into five parts:

- The production and distribution of e-books
- Planning and developing an e-book collection
- Delivering e-books to library readers
- Engaging readers with e-books
- The future of e-books.

This book is a ready reference source for any library and information professional with an interest in e-books and their development. It is essential background reading for library managers wishing to develop an e-book collection from scratch or for those responsible for maintaining an existing e-book collection. It will also have plenty to interest publishers, who need to be aware of the issues faced by libraries managing e-book collections, and will be of great value to students of librarianship and information studies, and those on publishing related courses.

ISBN 978-1-85604-572-8